LIBRARY IN A BOOK

AIDS

THE FACTS ON FILE LIBRARY IN A BOOK SERIES

Each volume of the Facts On File Library in a Book series is carefully designed to be the best one-volume source for research on important current problems. Written clearly and carefully so that even the most complex aspects of the issue are easily understandable, the books give the reader the research tools to begin work, plus the information needed to delve more deeply into the topic. Each book includes a history of the subject, biographical information on important figures in the field, a complete annotated bibliography, and a carefully designed index—everything the researcher needs to get down to work.

LIBRARY IN A BOOK

AIDS

Stephen A. Flanders & Carl N. Flanders

Bibliographic materials prepared by
Dr. Ruth C. Shoge, D.L.S., Columbia University;
Reference Librarian and Assistant Professor, Upsala College

Facts On File
New York • Oxford

LIBRARY IN A BOOK: AIDS

Copyright © 1991 by Stephen A. Flanders & Carl N. Flanders

Facts On File, Inc.   Facts On File Limited
460 Park Avenue South   Collins Street
New York NY 10016   Oxford OX4 1XJ
USA   United Kingdom

ISBN 0-8160-1910-X

Library of Congress Cataloging-in-Publication Data
Flanders, Stephen A.
   AIDS / by Stephen A. Flanders & Carl N. Flanders : bibliographic
materials prepared by Ruth C. Shoge.
      p.   cm. — (Library in a book)
   Includes bibliographical references.
   Summary: Discusses the AIDS epidemic, including a chronology of
major events, a summary of important court cases, a biographical
listing of key individuals, and a reference guide to further
research.
   ISBN 0-8160-1910-X (acid-free paper)
   1. AIDS (Disease) [1. AIDS (Disease)]   I. Flanders, Carl N.
II. Title. III. Series.
RC607.A26F58   1990
616.97'92—dc20   90-42577

A British CIP catalogue record for this book is available from the British Library.

Facts On File books are available at special discounts when purchased in bulk quantities for businesses, associations, institutions or sales promotions. Please call our Special Sales Department in New York at 212/683-2244 (dial 800/322-8755 except in NY, AK or HI) or in Oxford at 865/728399.

Text design by Ron Monteleone
Jacket design by Nadja Furlan-Lorbek
Composition by the Maple-Vail Book Manufacturing Group
Manufactured by the Maple-Vail Book Manufacturing Group
Printed in the United States of America

10 9 8 7 6 5 4 3 2 1

This book is printed on acid-free paper.

CONTENTS

Contents

ACKNOWLEDGMENTS

The authors would like to thank the following organizations and individuals for their assistance: the Centers for Disease Control; the American Foundation for AIDS Research; Project Inform; the Sprague Library at Montclair State College; the Seton Hall Law Library; and Eleanora von Dehsen and Nicholas Bakalar at Facts On File.

INTRODUCTION

The purpose of this book is to provide a one-stop source for reference information about AIDS. The first part of the book is an overview of the AIDS epidemic, designed to give the reader a basic perspective of the many issues involved with AIDS. It includes a general introduction, a chronology of major events, a summary of important court cases and a biographical listing of key individuals.

Once acquainted with the subject of AIDS, the reader can turn to the second part of the book for a comprehensive guide to reference materials on the topic. A broad spectrum of resources is identified for use in further research. To assist the reader, at the end of the book are a listing of acronyms used throughout, a glossary of key terms and a description of the federal government's public health system.

Our knowledge about AIDS is constantly evolving. This book is current through December 31, 1989. Readers are encouraged to consult the reference sources in the second half of the book for developments subsequent to this date.

PART I

OVERVIEW OF THE TOPIC

CHAPTER 1

INTRODUCTION TO THE AIDS EPIDEMIC

Since 1981 a mysterious disease has claimed more than 70,000 lives in the United States. The killer is a contagious, incurable and ultimately fatal condition that medical science has named *acquired immunodeficiency syndrome*, or *AIDS*. Although much is now known about AIDS, many puzzling aspects of the disease continue to confound experts. The emergence and spread of this lethal new disease in the past decade has had a dramatic impact on virtually every facet of American life. AIDS is now a household word. It is also a complex and difficult social, political and scientific reality.

The subject of AIDS can be examined at three different levels. There is, first of all, the disease itself. Medical research has focused much of its efforts at this level in trying to discern the nature of the enigmatic disease syndrome. The next level investigates AIDS as an epidemic. Estimates are that up to 1.5 million Americans carry the virus that causes AIDS. The health system has been challenged to care for those who are infected, while the larger society seeks ways to halt the precipitous increase in the number of new cases. There is, finally, the more abstract level of dealing with how the AIDS epidemic has influenced American behavior and institutions.

For many, the AIDS epidemic is made more difficult because it involves issues of human sexuality and, specifically, homosexuality—issues with which they are uncomfortable. Much debate over the course of the epidemic centers on the best way to discuss graphic and elemental aspects of AIDS.

3

This introduction to the AIDS epidemic consists of 10 sections. The first two, Medical Background and Health Care Issues, place the AIDS epidemic within a medical framework. Private Sector Involvement and Government Involvement then review responses to the epidemic in both the private and public arenas. AIDS and Politics, Legal Issues, AIDS and Society and AIDS and Culture address the repercussions of the epidemic in each of these areas. The international scope of the epidemic is assessed in Worldwide Perspective. The final section, AIDS and the Future, encapsulates the best guess projections of the experts about where the AIDS epidemic will go from here.

MEDICAL BACKGROUND

This medical overview of AIDS is divided into three sections: Emergence of a New Disease describes how AIDS first appeared and the subsequent, successful efforts to discover its cause. Current Knowledge about AIDS reviews what has been learned about the disease to date. Medical Responses to AIDS identifies the steps taken by health professionals to care for those with the disease and to bring the epidemic under control. Nine years after its emergence, there is now a relatively clear picture of what AIDS is, how it spreads and how it affects its victims. Scientists are in general agreement that it may take at least that long again to develop either a vaccine or cure for the disease.

EMERGENCE OF A NEW DISEASE

In the spring of 1981, a vexing pattern of disease began to appear among a small number of patients in San Francisco, Los Angeles and New York City. Previously healthy young homosexual men were diagnosed with symptoms of uncertain ill health, including night sweats, fevers, diarrhea, weight loss and swollen lymph nodes. Over time, as their clinical conditions worsened, these patients fell victim to a range of unusual and ultimately deadly infections. The most frequent were a rare form of pneumonia called *Pneumocystis carinii pneumonia* (PCP) and the skin cancer *Kaposi's sarcoma* (KS). Existing medical treatments were ineffective against these lethal illnesses. In due course, medical researchers would come to designate this new, complex disease acquired immune deficiency syndrome. The acronym AIDS was quickly adopted.

Puzzled physicians could not at first account for the sudden emergence of these fatal afflictions. The diseases were known. But they ordinarily struck only persons with genetic flaws in their immune systems or individuals whose natural disease-fighting abilities were compromised by other recognized medical conditions. These opportunistic infections were no threat to persons with normal immune capabilities.

Laboratory tests of blood samples from the first victims in California and New York revealed that a key element in their immune systems was depleted for no apparent reason. All had reduced numbers of the white blood cells called *T lymphocytes*, which perform important functions in protecting the body against microorganisms that cause disease. More detailed studies showed that one particular subset of T lymphocytes, called *T helper lymphocytes* or *T4 cells*, was particularly diminished in people with AIDS. This finding of immune deficiency provided an apparent explanation for the susceptibility of the initial AIDS patients to certain deadly infections.

From 1981 on the number of reported AIDS cases in the United States doubled about every six months. As the disease spread through major urban homosexual communities, theories about the cause of the syndrome emerged. The possibility of an unknown infectious agent was considered. One group of experts suspected an as-yet-unidentified microorganism that attacked the disease-fighting apparatus of the human body and exposed it to devastating infections. While this suspicion later proved correct, early laboratory studies did not provide confirming evidence.

Drug use was also viewed as a potential cause. In February 1982, scientists with the National Institutes of Health (NIH) found immune system defects linked to the use of nitrites, a drug popular among some homosexual men as a sexual stimulant. The NIH thought nitrites might cause immune suppression in the presence of repeated viral infections, but later studies did not confirm this.

The initial appearance of AIDS exclusively in gay men strongly suggested that the disease was infectious and transmissible. In July 1981 the Centers for Disease Control (CDC) set up studies in San Francisco, New York and Los Angeles to examine risk factors for the disease. The lifestyles of afflicted patients were compared with those of healthy homosexual men. The CDC hoped to highlight any differences that might account for vulnerability to the new disease. The studies yielded several important findings.

AIDS victims were far more sexually active than the matched group of healthy homosexuals. Afflicted patients had averaged over 1,000 sexual partners in their lifetimes. Researchers thought that numerous infections acquired during hundreds of sexual encounters may have overwhelmed the T4 cells in these patients and left them unable to fight disease.

Even prior to the appearance of AIDS, scientists had identified a set of health problems prevalent among gay men who had engaged in intimate sexual relations with great numbers of partners. The widespread outbreak of the viral disease hepatitis in the late 1970s in gay men in New York and San Francisco was tied to their repeated exposure to infectious microorganisms as a result of promiscuous sexual activity.

In addition, the CDC researchers established direct sexual connections between several of the patients under study. Of the first 19 reported cases of AIDS in Los Angeles, 9 were linked, through sexual contacts, to a single individual. The CDC case-control studies lent support to the evolving theory that AIDS was caused by an infectious agent and that the disease could be spread through sexual contact.

Early in the epidemic it became clear that other high-risk groups for AIDS could be identified. In the first quarter of 1982 the disease began appearing among heterosexual men and women who were intravenous (IV) drug users. Physicians noted the characteristic disease patterns of immune incompetence and devastating opportunistic infections.

Epidemiologists with the federal government tracked these cases, looking for factors that would explain the incidence of the disease in this new group. Lifestyle patterns were examined. Studies by the CDC revealed that a majority of the patients had shared unsterile needles with other, often anonymous IV drug users. Moreover, the CDC was able to directly link individual cases through this specific activity.

Public health experts were already aware of a general history of multiple infections in IV drug users associated with the common use of dirty needles. In previous outbreaks of infectious disease, needle sharing had permitted germs and microorganisms to be transmitted from one individual to another through the exchange of human blood.

Researchers saw parallels between these previous outbreaks and the appearance of AIDS in IV drug users. The implication of needle sharing as a high-risk behavior meant that blood-borne transmission of AIDS might be possible if, in fact, the syndrome was caused by an infectious agent.

The subsequent recognition that hemophiliacs were at high risk heightened concerns about blood's connection to transmission. In July 1982 the CDC received reports of three cases of AIDS in hemophiliacs who had been treated with clotting-factor concentrates to prevent bleeding. These patients had not engaged in the high-risk activities associated with the disease in gay males and IV drug users. Scientists speculated that the hemophiliac victims had contracted the disease through transfusions of blood-clotting agents.

Further evidence of a specific agent transmitted by sexual contact and blood products accumulated in late 1982 and early 1983. In May 1983 the CDC reported cases of AIDS in persons who had received whole-blood transfusions. These individuals had no other known risk factors in their backgrounds.

By the close of 1982, scientists in the United States and Europe had stepped up the search for the cause of AIDS. The urgency of the problem was evident. Known medical treatments could not halt the progression of the disease, and the number of reported cases was increasing dramatically. Some investigators thought the syndrome might simply be a new manifestation of a known virus. Others suspected that the disease might be caused by infection with two or more microorganisms. Finally, research teams began looking for an entirely new viral pathogen.

The idea that a virus was involved in AIDS crystallized in 1983. More specifically, the attention of researchers came to focus on a unique kind of virus called a *retrovirus*.

The discovery of the first human retrovirus, isolated from the cells of a leukemia patient, had been reported by Dr. Robert C. Gallo at the National Cancer Institute (NCI) in 1980. Gallo showed that this retrovirus had a distinct tendency to infect T helper lymphocytes, the white blood cells that control cell-mediated immunity. Gallo labeled the retrovirus *human T-cell leukemia virus*, or *HTLV*. The subsequent isolation of a distinct, but closely related, virus from a leukemia patient led to the scientific designations HTLV-I and HTLV-II.

By the time these findings were confirmed, the AIDS epidemic in the United States was in full swing. It was apparent that there might be some relationship. The immune deficiency that left AIDS patients so susceptible to infection involved loss of the same T-cell subset that led to the leukemia of HTLV-I. The suspected modes of transmission of AIDS, through blood products and sexual contact, appeared identical to those of HTLV-I.

Efforts to isolate the AIDS virus proved difficult. Scientists could occasionally detect retrovirus activity in T4 cells taken from AIDS patients. But the results of these tests were not reproducible. Researchers seemed unable to maintain the T4 cells in laboratory cultures. Investigators learned later that the virus was killing the cells before the researchers could finish their analysis.

The first isolation of the virus later shown to be the cause of AIDS was reported in May 1983 by Dr. Luc Montagnier and colleagues at the Pasteur Institute in Paris, France. They named the virus *lymphadenopathy-associated virus* (LAV) because it had been isolated from the lymph nodes of a patient with the AIDS-related condition of lymphadenopathy syndrome. During the following months, similar retrovirus samples were isolated by the Pasteur group from the blood of AIDS patients. But the

7

research team continued to have problems with sustaining samples of the virus in a laboratory environment.

Other investigators were on a similar track. In May 1984 Dr. Robert C. Gallo and his staff at the NCI reported the isolation of a new retrovirus from 48 AIDS patients. They named it HTLV-III. The meaning of HTLV was changed from human T-cell leukemia virus to human T-cell lymphotropic virus to reflect the fact that all members of the HTLV family showed an attraction to T lymphocytes. The NCI team then discovered a tissue culture cell line that allowed for production of large quantities of the virus.

Another virus isolate was described in August 1984 by Dr. Jay Levy at the University of California at San Francisco. He labeled the virus *AIDS-associated retrovirus*, or *ARV*.

These three independent discoveries led to often bitter legal and scientific controversies about who had actually found the AIDS agent and what it should be called. The Pasteur team even accused Gallo of virtual theft of its pioneering work. After a protracted dispute, detailed molecular comparisons of HTLV-III, LAV and ARV demonstrated that they were all variants of the same virus. Finally, in May 1986, an international committee of scientists designated a single name for the AIDS virus: *human immunodeficiency virus (HIV)*. As a legal resolution, Montagnier and Gallo were credited as codiscoverers of the viral agent.

Once the AIDS virus had been isolated, researchers were able to develop tests that would screen a person's blood for its presence. These tests detect not the virus itself, but the antibodies produced in response to infection with HIV. The most commonly used procedure is called the *enzyme-linked immunosorbent assay*, or *ELISA*, which employs a chemical method to indicate the presence of the antibodies. Another test, the Western blot, is frequently used to confirm initial ELISA findings and provide an added safeguard against potentially inaccurate results.

Much additional work was required to prove conclusively that HIV caused AIDS and was not simply another opportunistic infection attacking persons whose immune system defenses were deficient due to some other reason. Studies throughout 1984 consistently showed that the acquisition and transmission of HIV correlated with AIDS or AIDS-related conditions.

Blood recipients who developed AIDS and their donors provided an important piece of the puzzle. Blood bank records allowed researchers to track the natural history of the disease as it was spread from one individual to another. Identical virus samples could be obtained from blood recipients with AIDS and from the HIV-infected donors who supplied the blood. This enabled researchers to confirm the link between infection with HIV and the development of AIDS.

Although scientists have been able to determine what causes AIDS, the exact origin of the disease remains a matter of speculation. When the first cases were reported in the United States in June of 1981, scientists were fairly convinced they had detected a new disease. Evidence has been uncovered that HIV was present in Africa at least two decades before the first U.S. cases were diagnosed. Reviews of stored blood showed that antibodies to HIV were detectable in parts of Central Africa as early as 1963. The earliest reported evidence for the presence of the AIDS virus was found in stored blood serum obtained in Zaire, Africa, in 1959. Also, the records of people in Central Africa who had died from opportunistic infections have been examined retrospectively; these probes found individuals as far back as 1975 who would meet the current CDC definition of AIDS.

How the AIDS virus might have spread from Africa and reached the United States is a point of conjecture. A popular theory is that it may have come by way of Haiti. In the mid-1970s thousands of people travelled between the French-speaking nations of Haiti and Zaire. This contact would account for the spread of HIV across the Atlantic Ocean. Subsequently, the virus could have been carried from Haiti to New York by American homosexual men, for whom the island had become a popular vacation spot.

The natural history of the AIDS virus is open to question. Links have been explored between HIV and certain viruses that appear in monkeys. A syndrome called simian acquired immunodeficiency disease (SAID), found in macaque monkeys, closely resembles AIDS in its manifestations. The syndrome results from infection with a type of retrovirus that bears some genetic similarity to HIV.

Another retrovirus, isolated from African Green monkeys, also appears to share some genetic properties with HIV. These connections have lent support to the theory that the AIDS virus arose from mutated forms of a monkey virus that jumped species as recently as 30 years ago.

More recent research findings do not appear to support this hypothesis. Japanese scientists reported in June of 1988 that retrovirus in the African Green monkey lacks key genetic material present in the human AIDS virus. According to the researchers, if the virus had jumped from monkeys to humans in the last several generations, then isolates of the virus drawn from each species would be virtually identical. The mutation necessary to explain the differences they found apparently could not have occurred within such a brief time span.

The Japanese team speculated that an AIDS-like virus could have infected the common primate ancestors of humans and monkeys millions of years ago. As these primates evolved into humans and various species of monkeys, the parent AIDS virus assumed its current forms.

CURRENT KNOWLEDGE ABOUT AIDS

Medical research has pieced together much of the puzzle about acquired immune deficiency syndrome. AIDS is a fatal disease complex afflicting individuals whose immune systems have become severely deficient. It is characterized by a range of unusual and devastating diseases. These maladies result from opportunistic infections that ordinarily do not lead to illness in people with normal immune function.

Acquired suggests that AIDS is not an inherited or congenital condition. The immune deficit in AIDS patients that leaves them vulnerable to opportunistic infections is caused by a single viral agent scientists have named the human immunodeficiency virus (HIV). Because HIV is transmissible in only a specific number of ways, researchers have been able to determine those most at risk of contracting the virus. Infection with HIV does not necessarily mean a person has AIDS. Medical research has defined five categories of HIV-related conditions. These range from the cases of person who carry HIV but show no symptoms of immune deficiency to those of persons who have developed full-blown AIDS.

HIV

Viruses are microorganisms consisting of a core of the nucleic acids RNA or DNA surrounded by a protein coat. These microorganisms are capable of infecting the cells of almost all members of the plant and animal kingdoms. Viruses have no independent metabolism, so they are unable to grow on their own. Therefore, they are dependent on the cells they invade for reproduction.

Once a virus enters a cell of an animal or plant, it becomes activated. Then, fueled by enzymes in the host cell, it takes over the cell's internal equipment. Once a host cell is infected with an invading virus's genetic information—a blueprint for making more viruses—its own genetic instructions are changed or overcome by the new commands. An infected cell may be changed to such an extent that it makes copies of its new, flawed self. Or it can be forced to reproduce copies of the virus before finally dying.

Normally, viruses contain a DNA core, like most other living organisms. HIV, however, is unlike most other human viruses: It is a *retrovirus*. A retrovirus stores its genetic program in an RNA core. It issues a special enzyme, called *reverse transcriptase*, to copy its RNA program into

DNA. This unique feature allows a retrovirus to implant itself easily into DNA-formatted host cells. The retrovirus co-opts the genetic machinery of the host cell and turns it into a site for the manufacture of more viruses.

Among retroviruses, HIV has some distinctive characteristics. These features are part of the troubling nature of the AIDS virus. Studies of different isolates of HIV have revealed a high rate of mutation of its protein coat. This process of mutation is called *antigenic variation*. The protein coat is the protective wrapper that shields the core of the virus. Because it is on the outside, the wrapper is the most likely part of the virus to stimulate a response from the immune system. One stage of this response is the production of antibodies that recognize and fasten to specific parts of the protein coat. The fastening of antibodies then triggers other immune processes leading to the destruction of the virus. But because a virus like HIV can quickly change its coat, antibodies created against the protein envelope of one viral strain may not protect against another strain. Another notable quality of HIV is the startling pace at which new virus particles are produced. Researchers have identified a viral gene they think is responsible for this explosive replication. They call it the *trans-activator*, or TAT-3, gene. The gene appears to increase the speed and efficiency of RNA translation into new viral particles.

The Immune System

The human immune system consists of a variety of white blood cells and proteins in the blood and other body fluids, working together to recognize and destroy invading germs and microorganisms that cause disease. Two types of white blood cells vital to the normal functioning of the immune system are lymphocytes and macrophages. *Lymphoctyes* are responsible for orchestrating the immune system's reaction to an infectious agent. They are divided into two classes: B lymphocytes (B cells) and T lymphoctyes (T cells).

B cells respond to the presence of an invading microorganism by producing a type of protein called *antibodies*. Antibodies attach themselves to the pathogen, performing the key function of alerting other components of the immune system to the appearance of an alien organism. They also prevent the pathogen from binding to other immune system cells, and they assist in its elimination from the body. Scientists say antibody immune response is *specific*. In other words, antibodies produced against one microorganism will not work against another microorganism unless the two pathogens share a common molecular structure.

The immune system's response to an infectious agent is regulated by two specific kinds of T cells: The helper T lymphocyte, or T4 cell, plays

11

a critical role in this process by helping to initiate an immune response, signaling inactive B cells to produce antibodies. It does this by presenting them with bits of pathogenic matter. The T4 cell acts like a central dispatcher, directing the activities of those white blood cells that attack and eliminate invading microorganisms. To accomplish this, T4 cells produce chemical messengers that bring defender and killer white blood cells to the location of an infection. These cells are stimulated to multiply as necessary and kill the pathogen at hand. In this way, microorganisms are prevented from reproducing and spreading to other sites.

When a given immune response successfully runs its course, the system has a mechanism to, in effect, turn itself off. Suppressor T lymphocytes, or T8 cells, perform this function by deactivating the other cells. This deactivation prevents the possible damaging of healthy tissue.

Macrophages are a class of defender white blood cells present in the blood, the brain, mucous membranes, semen and cervical fluid. Macrophages fight infection by ingesting invaders such as bacteria and protozoa. Normally they do this after the T4 cells signal that these organisms have invaded the body. Macrophages also release proteins essential to the growth of healthy tissue throughout the body.

HIV does not appear to randomly attack the many components of the immune system. Instead, when the AIDS virus enters the body, it selectively targets the T4 cells. For a virus to enter a cell, its protein coat must match receptors on that cell's surface. Scientists have detected a specific molecule on the HIV protein envelope that they believe accounts for its preference for T4 cells.

Once the virus is inside the T4 cell, it becomes a virtual part of its host. HIV does not immediately disrupt immune function. The AIDS virus has a long incubation period. During this time, HIV is latent and the infected individual shows no evident signs of illness. Studies have revealed that the incubation period is four years on average, but may extend for as long as eight to 10 years. The virus is transmissible in this latent stage.

Eventually HIV begins to unleash its disruptive force on the T4 cells. Scientists are uncertain about what exactly triggers the onslaught. The invaded T4 cells, overcome by the genetic instructions of the HIV, produce more virus particles. These copies of the AIDS virus then spread out and target other T4 cells for infection. The process is repeated many times. The infected T4 cells are ultimately overwhelmed and destroyed. This reduction in the number of T4 cells is a characteristic indicator of the onset of AIDS. In the healthy immune system, the ratio of the quantity of T4 cells to T8 cells is about two to one. But the lethal impact of

HIV on T4 cells dramatically alters this ratio. In some instances the relationship may be reversed, so that T8 cells actually outnumber T4 cells by two to one.

When a sufficient number of T4 cells are infected or destroyed, other components of the immune system are disrupted. The cells and proteins that depend on T4 cells for direction are unable to function normally. The whole system of defenses is thrown off balance. The B cells react to this imbalance by producing either too few or too many antibodies. These distorted antibody levels hinder normal immune system responses. Those white blood cells that attack pathogens show a decreased capacity for destroying invading microorganisms.

The immune system attempts to fight back when confronted by HIV. Persons infected with the AIDS virus produce detectable levels of antibodies against the invader. The problem is that most of these antibodies are not able to neutralize or destroy the virus.

Depletion of T4 cells happens gradually. Vague symptoms of illness in the early stages of AIDS reflect the initial depression of the immune system. As greater numbers of T4 cells are overwhelmed, the immune response network is thrown into full decline. The individual is then vulnerable to the opportunistic infections that induce the fatal diseases associated with AIDS.

The scientific community's understanding of the microbiology of AIDS is constantly unfolding. Until recently, researchers focused on T4 cells in most studies because they are the cells most evidently targeted by HIV. Depletion of T4 cells is still considered fundamental to the development of AIDS, but scientists cite evidence that this alone is no longer sufficient to fully explain the disease. Evolving research indicates that the macrophages have an important role in the clinical course of HIV infection and AIDS. These findings are based on limited investigation. Scientists have cautioned against drawing premature conclusions and stress the need for further research.

Several recent studies suggest that macrophages may be the first or, in some instances, only cells invaded by HIV. The emerging picture is that HIV invades the macrophages first, spreading from them to the T4 cells. The virus kills the T4 cells, preventing them from properly alerting other macrophages to ward off infections. At the same time, infected macrophages do not combat invading microorganisms even if they are signaled by T4 cells. As a result, opportunistic infections are able to set in, and the individual progresses to full-blown AIDS.

The research on macrophages has yielded other interesting preliminary findings. Scientists now believe that infected macrophages do not secrete protein substances essential to the growth of a variety of body tissues. The result may be destruction of brain cells and the development of neurological symptoms of AIDS dementia in some patients.

Macrophages act as a reservoir for HIV. The virus multiples in them, but does not destroy them. Hundreds of viral particles can accumulate and lurk in the cells for indeterminate periods. The macrophages, while not killed, are incapacitated. It appears that virus particles may be transmitted to other components of the immune system, such as the B lymphocytes.

But in some instances infected macrophages seem to bypass the body's normal immune response network. In these cases, HIV is not passed on to the T4 cells or B cells. Thus, production of antibodies to the AIDS virus is not triggered. This finding may explain puzzling cases in which persons developed all the clinical signs of AIDS yet formed no detectable antibodies to the virus and showed no traces of the virus in their T4 cells. In fact, HIV has been isolated from the macrophages of some AIDS patients who had not produced antibodies and in whose T4 cells no virus was present. There are other reported cases in which carriers of the AIDS virus did not form antibodies for more than a year. Scientists believe the HIV could have concealed itself in the macrophages of these persons, then finally emerged and stimulated antibody production.

Disruption of macrophages by HIV infection may provide a clue to the prevalence of certain opportunistic infections in AIDS patients. The infections typical of AIDS primarily involve organisms that invade and kill body cells. These are exactly the class of organisms normally destroyed by macrophages.

One troubling implication of the macrophage research is clear: Persons who had been declared free of the AIDS virus by existing blood tests, based on the detection of antibodies made in response to HIV, may in fact be infected. HIV could be present in their macrophages. In addition, the blood supply could face new hazards. Blood banks screen donated blood for the presence of HIV by looking for virus antibodies.

A new test under development detects HIV in macrophages. The test involves a process called *polymerase chain reaction* (PCR), in which actual genetic material from the virus is magnified from blood and tissue samples.

Opportunistic Infections

Without adequate immune defenses, AIDS sufferers are susceptible to opportunistic infections and the diseases they engender. The infections connected with AIDS are a diverse group of pathogens: viruses, bacteria, fungi and protozoa. Even though everyone is exposed to them daily, these infectious agents do not normally cause illnesses in those whose immune systems are healthy. In AIDS patients, they are devastating and lethal.

The clinical courses of the opportunistic infections vary in severity. Some may recede after an initial manifestation, only to reappear soon after, perhaps in a more virulent form. Certain maladies respond to drug therapies and may be brought under control for a time. However, AIDS patients are ordinarily afflicted with multiple infections at the same time. Thus, even if one is temporarily treatable, another will continue to ravage the body. The areas of the body most often targeted by opportunistic infections include the lungs, skin, gastrointestinal tract, eyes, lymph nodes and brain.

Following are some of the opportunistic infections frequently diagnosed in AIDS patients:

Pneumocystic carinii pneumonia (PCP): A parasitic infection that afflicts the lungs, it is the most common life-threatening condition in AIDS patients. The initial signs of this disorder are difficulty in breathing, dry cough and fever. It occurs at least once in more than two-thirds of all AIDS sufferers. With early diagnosis and drug therapy, approximately 90% of AIDS patients survive their first bout of this disease. One problem in treating AIDS patients with PCP is that a large number react adversely to drug therapies. Early and aggressive treatment with aerosol pentamadine has proved effective in preventing the pneumonia.

Cytomegalovirus (CMV): This virus is a member of the herpes virus group. The most common sign of its presence in AIDS patients is spots on the retina, which can lead to blindness. CMV also causes pneumonia, esophagitis and colitis. It is the primary cause of death in some cases. CMV infections respond poorly to antiviral chemotherapy. Several new drugs have shown promise in clinical trials, particularly ganciclovir. Among AIDS patients, clinical improvements generally have been brief and relapses common.

Candida albicans: This yeastlike fungus initially manifests itself in whitish sores along the mouth. This can be one of the first signs of an immune system weakened by HIV. AIDS patients develop candidiasis lesions affecting the throat and brain. *Candida albicans* infections respond to antifungal therapy, but in AIDS patients the disease often reappears as soon as therapy has been completed.

Toxoplasma gondii: This parasite is the most common cause of inflammation of the brain in AIDS victims. Patients show some clinical improvement within weeks of the start of appropriate therapy, but relapses are common even after six months of treatment.

Cryptosporidium: This protozoan parasite causes severe diarrhea. In AIDS the diarrhea becomes chronic and may lead to malnutrition. Treatment of this disorder remains experimental.

Kaposi's sarcoma (KS): A previously rare cancer affecting older men of Mediterranean descent, it is included in the definition of AIDS because of its unusually high frequency in homosexual men with immune system compromises, even in the absence of opportunistic infections. The disease manifests itself clinically as painless purple-to-brown skin lesions on the legs and torso. Later, swollen lymph nodes develop, indicating spread of the cancer to the lymphatic system. KS is the second most common AIDS-associated disease, after PCP. The high incidence of KS in homosexuals with AIDS contrasts with a low incidence among IV drug abusers with AIDS. This implies that some factor responsible for KS is probably related to sexual contact. Although radiotherapy and some drugs, notably alpha-interferon, have had limited success in treating KS, most patients usually die of another irreversible opportunistic infection before completing the course of their treatment.

HIV-Related Conditions

Initially, the diagnosis of AIDS required the presence of an opportunistic infection or KS in the absence of other known causes of immune deficiency. Over time physicians noticed that other milder conditions related to AIDS, but clinically distinct from it, were appearing in the same risk groups for AIDS. When HIV was isolated and a test developed to screen for the virus, the means were available to suggest a range of HIV-related transmissible immunodeficiency conditions. These are the recognized conditions:

AIDS: The most extreme, it is fatal on average within two years of diagnosis. The collapse of the immune system allows lethal opportunistic infections to enter the body. Approximately half of all AIDS fatalities result from the otherwise rare form of pneumonia PCP. The federal CDC has set out these criteria for diagnosing the disease: (1) a positive blood test for antibody to HIV, or a positive cell culture for the virus; (2) a low number of T4 cells and a low ratio of T helper cells to T suppressor cells (T4:T8); (3) the presence of one or more designated opportunistic infections, or the appearance of Kaposi's sarcoma. These illnesses are indicators of underlying immune deficiency.

Roughly one-third of AIDS patients have had neurological disorders and symptoms of dementia. In some cases these problems have been attributable to opportunistic infections in the brain, or to depression. But in most instances, the problems appear to be a result of the direct effect of the AIDS virus on the brain, unrelated to opportunistic infections. Isolation of HIV from the brain cells and fluid of AIDS patients with neurological disorders lends support to this possibility.

The CDC classifies persons who have neurological disease linked to HIV as having AIDS, even when no opportunistic infections are present. Persons in this category may later develop an opportunistic infection and thus meet the standard criteria for diagnosis. Scientists have no set answer for why HIV appears to directly affect the brain in some patients. Speculation centers on the macrophages, white blood cells appearing naturally in the brain, in which the AIDS virus has been found.

AIDS-Related complex (ARC): While the CDC now effectively includes ARC under AIDS, much of the AIDS literature still distinguishes between the full-blown disease and a less-debilitating phase. Initial symptoms of ARC include weight loss, swollen lymph nodes, fever, diarrhea, fatigue and night sweats. Mild infections may also appear, such as oral thrush or the viral illness herpes zoster. As with AIDS, ARC is characterized by immune and blood abnormalities, including lower levels of T4 cells and an altered ratio of T4 to T8 cells. Persons with ARC have tested positive to exposure with HIV in blood or tissue culture tests. But the damage to the immune system is more moderate than is seen in AIDs. Most important, persons with ARC do not have opportunistic infections or KS. The clinical course of ARC is less severe than AIDS. Currently, the number of reported cases of ARC is 10 times greater than the number of persons with confirmed AIDS. The risk of a person with ARC eventually developing full-blown AIDS is unclear. Studies suggest that the configuration of ARC symptoms in a patient may indicate the risk of progression to AIDS.

Generalized lymphadenopathy syndrome (GLS): GLS is characterized by swollen lymph nodes over a course of at least three months. Individuals with GLS test positive for the presence of HIV antibodies. GLS does not involve opportunistic infections, KS or the general symptoms associated with ARC. Milder immune deficiency is a feature. Researchers are uncertain whether GLS is a definite precursor to AIDS, or a separate illness leading to AIDS in only some cases.

HIV antibody positivity (Seropositivity): Existing blood-screening tests detect the antibodies produced after exposure to and infection with HIV. Significant numbers of persons in high-risk groups test positive for the HIV antibody, indicating prior exposure to the AIDS virus. Infection with a retrovirus is lifelong. Individuals who test antibody-positive do not necessarily have AIDS or any of its other clinical conditions. It is not clear what proportion of those who carry the AIDS virus will eventually develop AIDS. Most seropositive persons appear healthy and are asymptomatic. Still, they are able to transmit the virus to others in this asymptomatic condition. Public health officials estimate that 1.0 to 1.5 million Americans are at present seropositive.

Acute infection: An acute illness marked by fever, swollen lymph nodes, lethargy and diarrhea manifests itself in some persons within 3 to 12 weeks after exposure to HIV. The condition is thought to be an initial reaction to infection with the AIDS virus.

Transmission

After extensive epidemiological studies, the CDC concludes that HIV is transmitted in the following ways: (1) through the exchange of blood, semen or vaginal secretions during intimate sexual contact; (2) from transfusions of HIV-contaminated blood products; (3) through the shared use of contaminated hypodermic needles; and (4) from an infected pregnant woman to her fetus. Medical experts also suspect mother-to-child transmission during breast-feeding, through either breast milk or possibly blood from cracked nipples, although this means remains open to question. Public health authorities insist that no case of transmission of the AIDS virus through casual contact has been conclusively demonstrated. HIV has been found in saliva and tears, but no instance of the virus spreading through contact with these bodily fluids has been proved.

Sexual contact: Sexual contact appears to be the most common way of transmitting HIV. Semen containing white blood cells infected with HIV comes into contact with tissue in the rectum and vagina. The virus can then enter the bloodstream of the host through perforations in the tissue surface. The risk of this happening is greatest in anal intercourse, either between two men or a man and a woman. The risk of transmission, though diminished, is also present in vaginal intercourse. Transmission of HIV by oral-genital contact has not been documented.

The lining of the anus is easily torn. Thus, the risk of infection among homosexual men is higher for the receptive partner. Homosexual men with many different sexual partners are at greater risk of infection because of the increased probability of exposure to an infected mate.

Because HIV is present in semen, it follows that men can transmit the virus to women through either anal or vaginal intercourse. Even though studies suggest that heterosexual transmission does happen in either direction between men and women, medical experts acknowledge that males convey the AIDS virus much more effectively than females. Female-to-male transmission can occur, but statistically the risk is reduced dramatically. There have been a scattering of such documented cases in the United States. HIV has been isolated from the vaginal or cervical secretion of women, but in amounts considerably less than that ordinarily found in infected blood and semen. Researchers believe that women infect men during vaginal intercourse when secretions carrying the virus reach the urethral lining of the penis.

Initial studies of female prostitutes fed speculation about heterosexual female-to-male transmission. At first, researchers found an alarming prevalence of seropositivity in prostitutes in the United States, as high as 25% in some urban centers, and numbers of infected heterosexual men without other prior risk factors reported contact with female prostitutes.

Subsequent studies, however, have suggested that HIV infection among prostitutes is not as widespread as initially presumed. These more-recent surveys revealed nationwide infection rates from 5% to 12% and found that the overriding majority of prostitutes carrying the AIDS virus were IV drug users. AIDS epidemiologists now surmise that the sharing of contaminated needles to inject drugs—rather than multiple sexual contacts—is the major factor behind the incidence of HIV infection among prostitutes. Scant evidence has emerged of female prostitutes sexually transmitting HIV to their male patrons.

Risk of heterosexual transmission appears to be less severe than what was being projected in the middle and late 1980s. The predicted explosion of the epidemic among the general heterosexual population (apart from IV drug users) has not occurred.

Exchange of blood: HIV is spread through a direct exchange of blood or blood products. This mode of transmission is most frequent among IV drug users who share injection needles. It includes, as well, hemophiliacs and other persons who receive blood transfusions, and fetuses of mothers who carry the AIDS virus.

IV drug users commonly share unsterile needles. These needles transmit HIV from the blood of one individual to the blood of another individual. In New York City it is estimated that contaminated needles are responsible for transmission in 90% of the cases of AIDS among heterosexuals. Exacerbating the problem, IV drug users are far less likely than other groups to engage in safe sexual practices. Experts predict this group will be hardest hit by the epidemic in the 1990s.

Hemophiliacs have been a high-risk group for HIV infection because of their medical need for transfusions of special blood products. Hemophiliacs, who are almost exclusively male, have an inherited bleeding disorder. They lack a single protein essential to normal coagulation. Factor VIII is a special blood-factor concentrate made from pooled blood. Hemophiliacs receive it through transfusions, and it permits normal blood clotting. Factor VIII is made from the blood plasma of thousands of different donors. Before the development of more effective blood-screening tests in 1985, the AIDS virus entered undetected into these blood-clotting agents. The first cases of AIDS among hemophiliacs were reported in July of 1982 among heterosexuals with no history of IV drug abuse.

In the United States, 2% of adults with AIDS have been infected with HIV through whole-blood transfusions. Among children with AIDS the figure is 10%. Current procedures for screening blood donors and donated blood will continue to restrict this mode of transmission.

The majority of children with AIDS contract the virus from their infected mothers in utero. In one scenario the mother may pass the virus in her blood across the placenta to the fetus. In another, HIV is transmitted through blood contamination of the fetus at delivery.

Casual contact: There is no demonstrated instance of the spread of the AIDS virus by casual contact. Public health officials say this point is borne out by comprehensive research on persons who have had extensive nonsexual exposure to individuals afflicted with the range of AIDS-related conditions, either as health care workers or as members of the same household.

Studies by the CDC indicate that HIV is rarely transmitted to health care workers even when they have had prolonged contact with AIDS patients. In most cases where transmission has occurred, health care workers accidentally stuck themselves with needles contaminated with the blood of a person who carried HIV. Statistical evidence suggests that the risk of infection in this manner is slight (about 0.4%). Several cases of transmission of HIV from a patient to a health care provider other than through a needle injury have been documented. But in these instances the individuals who contracted the virus apparently did not follow precautions recommended by the CDC.

The prevailing view in much of the medical community is that family members and housemates of seropositive persons who are not their sexual partners are not at increased risk of contracting the virus. Results of a comprehensive study of families of people with AIDS or ARC, in which there was considerable sharing of household items and facilities, indicated that HIV is not transmitted through casual contact. The CDC claims that no case of AIDS virus transmission has been documented among household members except sexual partners or persons in some independent high-risk group.

There has been public concern that seropositive children may infect healthy children in school or during play. The CDC holds that no reported case of HIV infection in the United States has been transmitted in school or at day care. The CDC recommends that children carrying the virus be allowed to attend school regularly, with the possible exception of a physically combative child, or one with open skin lesions.

Risk Groups

Over the course of the AIDS epidemic, the CDC has compiled cumulative statistics on reported cases in the United States. These have been classified into groups in an effort to track the epidemiology of the disease. The first established category was homosexual or bisexual men. As AIDS appeared in a wider range of groups, more categories were added. These groups permit health authorities to chart the incidence of the syndrome and describe the pattern of its spread. Reported cases can then be represented in terms of the percentage of the total that makes up each category.

By extension, figures on reported cases have been used to define groups at risk of infection with HIV. In this context, the significant, defining feature of a group is the lifestyle pattern or behavior in which its members engage. Not all homosexual or bisexual men are inherently at risk of infection. Instead, homosexual or bisexual men who participate in specific sexual practices, with increased number of partners, are at increased risk of contracting the AIDS virus. This reasoning applies to all groups.

After nearly a decade, the AIDS epidemiology is showing significant shifts. Increasingly AIDS is becoming a disease of poor, black and Hispanic heterosexuals in America's inner cities. Yet gay men still account for most reported cases and are thought to be the majority of those who carry the AIDS virus but are not sick. However, there are some statistical indications since 1988 that the rate of increase of new cases among homosexual men has flattened out. The apparent leveling could reflect the adoption of safe sex practices in the mid-1980s. Skeptics, cautioning against quick conclusions, say a slowdown in the growth of new cases among gay men could be temporary, or perhaps only a perceived lull due to underreporting.

IV drug users and their sexual partners and babies—concentrated in the inner cities—now account for one-quarter of all AIDS cases. Strong evidence suggests HIV is spreading fastest among these groups. Minorities are disproportionately struck: 4 of 5 AIDS cases arising from the sharing of contaminated needles occur among blacks and Hispanics. The problem of AIDS babies is also largely one of urban minority communities. More than 80% of afflicted infants are black or Hispanic. In the overwhelming majority of cases, their mothers used drugs or were sexually involved with drug abusers.

According to public health experts, the success with which America curbs the spread of AIDS among drug addicts and the urban poor will determine the epidemic's future course more than any other factor. Currently, the main problem is a continuing inability to halt the spread of HIV among IV drug users and their sexual partners. This task calls for drug treatment programs and education directed at young people in hard-hit urban areas.

HIV has spread slowly among heterosexuals who do not use IV drugs. This marginal expansion has occurred mainly among the sexual partners of drug abusers. The proportion of AIDS cases attributable to heterosexual transmission of the virus stands at roughly 4%. So far there has been no indication of AIDS spreading explosively among the general heterosexual population.

The CDC classification of risk groups is divided between adults and children under the age of 13 (see accompanying chart).

MEDICAL RESPONSES TO AIDS

Health professionals have taken a three-pronged approach to the AIDS epidemic entailing the treatment of those afflicted with the disease, preventive measures to control the spread of the disease and the search for a vaccine and cure. The fact that AIDS is both contagious and incurable poses special problems. Substantial resources are being devoted to the search for a vaccine capable of protecting those who are not infected, and a cure for those who are. In the absence of a vaccine, emphasis has been placed on educating the public about the dangers of AIDS high-risk behavior.

Treatment

Treatment of AIDS patients proceed on several fronts. The first line of care is directed at containing the deadly opportunistic infections. Drugs, chemotherapy and radiation treatment are used to combat the parasitic infections and cancers of AIDS. These measures can be temporarily effective. Responsiveness varies from patient to patient. In most instances

Introduction to the AIDS Epidemic

CDC CLASSIFICATION
(figures through December 31, 1989)

ADULTS (91% Male; 9% Female)

% of Reported Cases[a]	Group
61	Sexually active homosexual and bisexual men
21	IV drug users who share injection needles
7	Homosexual men who are IV drug users
4	Heterosexuals who have intercourse with people infected with HIV
1	Hemophiliacs receiving HIV-contaminated blood products
2	Other persons who have received transfusions of contaminated blood
3	Unable or yet to be classified into any existing risk group

CHILDREN (54% Boys; 46% Girls)[b]

% of Reported Cases[a]	Group
82	Born infected
10	Blood transfusion related
5	Hemophilia related
3	Unable or yet to be classified into any existing risk group

[a] Percentages may not add up to 100 because of rounding.
[b] Under the age of 13.

the clinical improvements are transient and brief. Relapses and continued decline are predictable because the incapacitating AIDS virus remains. The underlying immune deficiency virtually guarantees the resurgence of disease symptoms.

Still, AIDS researchers and clinicians have made important progress and are able to cite improved treatments for some of the diseases that afflict their patients. Aerosol pentamadine, granted limited approval by the FDA, has proved effective in helping prevent *Pneumocystis carinii* pneumonia (PCP), the leading immediate cause of death in AIDS patients. Another drug, ganciclovir, has yielded encouraging results in the treatment of cytomegalovirus (CMV) infections that cause blindness. Thus in March 1989 the U.S. Public Health Service (PHS) permitted its restricted distribution to AIDS sufferers even before clinical trials were completed.

Physicians are now combating wasting syndrome, which involves debilitating weight loss and diarrhea, with total parenteral nutrition, a highly concentrated intravenous solution that nourishes patients who otherwise are unable to eat. The solution can extend life expectancy by six months to a year but, at $300 to $400 a day, is very expensive.

Emerging treatment methods are aimed at confining HIV, halting its growth and preventing its spread to other cells. The focus is on a class of antiviral therapies. These disrupt the AIDS virus's ability to replicate and create more virus. Antiviral techniques work by interfering with the function of the reverse transcriptase enzyme.

Numerous experimental drugs are now under study as antiviral agents. In late 1985, the NCI started clinical trials to evaluate suramin. In several cases, this drug suppressed reproduction of the AIDS virus. But no long-term clinical benefit was proved. Preliminary laboratory research with ribavirin, HPA-23 and interferon showed these agents to be capable of inhibiting reproduction of the AIDS virus in lymphocytes. In follow-up clinical trials conducted by the NIH, these drugs so far have demonstrated no consistent ability to arrest the progress of the disease or to reverse the course of infection. And there is an added complication. These therapies have toxic properties. When given to AIDS patients experimentally, they frequently cause adverse side effects.

Azidothymidine (AZT), also called ziduvodine, is the most encouraging advancement in the antiviral strategy. The Food and Drug Administration (FDA) approved AZT in March 1987 for marketing in the United States, under the brand name Retrovir. It remains the only drug authorized by the federal government to treat AIDS virus infection. Since it became commercially available, AZT has been found to prolong AIDS victims' lives and partially rebuild their immune systems. The drug's capacity to leave the blood and enter the brain makes it unique among antiviral therapies, holding out some promise for treatment of AIDS dementia. Experts also note trials in which children with AIDS improved dramatically, albeit temporarily, when administered the antiviral drug.

Government-sponsored studies now show for the first time that AZT can significantly delay the onset of AIDS both in people who are infected with the virus but still asymptomatic and in those who are mildly symptomatic. Prior to late 1989, AZT was demonstrated to be effective only in patients who already had full-fledged AIDS. These latest findings, of course, suggest that AZT could benefit almost half of the estimated million or more Americans infected with HIV.

Optimism is tempered by several facts. The drug causes severe anemia and other debilitating side effects in some patients. In addition, researchers have detected strains of HIV that have developed resistance to AZT. Another promising antiviral drug treatment, dideoxyinosine, or DDI, has benefited patients in preliminary studies without accompanying toxic side effects. Encouraged researchers have rushed the drug into expanded tests to compare it with AZT.

The attempt to restore the weakened immune systems of AIDS patients is a further treatment approach. Researchers at the National Institute of Allergy and Infectious Diseases (NIAID) have tried to rebuild the damaged natural defenses of AIDS patients through a combination of bone marrow transplants and transfers of T lymphocytes. These efforts sometimes resulted in improved immunologic function. But patients showed no enduring clinical improvement.

Efforts to stimulate natural body defenses have also involved the experimental use of drugs that boost or restore immune response. In tests Isoprinosine improved the immune function of patients with AIDS. Alpha-interferon and gamma-interferon have been shown to inhibit growth of HIV and repress some AIDS-related tumors in laboratory and clinical trials. Interleukin-2 and Imreg-1 are immune system enhancers now undergoing human tests. In clinical probes, none of these substances have altered the deteriorating clinical condition of AIDS patients over time. As with their antiviral counterparts, immune stimulators tend to induce dangerous side effects in human subjects. Researchers are now exploring the possible benefits of combination therapies. In this approach, antiviral agents and immune system enhancers are used together.

The presence of only one generally approved drug treatment for the AIDS virus has led many AIDS victims to experiment with unapproved substances. The use of pirated forms of drugs like AZT and ribavirin is widespread. Some patients travel overseas for treatments either unavailable in the United States or whose American costs are prohibitive.

Two of the most commonly sought unapproved drugs are AL-721 and dextran sulfate. AL-721, a substance made from eggs and soybeans, reduces the level of cholesterol in the membranes of white blood cells. This makes the membranes more fluid, supposedly hampering the ability of the AIDS virus to fasten to and invade body cells. Dextran sulfate, also a cholesterol-lowering substance, appears to impede the reproduction of HIV in laboratory experiments. While no adverse side effects have been attributed to the use of AL-721 or dextran sulfate, medical experts are skeptical about the benefits of these and other unsanctioned treatments.

Scientists have created a synthetic version of the CD4 protein found on the surface of T4 cells. This is the receptor protein to which HIV attaches. In tests, the synthetic protein has acted like a sponge, attracting and absorbing HIV before it can invade cells. The new findings on macrophages may have ominous implications for treatment. Most current therapies have been targeted at the effects of HIV on T lymphocytes. There is concern that these substances will not have a collateral effect on macrophages infected with HIV.

Medical experts at the 5th International Conference on AIDS in June 1989 focused on the fact that AIDS has become a chronic disease, responding marginally, or better, to some therapies. In the developed world scientists will find more and more promising drugs. Life expectancy of patients from time of diagnosis will continue to improve. But it will be years before science yields a thoroughly effective treatment for HIV infection.

Prevention

As the AIDS epidemic has evolved, the search for medical solutions has accelerated. Rarely has the scientific community responded so quickly to a new medical problem. Yet there are inherent limits to the pace of progress. Development of safe and effective drugs for combating the disease is a time-consuming pursuit. Researchers face many obstacles in their search for a vaccine against HIV. Until antiviral therapies and a vaccine are available for widespread use, physicians and public health officials point to prevention as the best means at hand for curbing the spread of the AIDS virus.

Transmission of HIV is primarily attributed to high-risk sexual behavior or intravenous drug abuse. Immediate control of the epidemic depends on education and other public health measures to discourage or change these behaviors. Risk-reduction education is the cornerstone of the preventive public health strategy. Initial efforts were directed mainly at members of high-risk groups because their lifestyle patterns placed them in the clearest danger of either contracting or transmitting the virus.

Expanded educational initiatives now include campaigns directed at the general population. While risk reduction is a central focus, the larger aim of these efforts is to enhance the public's fundamental understanding of the disease. Public schools increasingly are including AIDS instruction in their health curricula. Former U.S. Surgeon General C. Everett Koop pioneered a leading role for the federal government in providing explicit information to the public in pronouncements, printed materials and nationwide mailings.

Education is supplemented by public health measures for containing the disease. The CDC has provided guidelines for preventing transmission of HIV in the workplace. These recommendations are directed especially at health care professionals involved in the treatment of patients with AIDS-related conditions.

The FDA, in conjunction with blood banks and the blood-products industry, has taken steps to safeguard the nation's blood supply. Since the development of tests for detecting exposure to the virus in early 1985, all donated blood has undergone screening for evidence of contamination with HIV.

Vaccine

Public health education and the development of treatments to suppress the virus are the short-term goals in the fight against AIDS. The one hope for halting the spread of the disease completely is widespread immunization of uninfected persons. Inoculation with a vaccine gives a person immunity from the disease.

A vaccine is a virus or part of a virus that has been physically altered so that it loses its disease-producing properties. At the same time, it retains enough of its unique chemical structure to be able to stimulate an immune response when administered to a human subject. This resulting response is able to protect the person from the live virus. In this way vaccines act like a natural infection in their effect on immunity. They induce lasting resistance to the virus by stimulating the recipient to produce and accumulate specific antibodies and cells that can mount an effective defense when challenged by later exposure to the actual virus. Again, the development of a safe vaccine assumes that the part of the virus used to provoke an immune reaction has been rendered unable to cause disease.

The search for a vaccine is an expanding frontier in AIDS research. The task is formidable. Within a scientific time frame, AIDS is a new disease. Scientists are still attempting to construct a profile of HIV that accounts for all of its characteristics. Complete understanding of the virus and its tendencies is essential to the discovery of a successful immunizing agent.

Vaccines are difficult to design and adequately test. Before a new one can be safely given to human subjects, repeated laboratory trials must demonstrate that the vaccine itself will not cause disease. HIV has a long and variable incubation period. The interval between infection and the appearance of disease symptoms might be four or more years. This makes any assessment of a potential vaccine's utility and safeness difficult.

Clinical trials require hundreds of volunteer subjects from high-risk groups who are not infected. Following inoculation, they have to be monitored for long periods to determine the vaccine's impact and to detect any evidence of adverse reactions. Historically, experimental vaccinations have produced the very disease against which they were designed to provide immunity in at least some persons. HIV is particularly dangerous. Medical experts are sensitive to the possibility of an altered, weakened strain of the virus, in vaccine form, regaining its devastating capacity after it has been administered.

Scientists face other barriers in the development of a vaccine. The chemical makeup of the AIDS virus protein coat is variable and appears to mutate rapidly (antigenic variation). These features suggest that a vaccine protecting against one strain of HIV may not offer immunity against alternate forms. There is the added possibility that antibodies alone cannot protect against the course of HIV infection. Immunity may require a more complex response involving many immune system functions.

Half a dozen vaccines are in the early stages of testing, with some already showing promise in animal studies and limited human trials. An experimental vaccine called gp160 has received approval by the PHS for human tests. It is a purified protein derived from a portion of the HIV outer coat. Its developer, the MicroGeneSys Company, now reports that gp160 has induced an immune response in six subjects on a trial basis. Whether the test subjects developed a reaction that provides protection against HIV is yet to be determined.

A team of scientists in California led by polio vaccine pioneer Dr. Jonas Salk is attempting to develop an agent that would both prevent initial HIV infection and help those already infected by forestalling development of full-blown AIDS. Salk claims his experimental vaccine has wiped out traces of HIV in tests on AIDS-infected chimpanzees. But he cautions that the findings are only preliminary, noting that much more research and follow-up testing lie ahead.

A long process is expected before these efforts result in an effective, sanctioned product. Medical experts attending the 5th International Conference on AIDS in Montreal, Canada, offered a sober assessment. They indicated that a prototype vaccine against HIV will probably not be available for another 10 years.

Cure

Researchers are guarded about prospects for an AIDS cure in the foreseeable future. For people already diagnosed with AIDS and those who are seropositive, hope rests on the development of a way to eliminate HIV from the body. Characteristics of the AIDS virus magnify the challenge scientists face. The main complication is the way in which HIV inserts itself into the genetic machinery of infected cells and becomes fully integrated. The virus lacks a sufficiently complex and unique internal composition to differentiate it from the cell it invades. Once inside, HIV is structurally indistinguishable from the infected host cell. No current antiviral drug can selectively pick out and destroy the AIDS virus while leaving the surrounding cell intact and unharmed.

The search for a cure has led researchers to consider possibilities suggested by the advances made in molecular genetics. But this branch of science is not at the point where specific genes of a virus can be isolated in living cells and individually removed. This is what would be required to reverse the course of infection with HIV.

The isolation of HIV from brain cells and cerebrospinal fluid further complicates the quest for a cure. A functional barrier exists between the brain's blood vessels and other blood cells throughout the body. It is called the blood–brain barrier. It serves as a filter, preventing impurities and other substances in the bloodstream that might damage tissue from entering the brain. Scientists now speculate that HIV gains access to the brain by infected macrophages. These white blood cells, naturally present in the brain, are able to pass across the filter. Evidence that the brain and spinal cord are key locations for the AIDS virus suggests that any effective antiviral treatment for the disease must also be able to penetrate the blood–brain barrier.

HEALTH CARE ISSUES

The AIDS epidemic has raised difficult health care issues. These primarily include the strains AIDS places on the health care system; protection of the blood supply against HIV contamination; policies and procedures for HIV testing programs; and the provision of unproven new drugs to terminally ill patients.

The full parameters of the AIDS crisis are still not unalterably established. The brief clinical history of the disease has not been sufficient time for scientists to determine with certainty how many people carrying the AIDS virus will actually develop AIDS. Medical researchers are also not sure if less-severe immune deficiency conditions linked to HIV infection are a definite precursor to AIDS.

The actual number of people infected with HIV remains unknown. For the public health community, gauging the magnitude of HIV infection is critical. This figure is the basis for making statistical projections of the epidemic's future scope. The balance of estimates places it at between 1.0 and 1.5 million persons. Experts acknowledge that the number could be as low as 400,000 or as high as 4 million. There is likewise no totally reliable data on the rate at which new cases of infection are occurring.

A lack of solid answers to these questions has limited the ability of health authorities to fashion a comprehensive strategy for responding to the AIDS epidemic. Despite these uncertainties, health professionals agree that even the most conservative projections for HIV infection presage a massive national health crisis in the 1990s.

The AIDS epidemic has stretched the health care system, exposing gaps in existing facilities and resources as growing numbers of patients require a wider range of services. Medical facilities are challenged to deal with these growing numbers and the soaring cost of care they foretell. Those who have AIDS are often afflicted with rare infections requiring expensive specialized treatment. At the end of 1989, analysts calculated the average total cost of providing medical care to an AIDS patient at approximately $60,000.

The impact of AIDS on health care and the availability of services varies markedly by region and economic status. In cities with large case-loads, such as New York and San Francisco, municipal resources are severely stretched. Hospitals are increasingly filled with AIDS patients who often could receive less costly and more personalized care through other kinds of institutions, such as nursing homes, hospices and home-care services. But these alternatives are insufficient to meet current needs, much less the burgeoning future requirements. With improving medical treatments, many patients are deteriorating less rapidly and living longer. More and more patients require not acute hospital care but help with their daily lives at home.

Some communities have successfully initiated outpatient care services, opening AIDS hospices and nursing homes that have reduced costs and alleviated the demand for available hospital beds. Experts believe this kind of care, with its more personal atmosphere, improves the outlook and, by extension, the clinical condition of many AIDS patients.

Human resources are also a factor. Government and private studies have identified the immediate need to expand the pool of trained health care specialists. Medical facilities in New York City report that their ability to handle the rising caseload is already jeopardized by severe staff shortages.

Still greater economic strains lie ahead for the patchwork of local, state and federal programs now contending with the AIDS financial burden. Federal health officials project that 172,000 diagnosed AIDS patients will require medical care by the end of 1992. If current epidemiological trends hold, one-quarter or more of new AIDS cases will be IV drug users or their sexual partners—groups most likely to need some form of public assistance. Even middle-class patients are sometimes forced to rely on Medicaid, the federal government's health insurance program for the indigent, to pay enormous AIDS medical bills. Federal authorities calculate that 60% of AIDS patients end up receiving Medicaid funding.

Recent studies indicate that most of the estimated million or more Americans infected with HIV who are either mildly symptomatic or asymptomatic can benefit from taking the drug AZT. This finding is certain to have major consequences for the health care system. Experts forecast billions of dollars in new costs. These outlays would be necessary to fund expected surges in AIDS virus testing and to pay the AZT bill for dramatically greater numbers of people.

Insurance companies have eyed with concern the potentially staggering expense of providing health insurance coverage to persons infected with HIV. Industry analysts estimate that the total cost of caring for AIDS patients will run between $5 billion and $13 billion by 1992. Some states require insurance companies to offer coverage to HIV-infected persons. Many of these individuals, however, cannot afford the steep premiums involved. State and local officials in those regions hit hardest by the epidemic, facing escalating budget outlays, have called for increased assistance from the federal government. But such calls come at a time when all levels of government are grappling with deficits and limited fiscal resources.

CDC guidelines have proved effective in protecting health care workers from accidentally contracting HIV. The concern now is for the many health care professionals facing burnout from the emotional demands of working with so many terminally ill patients. Several hospitals have initiated counseling programs for their personnel.

In New York City, new AIDS cases among IV drug users have surpassed those reported among homosexuals since the first quarter of 1988. This development reflects a nationwide trend. Health officials now generally acknowledge that IV drug abuse represents the most serious threat for the spread of the AIDS virus.

In June 1988 government health experts, at an AIDS long-range planning meeting convened by the PHS, identified expanded and improved drug treatment programs as essential for slowing the AIDS epidemic. Similar recommendations were presented the same month in reports prepared by the National Academy of Sciences (NAS) and the president's commission on AIDS.

In 1988 New York City pioneered a controversial program to distribute free, clean needles to drug addicts to stem the spread of the AIDS virus. Critics contended that the step promoted the use of illegal narcotics and undermined the war on drugs. They called the program an insensitive substitute for more drug prevention education and treatment centers in minority neighborhoods. City officials explained that they authorized the experiment as part of an effort to halt transmission of the AIDS virus by IV drug users who share contaminated hypodermic syringes. This program, under fire and poorly used, was discontinued at the end of 1989. Scores of other programs nationwide have yielded mixed findings on the effectiveness of needle-exchange efforts. Some experts now speculate that a number of these campaigns have failed to curb transmission of HIV because they overlook other routes of infection.

Public confusion about the risks of contracting AIDS through contaminated needles led to a marked decrease in blood donations during the early and mid-1980s. Health officials were able to make the case that the process of giving blood posed no danger whatsoever to the donor, and contributions gradually returned to normal levels.

The public faced a very real danger because donations by persons in high-risk groups had introduced the AIDS virus into the nation's blood supply. By the end of 1982, health authorities had documented several cases of individuals who had become infected with HIV through blood transfusions. These findings carried troubling implications, and made it clear that action was necessary to protect the safety of blood products.

Researchers had not yet found the cause of AIDS; thus, no test existed that could detect the presence of the still-unknown agent in blood. In March 1983, acting on recommendations from the PHS, the Red Cross and other blood services announced they would screen for high-risk blood donors. Voluntary restraint by persons in high-risk groups was urged. In response to public fears about the blood supply, a number of private organizations emerged that arranged for persons to store their own blood for future use. The issue was largely resolved with the discovery of the AIDS virus and subsequent development of procedures to screen for its presence. In October 1984 the FDA approved the first HIV blood test. The following February the agency ordered blood banks to screen all donated blood products for the AIDS virus.

The ability to test for HIV infection gave health authorities the tool they needed to chart the course of the AIDS epidemic. Much debate, though, has centered on the ways in which testing for the AIDS virus should be conducted.

Because HIV infection is believed to be concentrated in certain high-risk groups, health experts have maintained that widespread testing of the general population is unnecessary. Mandatory testing has been limited to a small number of groups where unique requirements exist for knowing an individual's medical status. Groups now tested include the military, foreign service personnel, immigrants and prisoners.

The vast majority of those involved in AIDS issues has favored voluntary rather than mandatory HIV testing programs for persons in high-risk groups. Legal experts have noted the civil rights issues raised by involuntary blood-screening programs. Health professionals, citing their concern that individuals at high risk will not come forward for testing if they fear results will be disclosed, have stressed the need for strict confidentiality assurances.

The psychological and emotional toll on persons who learn they are infected with HIV can be devastating. Suicide rates for individuals with AIDS far exceed the demographic norm. It has become standard practice for individuals who test seropositive to receive professional counseling at the time they are informed of their status.

The desperate plight of many AIDS patients has been a source of sustained controversy over federal rules and regulations governing the approval of new medical drugs. FDA guidelines call for extensive testing and clinical trials of drugs prior to their licensing for patient use. This standard approval process takes a minimum of several years. The intent is to ensure the drugs are effective and do not cause harmful side effects.

For AIDS patients facing clinical deterioration and death, these precautions are academic. The paucity of AIDS drugs has led many patients to circumvent the U.S. drug approval system. Since the mid-1980s an underground network to provide AIDS patients with experimental drugs from abroad, where licensing requirements are less strict, has functioned.

The medical community has debated the extent to which dying patients should be allowed access to unproven new drug therapies. The general concurrence has been that different rules should be applied in circumstances where patients have no hope of survival. In 1987 the FDA instituted a program to speed experimental drugs to the terminally ill. Since then, under pressure from AIDS advocacy groups and in light of encouraging developments on the early and preventive treatment fronts, the agency has further adjusted its drug-approval policies. It now allows individual AIDS sufferers to import selective experimental therapies from other countries for their own use. In addition, the FDA is making other drug treatments available even before clinical trials in the United States are completed.

In the spring of 1988, public health officials in states along the East Coast from Maryland to Massachusetts confronted a new AIDS health issue. AIDS-contaminated medical waste that had been dumped in the ocean started washing up on beaches in the region. Local authorities moved quickly to implement measures that would preclude a recurrence of the problem. Many beaches had to be closed to the public for extended periods, resulting in a great loss of revenue for oceanfront communities.

In November 1988 President Reagan signed into law a measure instructing the Environmental Protection Agency (EPA) to set up a program for tracking the disposal of medical waste in New York, New Jersey, Connecticut and the Great Lakes states. Under the legislation, the EPA is required to report regularly to Congress on the health threat posed by such medical debris as needles, vials and blood bags.

PRIVATE SECTOR INVOLVEMENT

AIDS did not emerge as a full-scale epidemic. It started slowly, with isolated cases appearing in homosexual communities in New York and California. The number of cases reported at the end of 1981 was slightly more than 150. The pace of new cases gradually accelerated, and by December 31, 1984, the CDC had recorded 7,699 Americans with the disease. After 1984, the precipitous rate of increase in newly diagnosed cases would quickly make the AIDS epidemic the health issue of the decade.

Private sector responses to the AIDS epidemic have followed a similar pattern. Initially, concerns about the emerging disease were confined to members of the gay community and a handful of medical professionals. This changed as the potential scale of the epidemic became apparent. As time went on, growing numbers of private organizations, institutions and individuals became involved in the AIDS crisis.

Homosexual groups, confronted with a lethal new medical condition sweeping through the gay neighborhoods in San Francisco and New York City, were the first to mobilize against the mysterious affliction. They were joined by local physicians and other health professionals struggling to cope with the outbreak of the disease. In both cities, clinics were established to handle the rising number of AIDS cases. As the epidemic evolved, spreading out from these coastal centers to locations in between, gay communities nationwide similarly organized to meet this new threat.

Homosexual organizations increasingly turned their attention to the expanding health crisis. Gay leaders, perceiving a need for specific action to deal with the impending epidemic, formed new agencies. Together these became a key element of the private response in America. In January 1982 the Gay Men's Health Crisis (GMHC) was established in New York City to coordinate fund-raising efforts for AIDS programs and to provide outreach services to AIDS patients. In subsequent years, organizations such as People With Aids were formed to furnish support services to mounting numbers of AIDS sufferers and to spearhead a campaign to accelerate the availability of experimental AIDS drug therapies.

Since 1986, the AIDS Coalition to Unleash Power, or ACT-UP, has been active politically and culturally in pressuring all levels of government and the medical establishment to respond to the AIDS crisis with funding and other concrete actions. The groups' aggressive protest tactics have sometimes drawn sharp criticism, but members defend their methods as being necessary to keep leaders focused on the epidemic and its consequences.

As the first AIDS cases were reported to the CDC in Atlanta, the federal public health system was energized to track, describe and control the new epidemic. The burden of caring for AIDS patients fell primarily on the private medical community. Several major university research facilities undertook studies of the new disease, either independently or in coordination with public health authorities.

Resources were frequently scarce. Many physicians and scientists were frustrated by the bureaucratic delays and complicated review processes involved in securing federal research grants and assistance. In response, medical professionals also turned to private fund-raising enterprises. In June 1983 Dr. Mathilde Krim organized the AIDS Medical Foundation to help finance private AIDS research and treatment programs.

Established national gay organizations revised their priorities as AIDS became the preeminent item on the homosexual community's agenda. The National Gay Task Force (NGTF), with headquarters in Washington, D.C., assumed a prominent role in AIDS political issues. The National Gay Rights Advocates (NGRA) and LAMBDA Legal Defense and Education Fund concentrated their expertise on the difficult legal issues raised by the epidemic. The first private conference on AIDS was held in August 1982 as part of a meeting of the National Lesbian and Gay Leadership Conference.

A sense of urgency over the possible consequences of a new and apparently contagious condition was not shared uniformly throughout the gay community in the first years of the epidemic. Homosexual leaders were sharply divided over the impact and meaning of the new disease.

By the spring of 1982, medical researchers were convinced AIDS was transmitted by certain kinds of sexual activity in which homosexuals commonly engaged. Studies indicated that chances of contracting the disease increased proportionally with the number of sexual partners. That summer, the GMHC published a newsletter on measures gay men could take to reduce the risks of getting AIDS. The newsletter's message generated controversy. Numerous gays felt that, after the struggles of the 1960s and 1970s, homosexuality had finally entered a more liberated era. Many resisted the suggestion of new restraints on homosexual lifestyles, arguing that evidence on AIDS transmission was inconclusive. Those who advocated curbing more promiscuous sexual behavior were labeled as either alarmist or reflective of the homophobic tendencies of the society at large.

In March 1983, the playwright and gay activist Larry Kramer published an article in the *New York Native*. Entitled "1112 and Counting," in reference to the number of reported AIDS cases, it was a forceful articulation of the need for the homosexual community to realize that AIDS was not a question of sexual politics but a matter of survival. The article is credited with having changed the way in which AIDS was debated in the gay community.

Surveys at the time indicated that an increasing number of gays were refraining from sexual behavior that placed them at high risk of catching AIDS. The debate over sexual lifestyles finally culminated in the issue of homosexual bathhouses. To many, the bathhouses were a symbol of newly won sexual freedom. Local health authorities and gay leaders involved in the AIDS crisis saw the bathhouses as facilitating sexual practices that furthered the rapid spread of the disease. By 1985, over strong opposition from gay rights activists, municipal authorities in New York and San Francisco had undertaken ultimately successful campaigns to close these establishments.

The watershed year in the AIDS epidemic is generally considered to be 1985. Prior to then, a loose coalition of gay organizations, medical professionals and local civic and political leaders had come together to press for greater public awareness of the pending AIDS crisis. Much of the public, however, continued to perceive the disease as a gay issue. The epidemic was not seen as having a direct impact on mainstream American life.

This perception began to change with the revelation in the summer of 1985 that the actor Rock Hudson had AIDS. The announcement resulted in extensive press coverage of the epidemic. News stories highlighted the terrible human cost of the disease and the impediments researchers faced in trying to find a vaccine and cure. Coverage of the progressive upsurge in the number of new AIDS cases reinforced the fact that the epidemic was a national problem. Public concerns were heightened by the appearance of reports exploring the risks of heterosexual transmission of AIDS.

A number of Rock Hudson's colleagues in the entertainment industry were inspired to take part in AIDS activities. In September 1985 Elizabeth Taylor was named director of the just-created American Foundation for AIDS Research (AmFAR). With the support of artists and celebrities, the organization has raised millions of dollars for private medical research.

Professional organizations representing fields affected by AIDS have entered into the public discourse over the disease. The American Medical Association (AMA) and the American Bar Association (ABA) have had to confront the complex clinical and legal issues raised by the epidemic. The National Academy of Sciences (NAS), in successive reports on the federal government's response to the AIDS epidemic, has stressed the pressing need for accelerated government action in the battle against the epidemic.

GOVERNMENT INVOLVEMENT

Government involvement in the AIDS crisis has grown as the size and impact of the epidemic have increased. Public officials at federal, state and local levels have struggled to implement effective policies for dealing with the new disease. The federal government has defined AIDS as the nation's top health priority. Government spending on AIDS now totals in the billions of dollars and encompasses treatment programs, research activities, prevention and education measures, and the development and testing of drugs and vaccines.

The first federal government agency to become involved in the AIDS epidemic was the CDC. In June 1981, the CDC formed the Kaposi's Sarcoma and Opportunistic Infections (KSOI) Task Force to investigate the recent incidence of KS and PCP cases in New York and California. The task force's inquiry revealed that these cases were the precursor of a new epidemic.

Other agencies in the PHS were enlisted in response to the emerging health crisis. Federal laboratories at the NIH initiated preliminary research on AIDS. The FDA was engaged in efforts to safeguard the nation's blood supply from AIDS contamination. In June 1983, Department of Health and Human Services (HHS) Secretary Margaret M. Heckler officially characterized AIDS as the department's number-one health priority.

The federal health system's involvement in the AIDS crisis rapidly expanded. The KSOI Task Force's activities broadened and underwent several reorganizations. While continuing to track the epidemiology of the disease, the CDC has issued extensive guidelines on AIDS health issues. These include measures persons should take to reduce or eliminate the risks of contracting AIDS, precautions health care workers should follow to prevent accidental infection and procedures for the education and care of children with AIDS.

National research laboratories concentrated first on finding the cause of the new disease syndrome. With the discovery of the AIDS virus in 1984, scientists turned to the more difficult tasks of developing a vaccine and a cure. The urgent need for medicines to treat both the opportunistic infections associated with AIDS and the AIDS virus itself forced the FDA to reexamine its procedures for approving new drug therapies. Since 1987 the agency has revised its policies, allowing AIDS patients to import unapproved drugs from abroad for personal use and accelerating the approval process for promising experimental AIDS therapies. Considerable research emphasis at the NIAID is placed on the testing of drugs for AIDS-related conditions.

At first, federal funding for AIDS programs was drawn from existing health agency budgets. Activities such as the KSOI Task Force were initially financed through monies already allocated to the PHS. In late 1982 and 1983 Congress authorized several supplemental appropriations to augment PHS efforts to mobilize against the disease. In subsequent years, designated AIDS expenditures have been incorporated into the federal budget.

Since 1982, federal allocations for AIDS have risen substantially. In 1985, total federal spending on AIDS—including research, education and prevention programs and medical care for the sick—just exceeded $200 million. Total government outlays in 1989 were approximately $2.2 billion, of which the PHS received $1.3 billion for its research, education and prevention efforts. Resources committed to AIDS in 1990 roughly equal those allocated to the war on cancer. Cumulative AIDS expenditures at the federal level from 1982 to 1989 totaled $5.5 billion. Based on spending trends and projected costs by federal agencies, annual federal spending should reach $4.3 billion in 1992. Although this would represent continued growth in AIDS funding, some critics contend it still is not adequate in light of the widespread effects of the disease.

Congress took an early interest in the AIDS epidemic. In April 1982 Representative Henry A. Waxman (D-CA), chairman of the House Subcommittee on Health and the Environment, conducted the first of many congressional hearings on AIDS. The subcommittee became a strong advocate for greater federal involvement in the AIDS crisis. In December 1983, Representative Theodore S. Weiss (D-NY) released a report by his House Subcommittee on Intergovernmental Relations and Human Resources of the Committee on Government Operations charging that HHS AIDS spending levels were dangerously inadequate.

Lawmakers on both sides of the aisle in the House and Senate have pressed for greater AIDS outlays. Much of the substantial increase in federal AIDS expenditures has come because of congressional involvement. Congress has consistently sought higher AIDS spending levels than those requested by the executive branch. Late in 1988 lawmakers passed an omnibus health bill containing the first significant federal policy outlines for managing the AIDS epidemic. The provisions of the legislation set out minimum spending levels over several years for AIDS education, anonymous blood testing and counseling, and home- and community-based health services for AIDS patients. The law earmarked funding for a new National AIDS Commission to coordinate the fight against the epidemic and expedited federal AIDS research activities.

As the epidemic evolved into a major health crisis, leaders in and out of government perceived a need for a national AIDS strategy. In September 1985, the PHS presented its long-range plan for controlling AIDS. The plan established milestones for achieving a steady reduction in the incidence of HIV infection. The ultimate goal was to halt the spread of the disease by the year 2000.

Although the plan was hailed as an important step, many felt it did not go far enough in devising a comprehensive policy for responding to the AIDS crisis. The formulation of this policy, however, was complicated by the widely divergent opinions held by different groups and individuals on issues such as homosexuality and HIV testing.

In February 1986, President Reagan directed Surgeon General Dr. C. Everett Koop to prepare a "major report" on the AIDS epidemic. The surgeon general completed his report in October 1986. Identifying AIDS as a national health problem, the report discussed AIDS high-risk sexual behavior in explicit terms, outlined preventive measures including the use of condoms and called for AIDS education starting in elementary school.

Koop became the administration's leading spokesman on AIDS health issues. In May 1988 he supervised the mailing of the brochure "Understanding AIDS" to every American household. Part of an AIDS-prevention campaign, the brochure presented the most current information available on the disease and ways to stop its spread.

The surgeon general's report had addressed AIDS from a health perspective. At the urging of top domestic policy advisors, in May 1987 President Reagan appointed a presidential commission on AIDS. Formally titled the Presidential Commission on the Human Immunodeficiency Virus Epidemic, its charter was to advise him on the public policy aspects of the AIDS crisis. When the panel's head, Dr. W. Eugene Mayberry, resigned amid growing controversy over the commission's competence, President Reagan named retired Admiral James D. Watkins to take his place.

The commission submitted its final report containing almost 600 recommendations in June 1988. The greatest priority was given to the immediate enactment of national measures to protect HIV-infected persons from discrimination. The panel also highlighted the need for a significant increase in the allocation of resources to the FDA for accelerating the approval of AIDS drugs and for drug treatment programs to arrest the spread of the AIDS virus among IV drug users.

President Reagan responded to the report with a 10-point plan outlining his administration's policy on the epidemic. In this AIDS action plan, Reagan directed the FDA to take steps to better protect the nation's blood supply and ordered the HHS secretary to conduct studies on the key public health issues related to AIDS. Despite the AIDS commission's forceful call for a law barring discrimination against those infected with HIV, Reagan stopped short of endorsing federal antidiscrimination legislation. Instead he ordered federal agencies to adopt guidelines that would prevent workplace discrimination against employees carrying the AIDS virus.

State and local governments, especially in those areas hit hardest by the epidemic, have been at the forefront of debates on public policy responses to AIDS. As early as 1982, San Francisco had appropriated monies in its municipal budget for an AIDS clinic. A full range of AIDS services soon followed. New York, facing a parallel upsurge in new AIDS cases, instituted similar programs. By 1987, health authorities in both cities had developed five-year plans for coping with the AIDS crisis into the next decade. The U.S. Conference of Mayors, noting that the AIDS burden is especially heavy on cities, has called for heightened federal assistance. State legislatures nationwide have passed AIDS antidiscrimination laws. Many now fund AIDS treatment, prevention and education programs. Increasingly, state boards of education are requiring AIDS instruction in their public classrooms.

The military has confronted a number of AIDS issues. In August 1985 the Department of Defense (DOD) announced that it would screen all prospective recruits for HIV infection. In October of the same year, HIV testing was expanded to include all active-duty personnel.

The DOD explained that its AIDS policy was based on certain unique requirements of military service. Wartime conditions could necessitate battlefield person-to-person blood transfusions. In preparation for possible overseas deployment, military personnel receive vaccinations that could prove harmful to persons with weakened immune systems. For these reasons, recruits who tested seropositive would be medically disqualified from enlistment. Seropositive individuals on active duty would undergo periodic medical evaluations. Those found otherwise fit for duty would have the option of remaining on active service, but would be classified as ineligible for assignment overseas or into a combat zone. Persons who developed more severe HIV-related conditions would be medically retired. Selected military medical centers and Veterans Administration hospitals have instituted AIDS treatment programs. The military health system has undertaken a number of AIDS research projects.

The Federal Bureau of Prisons began the systematic testing of inmates for the AIDS virus in June 1987. Most state and local prison systems have initiated similar programs. A disproportionate number of prisoners were IV drug users prior to incarceration. Test results, as expected, have shown a correspondingly high rate of HIV infection in the inmate population.

Dealing with AIDS in a prison environment has posed special problems for correctional authorities. Prisons are recognized as a difficult setting in which to maintain confidentiality. Prisoners identified as carrying the AIDS virus have been subjected to abuse and attacks from fellow inmates. Many prison systems were not prepared to handle the sudden influx of AIDS cases in the mid-1980s.

Most prisons have decided not to isolate seropositive inmates. Segregation is seen as clinically unjustified, while it risks stigmatizing infected prisoners with their peers. Those inmates who progress to full-blown AIDS are transferred to special prison wards or hospitals.

Recent studies show that the rate of new cases of HIV infection among prisoners is now lower than in the population as a whole. It is believed that the strict controls imposed on inmates, particularly those who are IV drug users, serve to limit the spread of the disease. These findings contradict the widely held impression that prisons are a breeding ground for AIDS.

AIDS AND POLITICS

In its first nine years the AIDS epidemic has progressed from an almost exclusive concern of those most directly involved with the disease to a mainstream political issue. Polls conducted during the 1988 presidential campaign indicate that a majority of voters considers AIDS among the nation's most urgent problems. But as late as 1985, the issue was still on the periphery of the American political landscape. Since then, the scope of the crisis has become better understood; individuals and groups across the political spectrum have advanced positions on virtually every aspect of the epidemic.

Political debate continues to center on the nature and extent of the government's role in responding to the AIDS epidemic. At issue are funding levels for AIDS treatment, research and educational programs;

testing of persons for infection with HIV; and safeguards against discrimination for those who carry the AIDS virus.

The debate is complicated by divergent attitudes in the political arena regarding homosexuality. Political initiatives to deal with the AIDS crisis frequently have become enmeshed in broader, divisive debate over homosexuality and its place in society. Gay activist organizations, such as the NGTF and the GMHC, have been politically involved since the initial appearance of the disease in 1981. Determined to draw attention to the AIDS crisis, gay political action has often taken the form of marches, vigils and protests. Legislative lobbying and fund-raising for candidates who support expanded government AIDS policies are now standard political tactics.

The gay political movement has pushed for civil rights laws to guarantee homosexuals protection against discrimination. Gay leaders argue that such legislation would encourage many gays who potentially carry the AIDS virus to step forward and seek the counseling and treatment they need without fear of reprisal.

In opposition of these views, assorted conservative political and religious groups have focused on questions of sexual morality. They stress that efforts to combat AIDS, especially government sector initiatives, should not imply an endorsement of homosexual lifestyles. They consistently have opposed measures they claim would legitimize or promote homosexuality—measures such as the public funding of gay organizations involved in health and outreach programs.

The AIDS epidemic emerged over the course of the Reagan presidency. There was sustained political division between the administration and its critics, who claimed the White House had consistently fallen short in its response to the AIDS crisis. The debate generally pitted those favoring an ideologically conservative approach to AIDS issues against those advocating a more liberal one.

Until recently, relatively few national political figures have taken a consistently high-profile stance in the AIDS debate. The positions of those who have been involved often reflect their personal perspectives more than party affiliation. Sharp disagreements with the Reagan administration over specific policy initiatives were well publicized. Strong differences arose over federal budget appropriations. The Reagan administration was widely criticized by state and local officials and members of Congress for not allocating sufficient monies to the fight against AIDS. They contended that far more could be done to advance research efforts, improve education and help local communities absorb the rising costs of AIDS treatment programs.

The administration consistently maintained that adequate funds had been dedicated to these areas. Administration officials noted that from 1984 to 1988 there were exponential increases in the executive branch's budget requests to Congress for AIDS spending. Partisan camps continued to argue over whether these increases resulted from outside political pressures or from the administration's own recognition of the problem right through the end of the Reagan second term.

The debate has explored not just desired AIDS spending levels but also the closely related question of budget priorities. In June 1988 both an expert panel of the NAS and the president's commission on AIDS called for substantial additional funding for AIDS programs. Today policy makers face difficult political choices as they seek more money for AIDS at a time of tighter budgets and burgeoning federal deficits.

A general consensus has emerged that mandatory testing of broad segments of the public for HIV infection is neither necessary nor advisable. Such testing, while doing little to solve the AIDS crisis, would raise serious constitutional issues concerning individual privacy rights. There is considerable disagreement over the extent involuntary testing should be implemented for selected groups.

The government's testing of military and foreign service personnel to ensure their fitness for duty has received widespread political backing. However, proposals to require the screening of individuals with high-risk profiles, such as prostitutes, have encountered strong opposition. Other proposals for expanded testing have been advanced as a means of stopping the spread of the AIDS virus. Critics contend that these plans risk violating the confidentiality rights of those who are tested and that disclosure of positive test results would leave persons vulnerable to discrimination.

Similar reservations are expressed about voluntary testing efforts. Health care professionals almost unanimously agree that such programs, essential to tracking the AIDS epidemic, will not work unless strong guarantees of confidentiality are enforced and safeguards against discrimination extended for those found to carry HIV. Otherwise these individuals at high risk for AIDS will not come forward for fear they will risk losing their employment, housing and insurance. The president's commission on AIDS identified the lack of a national policy containing effective remedies against discrimination in both the public and private sectors are the most significant impediment to progress in controlling the epidemic.

The federal court system has ruled that the Rehabilitation Act of 1973 prohibits discrimination against persons with AIDS in instances where federal monies are involved. In response to calls for further federal legislation, the Reagan administration reaffirmed its belief that additional measures should be enacted at the state level. President George Bush has indicated he would support stronger federal initiatives to protect AIDS virus carriers from discrimination.

Recognition of the expanding dimensions of HIV infection among IV drug users has led health authorities to link the control of AIDS with the war on drugs. The intersection of these two issues has precipitated a renewed emphasis on expanding treatment centers and programs for drug addicts. Again, budget constraints will play a key part in defining the extent of federal action in this area.

Analysts have observed that the AIDS crisis came of political age with its entrance into the 1988 presidential campaign. Until then, it had primarily been an issue in local elections in those areas where the concentration of AIDS cases was the greatest. Elections in California and New York, in particular, have included debates on gay bathhouses and homosexual lifestyles, antidiscrimination provisions and local AIDS budget levels.

LEGAL ISSUES

The AIDS epidemic has engendered a significant number of legal actions. Courts have been called on to resolve disagreements between groups with different ideas about how to respond to the epidemic. The rights of persons with AIDS have been a matter of particular controversy. Persons with AIDS have turned to the courts both to secure specific rights and to redress alleged instances of discrimination. Individuals and groups fearful of AIDS have asked the judiciary to uphold measures designed to protect them and the community-at-large from the spread of the disease. AIDS poses difficult legal questions. The judicial system has been challenged to consider criminal charges brought against those who deliberately tried to infect others. Individuals who inadvertently contracted the disease have filed civil lawsuits seeking damages.

Much of the legal debate about AIDS has revolved around the question of how the disease is transmitted. This debate has often taken place amid widespread and highly emotional concerns about possible infection. Many in the legal profession have commented that possibly the greatest service the judicial system has performed during the AIDS epidemic has been to provide a forum for the measured and rational examination of the actual risks of AIDS transmission.

Legal issues arising from the AIDS epidemic can be divided into four broad categories: the rights of persons with HIV; the duties of persons with HIV; the rights of uninfected persons; and the rights and duties of health care professionals. In each of these areas there is now a basic legal framework in place. There are, as yet, many unresolved questions.

The rights of persons infected with HIV have gradually emerged from a series of court actions dating almost from the inception of the AIDS epidemic. Both federal and state courts have ruled that AIDS is a handicap. The courts accordingly have tended to interpret existing federal and state laws prohibiting discrimination against the handicapped in favor of persons with AIDS. These statutes have been the basis for extending legal safeguards against discrimination to individuals afflicted with the disease. Whether these protections extend to persons who are infected with HIV but exhibit no disabling symptoms of illness remains under some debate in legal circles. But in the most important decision to date on the issue, a federal court in California ruled that the 1973 federal law barring discrimination against the handicapped indeed covers healthy carriers of the AIDS virus as well as those who have actually developed the deadly disease.

As handicapped persons, those suffering from AIDS and ARC have certain rights to nondiscrimination in employment, housing and education. In general, they can be denied employment only if it is unequivocally shown that their condition either impairs their work performances or places others with whom they come into contact at risk. The same rules hold true for housing, although their application has frequently been complicated by local zoning ordinances. The clearest arena is education. A combination of local court rulings and state policy initiatives has established an increasingly common standard for allowing children with HIV access to schools.

Intense controversy has surrounded the debate over the ability of HIV-infected persons to obtain insurance. Courts have had to weigh complaints of discrimination by those unable to obtain coverage against arguments by insurance companies that they simply cannot afford the prohibitive costs involved. AIDS virus carriers, and even those suspected of HIV infection, have encountered great difficulties in securing and keeping health, disability and life insurance coverage. Legal experts note that some insurance restrictions targeting people with AIDS have skirted laws or violated the industry's ethical standards. But the insurance companies' AIDS guidelines stem for the most part from their need to control costs by limiting risks to survive financially. The insurance industry has won the right to require that all applicants for individual health policies be tested for AIDS in 49 states. Those found seropositive are commonly denied coverage.

The rights of HIV-infected individuals to confidentiality about their medical status also hinge on federal and state regulations. The courts have strongly supported confidentiality rights while acknowledging the necessity for disclosure of information about contagious persons to appropriate public health authorities.

Persons with HIV have been held to have a duty under the law to not willfully or negligently expose others to the virus. Those who do so are subject to both criminal and civil statues. Some states have passed laws specifically making it a crime to deliberately attempt to infect others with the AIDS virus, but most jurisdictions have relied on existing offenses of attempted homicide and assault to prosecute these cases. Civil law governing noncriminal behavior have increasingly placed the burden of exercising ordinary caution in protecting sexual partners against a contagious disease on infected persons. Failure to do so is considered grounds for a civil suit for damages. HIV-infected persons also have a responsibility to not knowingly donate contaminated blood.

The rights of uninfected persons are, in large part, the converse of the obligations of persons infected with HIV not to transmit the virus. But bitter conflict has often arisen. The persons carrying the AIDS virus have clashed with uninfected persons claiming their right not to come in contact with those who are infected. Citing current medical evidence unambiguously stating that AIDS cannot be spread by casual contact, courts have ruled that the rights of infected persons can only be constrained when it is proved that their presence constitutes an actual threat to others. Uninfected persons have been deemed to have other rights to protection. They are entitled to assume that they are receiving safe blood products and that they will be warned by health authorities of health risks outside their own control.

Public health authorities are vested with certain legal powers to control the spread of contagious diseases. These powers or rights vary according to the level of government and the jurisdiction involved. They generally include the ability to order persons into quarantine and to direct compulsory testing of selected groups. Both health and legal authorities agree that the quarantine or isolation of persons with HIV should only be contemplated if these persons continue to engage in conduct dangerous to others despite warnings from public officials. Legal authorities concur that the involuntary screening of well-defined groups for the AIDS virus is justified. The courts have been reluctant to endorse the involuntary testing of specific individuals if the intent is possible prosecution.

Many health care professionals have expressed concern about working with HIV-infected persons. Health care professionals have a right to a safe working environment, and the health community has stressed the use of protective measures and procedures to avoid accidental infection.

The question of whether a health care worker has a duty to treat HIV-infected persons has no simple answer. There is wide agreement in the professional medical establishment that, at the very least, they have an ethical responsibility to do so. Whether they are legally required to provide care in all instances has not been fully tested. This issue may be resolved without extensive court involvement. There is growing acceptance among health care professionals that working with HIV-infected persons poses no unmanageable risks of infection.

AIDS AND SOCIETY

Since it appeared in 1981, the AIDS epidemic has been variously described as God's punishment of homosexuals, the end of the sexual revolution, and a 1980s version of *The Andromeda Strain*. Each of these characterizations reflects the impact of AIDS on American society, illustrating the intense fears that have surrounded the AIDS epidemic—fears that by the end of the 1980s seemed to be subsiding in the face of improved public understanding of the disease.

In the first years of the epidemic, many Americans shared a common desire not to come into contact with persons afflicted with AIDS. They feared exposure to a strange new medical condition that was somehow contagious and apparently incurable. People with AIDS frequently were ostracized or treated as untouchables. This general fear of AIDS has diminished as medical science has been able to establish that the risk of infection through casual contact is virtually nonexistent. Public debate about how to respond to persons with AIDS has moderated amid growing awareness and acceptance that their presence does not constitute a health menace to others.

Those who have AIDS face continuing social condemnation for their lifestyles. AIDS is primarily identified in the public's mind with homosexuals and, to a lesser extent, IV drug users. Although the AIDS virus can be transmitted through heterosexual activity, the basic perception has not changed noticeably. Many segments of American society have expressed deep antipathy to both homosexuality and drug addiction. AIDS patients have had to struggle not only with their fatal disease but also with the stigma associated with their condition.

In the early 1980s, gay leaders felt they were at the threshold of achieving real progress in their struggle for homosexual rights. The previous decade had seen the development of an increasingly effective homosexual movement. AIDS changed this. It quickly became the top, if not the exclusive, issue on the gay agenda. Gay leaders note that much of the earlier enthusiasm and momentum has been consumed in the homosexual community's desperate fight against the disease. Efforts to portray homosexuality as an acceptable alternative lifestyle to the population-at-large have not been enhanced by the images of gay bathhouses and sexual practices highlighted by the AIDS epidemic. At the same time, many gay leaders sense that the ability to mobilize and respond to the AIDS crisis has actually strengthened and unified the homosexual movement.

Some gay organizations contend the AIDS epidemic has instigated a new wave of homophobia in America. They cite statistics indicating an increase in the number of attacks on homosexuals. Actions such as the Supreme Court's decision against homosexual sodomy are viewed as a reflection of a renewed intolerance of gay lifestyles.

It is almost an article of faith with many gay leaders that efforts to mobilize against the AIDS epidemic in its early stages were met by widespread public indifference because it was a "gay disease." To what extent hostility toward homosexuality actually affected the public's initial response to the AIDS epidemic is difficult to gauge. It is generally agreed that AIDS did not become a pressing issue for most Americans until the news in the summer of 1985 that actor Rock Hudson had the disease. Public health authorities, though, point out that by the time that the Rock Hudson story broke, AIDS had been declared the nation's number-one health priority, the AIDS virus had been found, a screening test developed and measures implemented to protect the blood supply.

Some fundamentalist religious leaders have interpreted the AIDS epidemic as the work of a wrathful God punishing homosexuals for their sinful behavior. The vast preponderance of religious denominations denounce this notion. The religious community has counseled compassion toward those suffering from the disease. Religious figures, most notably Mother Theresa, have often taken the lead in providing shelter and assistance to the afflicted.

Because of the fear of AIDS transmission, a number of individual churches have required their parishioners to practice tincture rather than drink from a common communion cup. In general, those denominations that celebrate the Eucharist have opposed these measures as both unnecessary and contrary to the spirit of communion. The Catholic Church, in keeping with its long-standing position against birth control, has resisted calls for the use of condoms to control the spread of AIDS and continues to advocate sexual abstinence outside of marriage as the way to halt HIV transmission.

The AIDS epidemic has forced the public discussion of many issues that historically have been considered private matters. In bringing these matters into the open, health and other government officials decided that halting the spread of AIDS outweighed offending the sensibilities of many Americans. This introduction of previously taboo topics has not been without controversy. Former Surgeon General Koop was both praised and criticized for his frank statements urging sex education and the use of condoms and his explicit descriptions of high-risk sexual behavior.

More conservative groups have seen public health efforts such as sex education in schools and condom advertising as promoting immorality. They argue that the correct way to respond to the AIDS epidemic is to stress the values of abstinence until marriage, and monogamy thereafter. Most of those involved in combating the AIDS epidemic describe this approach as unrealistic and out of step with existing social mores.

Awareness that AIDS may be transmitted through heterosexual intercourse has not signaled the end of the sexual revolution. However, studies indicate that many Americans have changed their sexual lifestyles because of AIDS. Persons are more inclined to exercise care in the selection of a sexual partner and to practice safe sex. Some dating organizations require their members to undergo periodic HIV testing. There is no evidence yet whether the fear of contracting AIDS has led to a decrease in prostitution.

Although any suggested connection between AIDS and the biological-experiment-gone-awry scenario of the novel *The Andromeda Strain* is refuted by the epidemiology of the disease, the AIDS epidemic remains a high-technology drama. As members of a generation accustomed to technological triumph, AIDS patients have struggled to understand why medical science cannot quickly find an effective treatment for their condition. Their sense of frustration is not mitigated by the fact that the discovery of the AIDS virus itself was made possible only by the rapid advances in microbiology of recent years. Many fight a desperate campaign to hold out as long as they can, hoping there will be a sudden medical breakthrough.

Other AIDS patients have turned to New Age ideas in an attempt to cope with the disease. Regarded as nonsense by traditional science, these approaches range from the use of crystals as healing devices to an emphasis on healing oneself through self-actualization and positive thinking.

AIDS AND CULTURE

AIDS has had a powerful effect on American cultural life. Members of the art and entertainment worlds have witnessed firsthand the terrible consequences of the disease. Perhaps no group is more aware of its deadly impact than the arts community, where AIDS has taken an especially hard toll. Their experiences are increasingly shaping both the substance and spirit of creative expression.

AIDS has been the topic of movies, plays and novels. It is the subject of paintings, photographs and other visual art forms. In a broader sense, critics note that the specter of death and despair associated with AIDS has influenced the creative imagination of many current artists.

The body of work in the performing and visual arts that refers to AIDS is growing. Much of this artistic expression is about the impact AIDS has had on the lives of its victims. Often the works are by artists who themselves have struggled with the disease. A common theme is the alienation from society and rejection by friends and family that persons with AIDS have suffered. Many literary works belong to the confessional genre. Paul Monette's *Borrowed Time: An AIDS Memoir* and Emmanuel Dreuilhe's *Moral Embrace: Living with AIDS* explore the authors' trials with the disease, one as the companion of an AIDS sufferer and the other as a victim himself. These and other accounts frequently explore the writers' lives, their relationships with others and their feelings about their own sexuality and mortality.

Among the most acclaimed dramatic works on AIDS is the play *As Is* by William M. Hoffman. First performed in New York City in 1985, it portrays the struggle of a homosexual couple to cope with the lethal disease. A televised version of *As Is* was shown on the Showtime cable station in the summer of 1986.

Some works have addressed openly and expressly the broad policy aspects of the AIDS epidemic. Larry Kramer's drama *The Normal Heart* documents the playwright's perception that both New York City and its homosexual community failed to deal decisively with the AIDS epidemic in its first years. In his 1987 book *And the Band Played On*, journalist Randy Shilts indicts a cross-section of American institutions for ignoring or downplaying AIDS at a time when prompt action purportedly could have saved many lives. Reviewers generally point out that both works, while containing many elements of truth, benefit from the wisdom of hindsight; both are credited with galvanizing greater action in the fight against AIDS.

The outpouring by visual and performing artists has at least equaled the literary production. Nicholas Nixon and Robert Mapplethorpe are photographers who focused on the disease from different vantage points. Nixon chronicled in several series of photographs the final months in the lives of AIDS patients, illustrating their progressive deterioration and eventual death. Mapplethorpe, who died from AIDS in March 1989, shot portraits, some of them self-portraits, filled with gaunt men and hollow-eyed skulls. These and others of his works, numbers of them explicitly homoerotic, appeared in a posthumous retrospective exhibit partly sponsored by the National Endowment for the Arts. This show sparked fierce public debate in the United States over the propriety of public funding for such graphic and controversial material.

Painter Ross Bleckner's metaphysical paintings draw on Christian imagery to explore the human toll of AIDS, while Joe Bassell's canvases, inspired by his work at an AIDS hospice, depict men alone and bedridden, their only companions shadowy figures of death.

By the late 1980s greater numbers of artists were responding to public fears and stereotypes by adopting a more militant tone in their work. These artists now view their roles not just as public mourners but as political activists reacting to a government and populace still uninformed about AIDS. They have concentrated on art forms, such as videotape and billboards, that can reach the largest audiences. Moreover, they have criticized much of the work memorializing AIDS victims as too passive.

Aside from newscasts, the major networks first broached the subject of AIDS in November 1985. NBC aired the television movie *An Early Frost* about a young homosexual with AIDS and the reaction of his family on learning of his condition. The movie was followed by a special news report designed to amplify points raised about the disease.

Dramas such as *An Early Frost* and *As Is* have served to inform audiences about AIDS. In their depiction of the human cost behind the generalities, they have influenced the ways people see the epidemic. AIDS is no longer an abstraction, but the very real situation of individuals confronting the uncertainties of potentially horrific illnesses and death.

Other television programs have faltered, drawing criticism for either insensitive or inaccurate portrayals. An episode aired in December 1988 of NBC's "Midnight Caller" series outraged AIDS activists by depicting a bisexual man as a murderer intentionally spreading the AIDS virus through sex with unsuspecting women.

In stage dramas and TV productions, AIDS has been portrayed as a problem confined to gay men, reinforcing perceptions of AIDS as a "homosexual plague" and of the arts community as mostly gay. Few artistic works have examined the ever-greater numbers of minorities and drug abusers in America's inner cities being felled by AIDS. Although AIDS is becoming predominately a crisis among the poor and those suffering from drug addiction, it would be impossible to glean this fact from the artistic and cultural response.

The entertainment industry has adapted to the changing sexual climate brought on by the AIDS epidemic. Television and movie producers have shifted away from plots involving extensive casual sex. Characters in contemporary drama often represent the values of commitment and fidelity. In a well-publicized example, *The Living Daylights*, released in the spring of 1987, featured a much more restrained James Bond than the notorious womanizer of earlier movies.

Hollywood has had to deal with AIDS in a more direct sense. After the news that Rock Hudson had the disease, a number of performers balked at participating in scenes requiring intimate contact such as open-mouth kissing with other actors they did not know. Guidelines were enacted that granted performers the right to refuse close personal contact with anyone they believed might have a communicable disease.

Among the most unusual artistic responses to the AIDS epidemic is the Names Project. It involves a campaign to provide a memorial to those who have died by creating a constantly expanding quilt made up of panels containing the names of the disease's victims. The quilt was unveiled in October 1987 at an AIDS rally in Washington, D.C. The inclusion of names such as the choreographer Michael Bennett and the performer Liberace on the tapestry testifies to the very direct impact AIDS has had on culture through the death of many important artists. The quilt appeared on public display for the last time in October 1989 after organizers decided that, at 13 tons, it had become too cumbersome to show in its entirety.

WORLDWIDE PERSPECTIVE

The impact of AIDS is felt globally. At the end of 1989, 177 countries or territories had documented at least one case of AIDS to the World Health Organization (WHO). AIDS cases have been reported from all major areas of the world: North and South America, Africa, Europe, Asia and Oceania. The AIDS epidemic constitutes a worldwide public health problem.

The pattern of the disease in Western Europe has mirrored that in the United States, although the actual number of AIDS cases has been considerably lower. West Germany and France have reported the greatest total number of cases. Transmission of the AIDS virus has occurred predominately among homosexual and bisexual men and IV drug abusers. Prospects for at least limited containment of the disease are enhanced because most of the West European nations can allocate adequate financial and medical resources toward this end. Europe has been the site of important AIDS research since the early 1980s.

In Canada and Australia the epidemiology has paralleled the U.S. and Western European examples. Experts now warn that some Central and

South American countries may be heading toward an epidemic of AIDS similar to that sweeping parts of Africa. AIDS in these nations seems to be spreading quickly from homosexuals to heterosexuals, placing many more people at risk of the disease. Information about AIDS in Asia is limited. HIV has recently appeared in that continent. The spread of the AIDS virus among individuals with multiple sexual partners is just now being documented.

Haiti has suffered an uncommonly high incidence of AIDS as a proportion of its total population. The Caribbean island nation became a focal point in the first years of the epidemic because of the presence of the disease among many recent Haitian immigrants to the United States. The CDC classified Haitians as a separate risk group for AIDS until April 1985, when researchers concluded that unique risk factors could not be identified. Studies have revealed large clusters of seropositive individuals around the Carrefour district of Port-au-Prince, a major center for male and female prostitution in Haiti. This finding suggests that the unusually high number of Haitians with AIDS is related to known factors of high-risk sexual behavior and exposure to nonsterile needles and syringes.

AIDS has become an extremely threatening presence in Africa, particularly in the central region of the continent. Epidemiologists now estimate that the annual incidence of the disease in Central Africa may be from 500 to 1,000 cases per million population (the incidence in the United States is currently about 55 cases per million population). Some studies indicate that between 5% and 10% of the total population of the region is infected with HIV.

The true scale of the epidemic in Africa is hard to assess. Reporting of AIDS cases is often delayed and incomplete. Large segments of the population have limited access to health care facilities where a diagnosis of AIDS can be made. Tests detecting either exposure to the AIDS virus or to many of the opportunistic infections which follow are generally lacking. In addition, some governments have been reluctant, until recently, to even acknowledge the existence of AIDS in their countries. The identification in Africa of a distinct AIDS virus called HIV-2 has complicated the picture. Until scientists can describe the clinical and epidemiological characteristics of the new virus more thoroughly, its implications for the future course of the AIDS epidemic will remain a troubling uncertainty.

Pinpointing where the AIDS virus first entered the human population is difficult. A significant increase in opportunistic infections characteristic of AIDS began appearing in Africa in the late 1970s. The syndrome of chronic diarrhea and weight loss common in Uganda and Tanzania became known locally as "slim disease." Scientists now believe slim disease is another form of AIDS. There is no treatment, and those afflicted ordinarily die within one year of diagnosis.

The pattern of AIDS in Central Africa differs in important respects from the one in the United States. Approximately half of African AIDS patients are women. Studies have found a direct association between HIV infection and heterosexual promiscuity, especially involving female prostitution. This data has led some researchers to conclude that heterosexual contact is the dominant mode of transmission in Central Africa. Others are less certain and point out the great difficulty of conducting cross-cultural studies of disease transmission in remote and underdeveloped areas.

It is thought that unsanitary health practices contribute to the high incidence of AIDS. Reusing hypodermic needles is endemic in rural medical settings. Many ritual practices and cultural customs involve cutting and scarring with unsterile instruments. Transfusions of contaminated blood are a recurring difficulty.

All indications are that the increase and spread of AIDS in Africa will continue unabated. Public health experts predict the development of perhaps millions of AIDS cases there within the next decade. Implementation of practical health and social policies for curbing AIDS virus transmission and treating the syndrome meets many obstacles. Unsanitary medical methods are long-standing and, hence, difficult to alter or discourage. The costs of widespread blood screening and adequate clinical care are prohibitively steep for African governments, whose resources are already stretched to the limit. Prospects for improved access to treatments and therapies developed in the West are severely inhibited by lack of money and effective delivery systems.

Accurate projections of the scope of AIDS in communist nations have been difficult to make. After initial denials and withholding of information, the Soviet Union has publicly confirmed several cases of the disease within its borders. It is believed that the AIDS virus entered Cuba via soldiers returning from service in Angola. The Soviet Union and Cuba now have some of the strictest laws in the international community for controlling the spread of AIDS. These measures call for mandatory testing of high-risk groups and empowering public health officials to quarantine infected individuals. Western physicians visiting Rumania have described that nation's problem with pediatric AIDS. Observers attribute the incidence of disease among Rumanian children to substandard medical conditions and an unprotected blood supply.

A growing number of nations have taken legal steps to deny entry to those infected with HIV. WHO counts at least 24 countries that have adopted immigration and travel restrictions for HIV-infected persons since 1985. This is the first time health officials around the world have implemented laws for a specific disease. The U.S. government, in response to the protests of AIDS groups and numbers of international organizations, has eased restrictions on the freedom of people infected with the AIDS virus to enter the United States and no longer stamps passports to indicate the holder is infected with HIV. Under rules passed at the end of 1989, infected people still must declare their condition when they apply for a visa and seek a waiver of rules barring them from the country. Since May 1989 the Immigration and Naturalization Service has permitted foreigners with AIDS to enter the United States on temporary visas to attend conferences or for medical treatment.

It is hoped that increased cooperation between countries will lead to improved public health measures and education to slow the spread of HIV. National AIDS control programs have been established throughout the world with the technical and financial support of the international community. Multinational organizations and international assistance agencies have supported the control of AIDS in developing countries. WHO is directing these efforts through its Global AIDS Strategy and Special Program on AIDS. But the outlook is grim. In a report issued in December 1989, WHO revealed that the epidemic is gaining momentum despite increased containment efforts and is spreading to new areas as well as among more people in already-infected areas. The cumulative number of reported cases worldwide through December 31, 1989, was slightly more than 203,000—a 50% rise from the figures at the end of 1988.

AIDS AND THE FUTURE

The AIDS epidemic promises to be a dominant international public health problem to the end of the century and beyond. Scientists will continue their search for effective medical remedies. After nine years, researchers' expectations are moderated by a sense of what is realistically achievable. Even the most optimistic do not anticipate a major breakthrough in the development of a vaccine or cure in under 10 years. Successful immunization may be a race against time. The disturbing possibility looms that the AIDS virus will mutate. If so, changes in its composition could render useless efforts now underway to find a vaccine.

Epidemiological models project that 20% to 30% of the estimated 1.0 to 1.5 million persons infected with HIV in the United States will progress to AIDS or AIDS-related illness within five years. The PHS predicts approximately 365,000 cases by the end of 1992. These numbers underscore the enormous challenge society faces in providing adequate care to those already afflicted. As the demand for health and supportive services escalates, the strain on existing resources will intensify.

There is encouraging evidence that preventive education and other precautionary measures have had some beneficial impact. Epidemiologists report an apparent decline in the overall rate of increase of AIDS virus infection in the United States. Hopes are blunted by the recognition that transmission of HIV is now accelerating among IV drug users in many inner cities. Public health authorities warn of the harsh toll AIDS will take on members of this group if the trend is not reversed. The worrisome possibility that HIV infection may spread sexually from IV drug users to the population at large also causes concern.

In the future, the most harrowing consequences of the epidemic could well be witnessed in the underdeveloped world. AIDS may completely decimate whole areas of Africa in the next 15 years. Experts note that massive international assistance will be necessary to change the course of the epidemic on the continent. Because AIDS can cross geographic boundaries with relative ease, eventual control of the epidemic must come through a coordinated, global effort.

AIDS has prompted allocation of considerable resources to branches of scientific research that may not otherwise have received such concentrated attention. The focus on genetic engineering in AIDS laboratory research could accelerate advances in this arena and lead to important breakthroughs with far-reaching and diverse applications.

CHAPTER 2

━━━

CHRONOLOGY

This chapter is a chronological account of the significant events in the first decade of the AIDS epidemic. It includes entries drawn from a broad spectrum of medical, legal, political, social and cultural developments.

The chronology is divided by year into nine sections. Within each section, individual entries are preceded by the month and day on which they occurred. The format for entries features two cross-referencing techniques: (1) court cases in emboldened print and events related to Ryan White are addressed in greater detail in Chapter 3; and (2) dates in parentheses at the end of an entry, e.g., (Dec 14, 85), indicate related items within the chronology.

The chronology begins in 1981, with the initial appearance of AIDS in New York and California. The first reported cases in the United States enabled the scientific and medical communities to recognize and describe the new disease complex. Evidence collected over the course of the epidemic now suggests that AIDS was present prior to 1981 in parts of Africa and Western Europe.

1981

January 31: Two young, homosexual men under Dr. Donna Mildvan's care at Beth Israel Medical Center in New York die in January from cytomegalovirus (CMV). She notes the patterns of age, sexual orientation and immune system depression among the patients.

February 28: Dr. Linda Laubenstein at New York University School of Medicine diagnoses her sixth case of Kaposi's sarcoma (KS) since December 1980, all among gay men.

AIDS

February 28: Two gay male patients are referred to Dr. Michael Gottlieb at the University of California at Los Angeles (UCLA). Both patients have *Pneumocystis carinii* pneumonia (PCP) and show evidence of T-cell depletion.

April 9: Dr. James Groundwater makes the first diagnosis of KS in San Francisco. The patient, Ken Horne, is a gay male. He is also diagnosed with the parasitic infection cryptococcus.

April 15: By the middle of the month the fourth case of PCP has appeared at UCLA. Dr. Michael Gottlieb sees an emerging pattern of immune system breakdown and high levels of cytomegalovirus in the blood among these gay male patients. Dr. Wayne Shandera of the Los Angeles County Department of Public Health locates a fifth case of PCP in Los Angeles.

April 24:
- Dr. Alvin Friedman-Kien of New York University School of Medicine briefs Dr. Marcus Conant and Dr. James Groundwater on the recent outbreak of KS among gay men in New York City. Connections are drawn to the first reported KS cases in San Francisco.
- Ken Horne's case of KS is reported to the Centers for Disease Control (CDC) in Atlanta. His is the first officially reported case of what is later designated acquired immune deficiency syndrome (AIDS).

May 18: Dr. Michael Gottlieb and Dr. Wayne Shandera submit a report to the CDC on their research/findings on PCP and other opportunistic infections afflicting gay men in Los Angeles.

June 5: The CDC publishes the Gottlieb and Shandera work in *Morbidity and Mortality Weekly Report* (MMWR) under the title *"Pneumocystis carinii* Pneumonia—Los Angeles."

June 9: The CDC establishes a special task force, named the Kaposi's Sarcoma and Opportunistic Infections (KSOI) Task Force, to look into the outbreak of KS and PCP in New York, San Francisco and Los Angeles. Dr. James Curran is appointed as director. Its initial focus is on finding the cause, or causes, of the maladies.

June 12: In Paris, Dr. Willy Rozenbaum reads about the findings of Drs. Michael Gottlieb and Wayne Shandera in MMWR and compares them with his own experiences treating PCP in gay men at Claude-Bernard Hospital. Rozenbaum begins to suspect that an infectious agent is the connecting piece.

June 16: Dr. Donald Francis, an epidemiologist with the CDC, and Dr. Max Essex at Harvard University discuss the reports on KS and PCP, in particular the pattern of T-cell depletion among the diagnosed cases. Francis speculates that a new virus—maybe a retrovirus—is the cause of the immune system compromise and disease in gay men. He suggests transmission is by sexual contact.

July 2:   Dr. Marcus Conant at the University of California at San Francisco (UCSF) proposes the establishment of a KS clinic for research and treatment in the San Francisco area. He emphasizes the need for a consolidation of efforts.

July 4:   The CDC publishes the first official report on the KS outbreak, entitled "Kaposi's Sarcoma and *Pneumocystis carinii* Pneumonia among Homosexual Men—New York and California." It appears in MMWR.

July 15:   CDC researchers set out a standard definition of the still-unnamed syndrome. The KSOI Task Force decides to undertake a case-control study in New York, San Francisco and Los Angeles. The announced intent of the study is to isolate and evaluate all causitive possibilities. Infectious agents (a virus or microbe), environmental factors (toxic substances or drugs) or a combination of the two are under consideration.

July 17:   Dr. Mary Guinan of the CDC begins the case-control investigation in New York. Her findings reveal cases of PCP among reportedly heterosexual intravenous drug abusers. Guinan also, for the first time, is able to directly link two gay male victims sexually. The possibilities of both sexual and blood-borne transmission are raised.

July 29:   Dr. Harold Jaffe initiates the CDC case-control study in San Francisco. His interviews with gay male sufferers of the disease provide two leads: a high number of sexual contacts and frequent use of nitrite inhalants.

July 31:   The CDC releases cumulative statistics for the United States: 108 cases reported nationwide; 43 deaths.

Oct 31:   In October the nation's first KS clinic opens in San Francisco, under the sponsorship of UCSF Medical Center and San Francisco General Hospital. Dr. Marcus Conant and Dr. Paul Volberding are the clinic's cofounders.

December 31:
- Dr. Jacques Leibowitch and Dr. Willy Rozenbaum in Paris, France, note a new link in the clinical profiles of several KS and PCP patients under their care: recent travel or residency in Central Africa.
- Dr. Arye Rubinstein at the Albert Einstein College of Medicine in New York diagnoses patterns of severe immune deficiency, lowered T-cell counts and opportunistic infections among infants of mothers who are intravenous drug abusers.

■ The KSOI Task Force case-control findings to date suggest that the instances of KS and PCP among gay men are part of a new infectious disease that is sexually transmitted. A direct relationship appears to exist between greater risk for contracting the disease and increased numbers of sexual contacts.

1982

January 10: Dr. Bruce Evatt of the CDC is notified about the case of a hemophiliac in Miami who died of PCP. The victim, who had regularly received transfusions of Factor VIII, a blood-clotting agent, fit no existing risk category for the KS/PCP epidemic. This suggested the possibility of an infectious agent capable of being transmitted in blood-clotting substances. Evatt notes the potential implications for hemophiliacs.

January 12: In New York, the Gay Men's Health Crisis (GMHC), a private fund-raising organization, is formed to raise money for research on KS. Paul Popham is named president.

January 15: By the middle of January, Dr. Jacques Leibowitch and Dr. Willy Rozenbaum have convened a French study group to track the epidemiology of the new diseases appearing in Paris.

January 31: By the end of January, gay-related immunodeficiency disease, or GRID, has become the generally accepted acronym among American researchers for the range of diagnosed disorders.

February 28: The CDC reports that 251 Americans have contracted GRID, with 99 recorded deaths.

March 3: In Atlanta, the U.S. Public Health Service (PHS) holds its first formal conference on GRID. Preliminary studies by the National Institutes of Health (NIH) on the significance of environmental factors in the emerging epidemic are reviewed. Dr. Donald Francis advances the theory that GRID is caused by a new viral agent. He sketches similarities between GRID, feline leukemia and hepatitis B.

March 4: Dr. Dave Auerbach and Dr. William Darrow of the CDC begin to investigate the first cases of GRID in Los Angeles. They determine that 9 of the first 19 reported cases can be linked, through sexual contact, to a single individual, a gay male airline steward named Gaetan Dugas. The Los Angeles "cluster study" reveals certain patterns: the incidence of GRID is tied to greater sexual activity; environmental factors seem unlikely as a probable cause; GRID has a long incubation period, and is transmissible during this time.

March 31: By the end of March, the CDC is receiving reports of cases of PCP, tuberculosis, KS and toxoplasmosis among Haitians living in

Miami, Florida. The KSOI Task Force investigates, and Haitians are made a new risk group for GRID. (Apr 9, 85)

April 2: The latest CDC statistics reveal that 300 Americans have contracted the disease, 119 have died.

April 13: Rep. Henry Waxman's (D-CA) House Subcommittee on Health and the Environment begins the first U.S. congressional probe into the GRID crisis. The emphasis is on the status of federal funding for research.

June 11: The nation's first documented hemophilia GRID case is reported in Colorado. Transmission through the blood-clotting agent is suspected.

July 13: A professional symposium on GRID opens at Mount Sinai Hospital in New York. The spread of GRID in the Haitian refugee communities of New York and Miami is highlighted. Dr. James Curran announces that hemophiliacs have been added to the list of risk groups by the CDC.

July 27: The NIH, Food and Drug Administration (FDA), blood industry representatives, gay organizations and hemophiliac groups meet in Washington, D.C. Recent evidence of transmission through blood-clotting products is assessed. Blood-screening procedures are reviewed, but no changes announced. All participants agree to designate the epidemic *acquired immune deficiency syndrome,* or *AIDS.*

July 31:
- In July, the San Francisco city government appropriates funds to create an AIDS outpatient clinic at a local county hospital. Reportedly, it is the first direct outlay of municipal monies anywhere in the country for AIDS care.
- The GMHC publishes a newsletter in New York advising gay men on measures they can take to reduce the risk of getting AIDS. It is the first nonscientific publication by any organization in the world on AIDS.

August 13: The first national AIDS Forum is held in Dallas, Texas, as an adjunct to the first National Lesbian and Gay Leadership Conference. The impact of AIDS on the gay community is addressed.

August 31: By the close of August, plans for the establishment of the San Francisco Kaposi's Sarcoma Education and Research Foundation are laid out by Dr. Marcus Conant, colleagues and gay community representatives.

September 27: A $450,000 supplemental appropriations bill is passed by the San Francisco city government to fund the world's first AIDS clinic and grief counseling program.

October 28: The CDC announces its most current epidemiological figures: 691 reported cases of AIDS; 278 deaths.

October 30:
- A major conference on the AIDS epidemic opens at UCSF. Dr. Arthur Ammann presents his findings on the incidence of pediatric AIDS. Ammann's report is the first retailed revelation of the presence of the disease among children.
- Dr. Harold Jaffee, in conjunction with Dr. Arthur Ammann and Dr. Selma Dritz, investigates what appears as possibly the first documented case of AIDS transmitted through a blood transfusion.

October 31: French researchers Dr. Francoise Brun-Vezinet and Dr. David Klatzmann, at the close of October, focus on two hypotheses: AIDS had come out of Central Africa; AIDS is caused by a human retrovirus.

December 10:
- The first public admission by the CDC that AIDS may be linked to the nation's blood supply appears in MMWR.
- An article appearing in the *Journal of the American Medical Association* reports on instances of unexplained brain disorders among certain AIDS patients.

December 17: _An article in MMWR reports on 22 cases of pediatric AIDS. These infants have no inherited immune defect. All are children of mothers in existing high-risk groups, either intravenous drug users or Haitians.

December 31: At the close of the year the Pasteur Institute in Paris initiates research on AIDS in its retrovirus labs, under the direction of Dr. Luc Montagnier and Dr. Jean-Claude Chermann.

1983

January 3: Dr Francoise Barre at the Pasteur Institute begins a study of lymph node tissue samples from gay male AIDS victims—the first step in an effort to find a viral explanation for AIDS. Conjecture centers on a retrovirus, such as human T cell lymphotropic virus (HTLV).

January 4: The U.S. PHS advisory committee meets in Atlanta to consult on the threat AIDS poses to the blood supply. The case for testing of all blood products is advanced, but no decision is made.

Chronology

January 5: The American Association of Blood Banks issues a statement emphasizing its opposition to comprehensive donor screening. Rights to privacy and individual choice are cited.

January 7: The first official report on the growing problem of AIDS in prisons, primarily among IV drug users, appears in MMWR.

January 31: Over the course of January, Dr. Francoise Barre measures strong levels of the enzyme reverse transcriptase, unique to retroviruses, in tissue samples from AIDS patients. The retrovirus behaves unlike HTLV. Evidence indicates it is a new human retrovirus.

March 3: The U.S. PHS announces recommendations for changes in blood-screening procedures. Voluntary restraint among high-risk groups is urged. The pronouncements on AIDS also include the first risk-reduction guidelines ever issued by the federal government.

March 7: "1112 and Counting," an article by the writer and gay activist Larry Kramer, is published in the *New York Native.* According to Gary Shilts in *And The Band Played On*, the article "irrevocably altered the context in which AIDS was discussed in the gay community and, hence, in the nation."

March 31: Dr. Marcus Conant holds a meeting with gay political and community leaders in San Francisco to discuss the scope of the AIDS epidemic.

April 10: Lenox Hill Hospital in New York holds a major symposium on AIDS. Dr. Kevin Cahill, the conference organizer, criticizes both the medical establishment and government responses to the AIDS epidemic.

April 11: The National Cancer Institute (NCI) Task Force on AIDS convenes in Bethesda, Maryland. Dr. Robert Gallo, task force head, spells out its commitment to finding the cause of AIDS. Like the French, Gallo suspects a retrovirus.

April 30: The GMHC holds a circus fund-raiser at Madison Square Garden in New York, raising $250,000 for AIDS education and research.

May 1: Dr. James Curran announces detection of an uncommon human T-cell leukemia virus in a third of the blood specimens of AIDS patients tested at Harvard University. He adds that there is no proof this virus causes AIDS.

May 4: Thousands participate in a candlelight march down Castro Street in San Francisco for AIDS sufferers.

May 6: An American Medical Association (AMA) news release says evidence suggests that AIDS may be transmitted through casual, household contact.

May 18: The federal Social Security System announces it will extend disability benefits to sufferers of the infections linked to AIDS.

May 24: Assistant Secretary of Health and Human Services (HHS) Dr. Edward Brandt says AIDS is the number-one priority of the U.S. PHS.

June 2: San Francisco Public Health Director Mervyn Silverman announces the required posting of AIDS warnings in the municipality's gay bathhouses.

June 3: Dr. Luc Montagnier gives the name *lymphadenopathy-associated retrovirus* (LAV) to the isolates of the human retrovirus discovered in the Pasteur Institute studies.

June 5: Rep. Ted Weiss (D-NY) alleges that the PHS resisted congressional efforts to track the cause of AIDS. He adds that federal CDC lack of cooperation blocks the work of the House subcommittee studying the course, treatment and prevention of AIDS.

June 14: In a speech to the U.S. Conference of Mayors in Denver, Secretary Margaret Heckler says the Department of HHS considers AIDS its number-one priority.

June 15: The second National AIDS Forum convenes in Denver to consider public policy issues, AIDS-prevention education and concerns about the blood supply.

June 16: The U.S. Conference of Mayors unanimously adopts a resolution calling for its members to promote research on AIDS. Allocation of more federal funds for combating AIDS is urged.

June 26: In New York, San Francisco and Washington, D.C., Gay Freedom Day parades draw historic turnouts, as marchers and rally organizers demonstrate their concern over the widening impact of AIDS on homosexuals nationwide.

June 27: In Manhattan, tens of thousands march in a parade commemorating the city's AIDS victims.

June 30: Dr. Mathilde Krim organizes the AIDS Medical Foundation. She aims to encourage the private medical community's involvement in AIDS research and treatment.

July 31: The CDC establishes its clinical definition of AIDS-related complex, or ARC.

Chronology

August 1: Rep. Ted Weiss (D-NY) opens his House oversight subcommittee's hearings on AIDS in Washington, D.C. Public health officials, researchers and blood industry representatives testify on the current status of the epidemic.

August 2: National Gay Task Force executive director Virginia Apuzzo, in congressional testimony, alleges there is no coordinated federal strategy for coping with AIDS.

September 17: Dr. Luc Montagnier presents the Pasteur Institute work on LAV at a conference of AIDS researchers at Cold Springs Harbor, Long Island.

November 22: AIDS experts convene at the World Health Organization's (WHO) headquarters in Geneva for a meeting on the international implications of AIDS. The focus is on the epidemiology of AIDS in Africa and Haiti.

December 6: Rep. Ted Weiss releases his subcommittee's report, "The Federal Response to AIDS." Weiss is critical of HHS funding levels for AIDS. The report is the first comprehensive congressional investigation of federal AIDS policy.

December 30: A statistical model developed by the CDC suggests that the average incubation period for AIDS is approximately 5.5 years.

1984

January 4: CDC and University of Miami researchers report new evidence that AIDS can be transmitted through heterosexual sexual contact, and that transmission can occur before a person exhibits outward symptoms of the syndrome.

January 6: The CDC reports that 3,000 cases of AIDS have been reported since the disease was recognized in 1981, with half of these cases reported since February 1983.

January 11: Federal health officials say that concern over possible transmission of AIDS through blood transfusions is supported by new data. The 60 reported cases of AIDS associated with blood or blood products represent 2% of the total number of AIDS cases to date.

February 11: A panel appointed by Governor Mario Cuomo awards 20 New York State grants totaling $4 million for research aimed at discovering the cause of and possible protection against AIDS.

March 1: Scientists at the University of California isolate a previously unknown virus that induces symptoms in monkeys resembling those of AIDS in humans. This finding adds support to the view of some researchers that the human syndrome is the result of an undetected infectious agent, possibly a virus.

April 4:   Cornell University researchers announce that they have conducted studies indicating interferon may be partially effective as an AIDS treatment.

April 9:   Dr. Mervyn Silverman, director of the city's Department of Public Health, declares a ban on high-risk sexual activity in San Francisco's gay bathhouses. The action is termed a precautionary public health measure. (Oct 9, 84; Nov 28, 84; Nov 11, 85)

April 17:   African, Belgian and American doctors estimate that the incidence of AIDS in Zaire, Africa, may be 10 to 20 times higher than in the United States. Concern over the future course of the epidemic in Central Africa are expressed.

April 22:   CDC Director Dr. James Mason says he believes that LAV—the reputedly new virus identified by Pasteur Institute researchers among AIDS patients in France—is the cause of AIDS. Mason also predicts eventual development of diagnostic and screening tests for AIDS.

April 23:   HHS Secretary Margaret Heckler at a major news conference announces that federal researchers, led by Dr. Robert Gallo at the NCI, have isolated the virus thought to cause AIDS. The virus is named HTLV-III. The NCI also reports that it has developed the means to mass-produce the virus in large amounts—a process considered essential to continuing research efforts on AIDS.

May 14:   The American Red Cross says it plans to begin evaluating the accuracy of a recently developed test for detecting the AIDS virus in blood donated for transfusions.

September 19:   Secretary of HHS Margaret Heckler says the federal government will collect 200,000 blood samples from healthy donors nationwide for AIDS research purposes. She indicates the samples will be drawn after a diagnostic test for the AIDS virus is available.

September 21:   Newport Pharmaceutical International announces that a new drug, Isoprinosine, has slowed or prevented the development of AIDS in clinical trials.

October 9:

New scientific findings suggest that the suspected AIDS virus HTLV-III may be transmissible through saliva. Researchers stress that no case yet reported can be directly linked to saliva transmission.

San Francisco Public Health Director Dr. Mervyn Silverman orders immediate closure of 14 homosexual bathhouses on grounds they allow indiscriminate sexual contacts that facilitate the spread of AIDS. (Apr 9, 84; Nov 28, 84; Nov 11, 85)

October 11: The NCI's Dr. Robert Gallo says important genetic variations have been found in samples of HTLV-III. These variations are described as a "potentially significant obstacle to the development of an AIDS vaccine."

October 22: The FDA grants approval to Abbott Laboratories for its diagnostic test ELISA to screen blood for antibodies to the suspected AIDS virus. (Mar 2, 85; Jun 1, 85)

November 28: A San Francisco Superior Court judge rules that the bathhouses closed in October can reopen, but only under limitations on sexual practices and behavior. (Apr 9, 84; Oct 9, 84; Nov 11, 85)

November 30: New York City Health Commissioner David J. Sencer, noting the continued increase in number of AIDS cases in 1984, characterizes the disease as the city's most critical health problem.

December 3: Researchers at the University of California say one of the first blood tests for detecting AIDS virus in humans will be used in as many as 10,000 random samples in 1985. These trials hope to determine the efficacy of the new procedure.

December 21: CDC researchers claim that in laboratory studies the drug ribavirin blocks the growth of the AIDS virus.

1985

January 3: Scientific studies show the presence of the AIDS virus in the brains of AIDS patients suffering memory loss, impaired concentration and other symptoms of dementia.

January 18: The *New York Times* reports that U.S. and French scientists independently claim to have made a complete analysis of the genetic material of the AIDS virus.

February 8: Pasteur Institute researcher Dr. Jean Claude Chermann offers evidence that a new compound drug, HPA-23, appears for the first time to have inhibited the reproduction of the virus believed to cause AIDS.

February 12: The FDA orders the nation's 2,000 licensed blood banks to begin testing all donated blood for antibodies to the AIDS virus. Federal officials stress that the test does not determine if a donor has or will contract AIDS.

March 2: HHS Secretary Margaret Heckler announces government approval of the new blood-screening test for AIDS virus antibodies. She says the ELISA test is now licensed for commercial production and will be available in the United States in two to six weeks. (Oct 22, 84; Jun 1, 85)

March 7: A second screening test for blood receives FDA approval. Studies demonstrate that the Western blot is a less sensitive, thus more accurate, indicator of possible exposure to the AIDS virus.

April 9: The CDC eliminates recent Haitian immigrants to the United States from the list of those groups considered at greatest risk of contracting AIDS. (Mar 31, 82)

April 14: The first International Conference on AIDS, sponsored by the CDC and WHO, opens in Atlanta. It is the largest conference ever held on AIDS.

April 21: Larry Kramer's play *The Normal Heart*, a dramatic treatment of the impact of AIDS on the gay community, has its preview performance at the Public Theater in New York. The production receives critical acclaim and stirs considerable controversy for its strong indictment of public policy responses to the epidemic.

April 25: The small town of Belle Glade, Florida, reports an uncommonly high incidence of AIDS since 1982. Experts claim the majority of its AIDS victims fit existing high-risk categories and see no connection to overcrowding and poor sanitation. (Sep 22, 86; Jan 7, 88)

May 15: A report appearing in the *New England Journal of Medicine* contends that the AIDS virus may persist without symptoms in infected people for more than four years.

May 18: Federal health officials claim that the risk of AIDS spreading among the general heterosexual population is minimal.

May 19: The Comic Relief benefit show for the AIDS Medical Foundation raises $500,000 for AIDS research.

June 1: The ELISA blood-screening method is patented for the Department of HHS by Dr. Robert Gallo and two colleagues. (Oct 22, 84; Mar 2, 85)

June 28: Scientists report the discovery of a previously unidentified gene in the AIDS virus. They speculate the gene is a key factor in the virus's ability to cause disease.

July 25: The American Hospital in Paris, France, acknowledges that American actor Rock Hudson is being treated for AIDS.

August 1: **Ryan White,** a 13-year-old hemophiliac with AIDS, is prohibited from returning to school in Kokomo, Indiana. School officials say they fear he could pose a health threat to other pupils. (Apr 10, 86)

August 16: NCI scientists reveal that the AIDS virus has been isolated in the teardrops of a female AIDS patient.

August 30:
- The CDC announces its initial recommended guidelines for the education and foster care of children infected with the AIDS virus.
- The U.S. Department of Defense (DOD) announces it will begin screening all prospective military recruits for possible exposure to the AIDS virus.

September 17: The drug HPA-23 receives FDA approval for experimental use in the United States. The drug has been shown to prevent the AIDS virus from reproducing.

September 19: A benefit for AIDS victims is held in Los Angeles. Entertainment industry stars Burt Reynolds, Elizabeth Taylor, Shirley MacLaine and Liza Minnelli are among the 2,500 who attend.

September 26: Dr. Mathilde Krim and actress Elizabeth Taylor announce the formation of the American Foundation for AIDS Research (AmFAR). Elizabeth Taylor is named its director.

September 28: WHO officials say they have gathered the medical and financial support to draft a worldwide plan for managing the AIDS epidemic. They aim to provide a centralized program for coordinated U.S. and European research.

September 30: The U.S. PHS unveils its long-range plan to control the spread of AIDS. Three goals are advanced: Halt the steady increase in the transmission of the virus by 1987; reduce the incidence of new AIDS cases by 1990; stop the spread of the virus by 2000.

October 1: A CDC study finds that the risk of transmitting AIDS by daily, casual home contact is "virtually non-existent."

October 9: Dr. Anthony Fauci, director of the National Institute of Allergies and Infectious Diseases (NIAID), reports some progress toward the development of drugs to treat AIDS. He says the drug suranim has been shown to block the AIDS virus's ability to reproduce itself in the human body.

October 18: The DOD announces it will screen all 2.1 million military personnel for exposure to the AIDS virus.

October 25: Arista Records releases "That's What Friends Are For," performed by Dionne Warwick, Stevie Wonder, Elton John and Gladys Knight to benefit AIDS research.

October 26: New York State health regulations authorize local health officials to close homosexual bathhouses and other places where AIDS high-risk sexual activities take place. (Nov 7, 85)

November 3: Entertainment personalities perform at a gala held at the Metropolitan Opera House in New York to raise money for AIDS research. The AIDS Medical Foundation and AIDS Resource Center are the beneficiaries.

November 7: New York City closes the Mine Shaft, a Manhattan bar frequented by gay men. It is the first of several establishments shut down under a continuing city campaign against places allowing high-risk sexual activity linked to AIDS virus transmission. (Oct 26, 85)

November 8: Researchers in Africa says AIDS is seemingly being transmitted in conventional sexual intercourse among heterosexuals there, and striking women approximately as often as men.

November 11:
- San Francisco Mayor Dianne Feinstein announces a city plan to close down homosexual bathhouses, saying they continue to encourage sexual activity that helps to spread AIDS. (Apr 9, 84; Oct 9, 84; Nov 28, 84)
- NBC broadcasts the made-for-television movie "An Early Frost," the first film drama to focus on AIDS aired on network television.

November 15: The CDC releases its initial recommended guidelines for preventing transmission of the AIDS virus in the workplace. The guidelines specifically address the risks encountered by health care professionals.

November 20: An auction at Sotheby's gallery in Manhattan raises $660,000 for the GMHC. The money is targeted for AIDS counseling and education.

December 11: The Florida Human Relations Commission rules that employment discrimination against AIDS sufferers violates the state's disability law. The ruling stems from the case of Todd Shuttleworth, who was released from his job after it was revealed he had AIDS.

December 14: The Pasteur Institute brings suit against the U.S. Government in a dispute over who initially isolated the AIDS virus. (Mar 31, 87)

1986

January 10: The first published estimate of the national economic impact of AIDS figures the initial 10,000 AIDS cases will cost $6.3 billion in hospital expenses and lost earnings due to disability and premature death.

February 6: The CDC reports the first known case in which a parent contracted the AIDS virus from a child with the syndrome.

February 11: New York City's policy of not automatically excluding all children with AIDS from public school classrooms is upheld by the New York State Supreme Court. **(District 27 Community School Board v. Board of Education of the City of New York)**

February 24: Channon Phipps, an 11-year-old carrying the AIDS virus, returns to class in El Toro, California, after a court order lifts a school ban on his attendance.

March 26: U.S. and French researchers contend, independently, that they have successfully isolated a new AIDS virus. The virus first appeared in two West African AIDS patients. (Nov 8, 86)

April 10: **Ryan White** goes back to school in Kokomo, Indiana, as a judge removes the final legal obstacle to his return (Aug 1, 85).

April 23: The federal government proposes to bar aliens diagnosed with AIDS from immigrating to the United States.

May 1: The legal dispute between American and French researchers over the discovery of the AIDS virus leads an international committee of scientists to designate a single name for the virus: *human immunodeficiency virus*, or *HIV*.

May 27: The Washington, D.C., city council approves legislation requiring life insurance companies to provide coverage for people exposed to HIV.

June 12: Federal health officials predict a tenfold increase in the number of reported AIDS cases and deaths in the next five years. Estimates of the total cost of care for AIDS patients by 1991 are from $8 billion to $16 billion.

June 20: The U.S. Department of Justice rules that federal civil rights laws provide limited protection to persons with AIDS. This interpretation of the legal rights of AIDS sufferers is narrower than that recommended by the Justice Department's civil rights division.

June 23:
- The Second International AIDS Congress opens in Paris to hear reports on the latest scientific and medical research.
- In a test of the military's policy of mandatory blood screening for all personnel, a Navy sailor who refused to submit to the test for exposure to the AIDS virus is found guilty of disobeying an order.

June 24: NIAID researchers say that for the first time a human immune system damaged by AIDS-related infections has been restored to apparently normal condition. Lymphocyte transfusions and an antiviral drug were used as treatment in the trial.

June 30: The Supreme Court rules in **Bowers v. Hardwick** that homosexuals do not have a constitutionally guaranteed right to engage in consensual sodomy.

August 2: The nation's first hospital dedicated solely to AIDS research and care is established in Houston, Texas. The facility is called the Institute for Immunological Disorders. (Dec 11, 87)

August 8: The Department of HHS finds that Charlotte Memorial Hospital in North Carolina violated the civil rights of an employee who had AIDS when it dismissed him from his position as a registered nurse. This marks the first time such conduct is characterized as discrimination by the federal government.

September 19: Assistant Secretary of HHS Robert Windom says the drug Azidothymidine (AZT) has been shown to improve markedly the health of one group of AIDS patients. He reports that thousands of AIDS victims will soon be provided access to the drug in the United States.

September 22:
- CDC scientists say blood test results indicate that African Swine fever is unrelated to the unusually high incidence of AIDS in Belle Glade, Florida. (Apr 25, 85; Jan 7, 88)
- Dr. Robert Gallo and Dr. Luc Montagnier, key scientific figures in the discovery of the AIDS virus HIV, are named as winners of the Albert Lasker Medical Research Award.

October 23: Paul F. Cronan returns to work at the New England Telephone Company after a Massachusetts State Court holds that employment rights of workers with AIDS are protected under the state's handicapped discrimination law.

October 24: A panel named by the National Academy of Sciences (NAS) looks into charges of sabotage and mismanagement in the AIDS lab at the CDC in Atlanta. (Dec 9, 86)

October 29: "Confronting AIDS," a report prepared by the NAS, describes the federal government's response to the epidemic as "dangerously inadequate." The report proposes the federal government allocate $2 billion annually for AIDS education and research.

October 31: The surgeon general's report on AIDS, mailed in late October, is scheduled to arrive in all U.S. households by the last day of the month.

November 6: NCI researchers say studies indicate HIV attacks different types of cells in the brain and central nervous system than in the immune system. The finding may complicate treatment of the deadly infection.

November 8: Dr. Luc Montagnier contends that the new AIDS virus found in West Africa may be as deadly as the original AIDS virus. (Mar 26, 86)

November 20: WHO announces a coordinated global effort to manage the AIDS epidemic. A WHO official calls AIDS a "health disaster of pandemic proportions."

November 27: The U.S. State Department reveals that Foreign Service personnel will be tested for exposure to the AIDS virus starting January 1.

December 9: An independent investigative panel of the NAS, while acknowledging that the AIDS lab at the federal CDC in Atlanta experienced some operational problems, finds no evidence of sabotaged experiments or suppressed data. (Oct 24, 86)

December 10: Bailey House, a supervised residence for homeless AIDS victims, is opened in Manhattan by the AIDS Resource Center.

1987

January 9: The drug ribavirin is reported to halt the progress of the initial forms of infection caused by the AIDS virus.

January 12: California health officials refuse to take part in a federal study on AIDS, asserting that blood-sample testing without a patient's consent violates the state's confidentiality laws.

January 16: A panel of FDA advisors recommends that AZT be licensed for sale despite uncertainties about the drug's safety and effectiveness.

January 20: In a speech at Liberty University, Surgeon General C. Everett Koop notes that approximately 100 million people may die from AIDS worldwide by the year 2000 if a cure or vaccine is not found.

January 25: Several nationwide newspapers and periodicals announce they will begin to accept condom advertising in response to the health threat of AIDS virus transmission.

January 29: HHS Secretary Otis R. Bowen, in remarks to the National Press Club in Washington, D.C., suggests that AIDS in time may rival such earlier epidemics as small pox and typhoid in terms of its impact.

___

February 10: Surgeon General C. Everett Koop says condoms are the most effective protection against sexual transmission of the AIDS virus for those who "will not practice abstinence or monogamy." He calls for televised condom advertisements.

February 19: The CBS and NBC television affiliates in New York announce they will accept condom advertising, but only when explicitly related to protecting against AIDS virus transmission. In addition, the stations say they will not run the messages before 11 P.M. The qualified decision reflects long-standing broadcast-industry misgivings about condom advertising.

March 3:

- The CDC reports that the risk of developing AIDS rises yearly after initial infection with the virus.
- The Supreme Court rules in ***School Board of Nassau County v. Arline*** that persons suffering from contagious diseases are entitled to handicapped status under federal law.

March 7: Dr. Robert Gallo and Dr. Mikulas Popovic of the NCI patent their method of producing the AIDS virus.

March 16: The Reagan administration issues a plan for AIDS education. The plan urges that specific information on how to prevent transmission of the AIDS virus be made available to all Americans.

March 20: The FDA approves the use of AZT, but stresses that the drug is not a cure for AIDS. AZT is the first drug approved in the United States for the treatment of AIDS.

March 24: Surgeon General C. Everett Koop urges all women to be tested for exposure to the AIDS virus before a pregnancy on a voluntary basis.

March 31: President Reagan and Prime Minister Chirac of France announce resolution of the legal dispute between American and French researchers over discovery of the AIDS virus. The settlement calls for joint recognition of the discovery and sharing of patent rights to the HIV blood test. (Dec 14, 85)

April 8: White House domestic policy advisors recommend to President Reagan that he establish a special commission for examining the AIDS issue. The commission would offer proposals about the federal government's role in contending with the epidemic.

April 15: The New Jersey Supreme Court upholds state regulations allowing children with AIDS or ARC to attend public schools.

April 30: The U.S. Senate Appropriation Committee votes $30 million to fund the cost of treating low-income AIDS patients with AZT.

May 1: Federal officials propose a revised definitions of AIDS, to include dementia and emaciation, that would increase the number of recorded cases by 20%.

May 4: President Reagan announces the formation of a special AIDS commission to advise him on public policy aspects of the epidemic.

May 7: Rep. Stewart B. McKinney (R-Conn) dies of AIDS, the first U.S. Congressman known to have died of the syndrome.

May 15: The U.S. PHS recommends mandatory testing for the AIDS virus of the 500,000 applicants seeking permanent residence in the U.S. each year.

May 28: Federal health officials report the first case of AIDS virus transmission through donated organs doctors had thought were safe.

May 31:
- President Reagan, in his first speech devoted exclusively to the AIDS epidemic, calls for extensive AIDS testing at the state and federal levels to gauge the spread of the virus across the population.
- St. Clare's opens in May in Elizabeth, New Jersey, the first group home in the United States for children with AIDS.

June 1: The Third International Conference on AIDS convenes in Washington, D.C. Vice President George Bush delivers the opening remarks. He calls for broader AIDS testing at state and federal levels, but emphasizes the need for confidentiality of test results.

June 5: HHS Secretary Otis R. Bowen says the federal government plans to draw 45,000 blood samples from randomly chosen individuals as part of a national study to chart the incidence of AIDS virus infection among Americans.

June 7: WHO says no evidence exists that the AIDS virus can be spread through tears, saliva or normal kissing.

June 10: AIDS is described as "one of the biggest potential health problems in the world" by leaders attending the seven-nation economic summit in Venice, Italy.

June 11: Governor Michael Dukakis of Massachusetts unveils the most comprehensive statewide AIDS education program in the nation.

June 24:
- A Minnesota prison inmate who tests seropositive for the AIDS virus is found guilty of assault with a deadly weapon after biting two guards.
- The National Gay Rights Advocates bring suit against the U.S. Government. The group seeks the enactment of rules to accelerate the testing and availability of drugs and therapies for treating AIDS.

June 25: President Reagan names Dr. W. Eugene Mayberry to lead the new presidential advisory commission on AIDS.

June 30: A month-long benefit sponsored by Art Against AIDS raises $1.25 million. It is the largest private AIDS fund-raising event to date.

July 23: President Reagan appoints the 12 members of his national commission on AIDS.

July 27: The federal government rules it will extend Social Security disability payments to AIDS sufferers who meet the expanded federal definition of deadly diseases. The decision affects those patients with AIDS-related dementia or emaciation.

August 4: The U.S. Congress votes to appoint a national commission on AIDS, composed of leading experts, to advise the House on the role of the government in AIDS research and treatment.

August 18: Federal officials and MicroGeneSys Co. announce plans for the first human trials in the United States of an experimental AIDS vaccine.

August 24: Richard, Robert and Randy Ray, hemophiliac brothers who are seropositive, return to public school in Arcadia, Florida, under court order and a police guard. (Apr 30, 88)

September 28: California Governor George Deukmeijian signs legislation providing for state testing of drugs for the treatment of AIDS. The bill allows for potential state approval of such drugs without the involvement of the federal government.

October 7: The senior leadership of the president's commission on AIDS abruptly resigns. Chairman Dr. W. Eugene Mayberry, Vice Chairman Woodrow Myers and Senior Staff Advisor Dr. Franklin Cockerill III all quit without comment. The resignations reportedly stem from disputes and rivalries within the commission and from frustrations over the panel's lack of progress.

October 10: Admiral James D. Watkins is named the new chairman of the president's AIDS commission. He pledges to get the panel reorganized.

October 11: In Washington, D.C., 200,000 people attend the largest gay rights march ever held in the United States.

October 19: Studies done in New York, Florida and California indicate women die significantly faster than men after they are diagnosed with AIDS.

October 24: Methodist Hospital in Houston, Texas, announces it will begin testing all entering patients for the AIDS virus. It is the most comprehensive AIDS testing program at a major hospital anywhere in the country.

November 12: The AMA issues a statement saying doctors are ethically obligated to treat patients with AIDS.

November 18: A federal appeals court orders the reinstatement of a California teacher with AIDS, the first time a federal court rules that discrimination against a person with AIDS is prohibited under federal laws protecting the handicapped.

December 2: A male Army soldier pleads guilty at his court-martial to charges resulting from his having sexual relations with three female soldiers without informing them he carried the AIDS virus. A second male soldier pleads guilty to similar charges in an unrelated case two weeks later.

December 11: The Institute for Immunological Disorders in Houston closes after losing $8 million in 14 months. It was the nation's first private hospital expressly for AIDS patients. (Aug 2, 86)

December 18: The DOD says military personnel testing seropositive will be transferred from some sensitive jobs. The department cites new evidence that the virus can impair mental function.

1988

January 7: Researchers say their study of the unusually high rate of AIDS in Belle Glade, Florida, reveals no evidence that the AIDS virus is transmitted by mosquitos. (Apr 25, 85; Sep 22, 86)

January 12: U.S. scientists report that their studies have not confirmed any connection between genetic factors and a susceptibility to developing AIDS.

January 28: Researchers at the University of Medicine and Dentistry of New Jersey say a West African woman diagnosed with AIDS is the first person in the United States found infected with HIV-2, a second variety of the AIDS virus.

January 28: Surgeon General C. Everett Koop outlines the plan of American health officials to screen every student at a major university as part of a study designed to help detect the rate of AIDS infection among young adults.

February 2: The nation's first outpatient treatment clinic for persons who test positive for the AIDS virus, but show no symptoms of AIDS, opens in San Francisco.

February 13: The Burroughs Wellcome Co. patents Retrovir, the commercial name for the drug AZT.

February 14: WHO reports that cases of AIDS have appeared in 160 nations since 1981. The number of cases worldwide is put at an estimated 150,000.

February 16: Federal health officials grant approval for the expanded use of the drug trimetrexate to treat AIDS patients with PCP.

February 19: Admiral James D. Watkins, chairman of the President's Commission on AIDS, says the FDA requires more money and staff to accelerate the approval of drugs to treat AIDS.

February 24:
- Admiral James D. Watkins recommends a national commitment of $2 billion annually for expanding drug abuse treatment programs and improving health care services to contend with the AIDS epidemic.
- The American Association of Blood Banks says new screening techniques under study may reduce even further the possibility of transmitting the AIDS virus through blood transfusions.

March 6: Dr. William H. Masters and Virginia E. Johnson publish their book *Crisis: Heterosexual Behavior in the Age of AIDS*. The book alleges that the AIDS virus is far more prevalent among heterosexuals in the United States than the medical community has maintained.

March 9: A bill is introduced in the New York State Assembly that would allow physicians to warn the sexual partners of AIDS patients they are at risk of infection, even when patients object to such disclosure. This is the first such measure introduced in the nation.

April 29: Dr. Anthony Fauci testifies before Congress that insufficient staffing at the NIAID has contributed to delays of up to one year in the human clinical trials of certain promising AIDS drugs.

April 30:
- Ricky, Robert and Randy Ray, three hemophliac brothers who contend they contracted the AIDS virus from blood-clotting substances, sue the two pharmaceutical companies that processed the clotting agents. (Aug 24, 87)
- The NIAID reports that the first test of an experimental AIDS vaccine in the United States has caused an immune system response in six volunteers. This is described as an important step toward the development of an effective vaccine.

May 15: Surveys of federal and state prisons suggest that the rate of increase in the incidence of AIDS in prisons has been less than in the general population.

May 16: A group of scientists in California claim they have developed a new AIDS virus test for detecting the presence of the virus prior to the development of antibodies. The new test locates actual genetic material of the virus in blood and tissue samples. Its creators describe it as a refinement of a similar test already developed by the Cetus Corporation of California.

May 18: William Masters and Virginia Johnson appear before the president's commission on AIDS to defend their controversial book *Crisis: Heterosexual Behavior in the Age of AIDS* against charges of irresponsibility and alarmism.

May 25: A new study predicts lower costs for AIDS patient medical care nationwide than some earlier projections. The study is the first ever to include the cost of treatment with AZT. The lower costs are attributed to two factors: shorter hospital stays and a decline in the estimates of the number of people who will develop AIDS.

May 26: Preliminary studies on the use of AZT in the treatment of children with AIDS yield promising results.

May 31: In May, the federal government mails "Understanding AIDS— A Message from the Surgeon General" to every household in the United States.

June 1:
- Researchers at Johns Hopkins University say they have observed four cases in which HIV stopped reproducing in the patients' bodies and became dormant.
- An expert panel of the NAS releases "Confronting AIDS: Update 1988." This report cites an "absence of strong Federal leadership in the fight against the AIDS epidemic." The panel forecasts the imminent need for $1 billion a year to pay for public health and education measures to limit the epidemic.

June 2: Japanese biologists report that studies they conducted indicate the AIDS virus probably did not pass from monkeys to humans. Instead, they speculate the virus may have infected common ancestors of humans and monkeys millions of years back.

June 2: Admiral James D. Watkins urges the enactment of new federal laws and directives to curb discrimination against people who are infected with HIV. He says the absence of such legal protection is "the most significant obstacle to progress in controlling the epidemic."

June 3:
- Scientists reveal they have identified and synthesized a protein fragment that in laboratory trials blocks the AIDS virus from destroying cells.
- At a meeting in Charlottesville, Virginia, government health experts recommend a major increase in drug abuse treatment programs as part of an effort to curtail the growth of the AIDS epidemic.

June 4: In a decision expected to influence similar lawsuits around the country, a Denver, Colorado, court clears a blood bank of liability for HIV-contaminated blood provided before the development of screening tests for the virus.

June 5: Researchers say they have found unusual cases in which the AIDS virus "hid" in one type of body cells called *macrophages*. In these instances, the virus was undetectable by commonly used blood- and tissue-screening methods.

June 8: The Cetus Corporation announces that its new AIDS virus test, which detects HIV in macrophages, should be available for commercial use in approximately two months.

June 9: Scientists report the findings of a study suggesting that the origin of the human AIDS viruses in their current form may be as recent as 40 years ago.

June 10: Dr. Jay Levy says a team of UCSF researchers have discovered two less deadly strains of the AIDS virus HIV-2.

June 12: The Fourth International Conference on AIDS opens in Stockholm, Sweden. Some 7,000 participants gather to hear more than 3,200 scientific presentations on current AIDS research.

June 14: Results of a new study reveal that a group of 18 men carrying the AIDS virus were infected for more than a year before they produced antibodies in response to the invading virus. The researchers stress that the study involved too few patients to accurately gauge how much time ordinarily passes between infection with HIV and development of antibodies to the virus.

June 17: A divided President's Commission on AIDS approves an antidiscrimination measure that Chairman James D. Watkins says is the key issue in the commission's final report to President Reagan. The proposal recommends that a federal law prohibiting government-supported programs from discriminating against persons with AIDS be strengthened to include the private sector.

June 24: The president's commission on AIDS officially submits its final report to President Reagan. The document contains over 600 recommendations for public policy approaches to the epidemic.

Chronology

June 28: Vice President George Bush, embracing the major recommendation of the president's AIDS commission, endorses legislation and other steps at the federal level to bar discrimination against AIDS sufferers. When questioned, Bush acknowledges he is out in front of President Reagan on the issue. On receiving the commission's report, Reagan declines to comment on its proposals.

June 30:
- The AMA urges doctors to warn the sexual partners of patients who are carrying HIV when no other way exists to alert them of the hazard. The policy statement, a departure from their long-standing tradition of confidentiality, also stresses the responsibilities of state governments to trace and contact sexual partners at risk.
- A federal court in California rules that the Federal Rehabilitation Act of 1973, which bars discrimination against the handicapped, protects healthy carriers of HIV as well as those who have actually developed AIDS. Previous court cases had suggested but never expressly stated that the law applied to healthy seropositive individuals.

July 23: Commissioner Frank E. Young, attending the Lesbian and Gay Health Conference and AIDS Forum in Washington, D.C., announces the FDA's plan to permit AIDS sufferers in America to import small amounts of unsanctioned drugs from abroad for their personal use. Young's decision follows protracted criticism of the FDA by patient advocates over the agency's reluctance to speed the availability of possible treatments to the terminally ill.

August 2: President Reagan, unveiling his administration's 10-point AIDS policy program, directs all federal agencies to enact guidelines barring discrimination in the workplace against employees with HIV. Reagan stops short of endorsing federal antidiscrimination legislation, the key recommendation in the June 1989 report of the president's AIDS commission.

August 10: City officials say 150,000 to 225,000 New Yorkers are infected with the AIDS virus. The projections, a refinement of the 200,000 figure announced July 19, represent a dramatic drop from the 400,000 figure cited by officials since 1986 and set off debate over the accuracy of the numbers and the impact they will have on AIDS programs.

September 19:
- Findings of studies conducted in New York City and nationwide indicate that HIV infection among female prostitutes is not as prevalent as experts had predicted. Researchers, confirming their suspicion, discover that most of the 12% who tested HIV positive were IV drug

users. In addition, the studied yielded almost no evidence of prostitutes sexually transmitting the AIDS virus to their patrons.

- Dr. Veronica Prego, once employed at Kings County Medical Center in Brooklyn, sues the hospital, New York City and two doctors for $175 million, contending their negligence led to her infection with the AIDS virus. Prego, who went on to develop the disease, says she was stuck by an HIV-contaminated needle left on an AIDS patient's bedding. The subsequent trial is the first of its kind in the nation. Prego eventually drops her suit, settling out of court for $1.35 million.

September 21: Scientists meeting at an international AIDS conference in Tanzania are informed that the worsening epidemic could reduce population growth rates in Central Africa to zero.

September 30: The three major television networks conclude an agreement with federal officials to broadcast public service announcements encouraging condom use to curb the spread of AIDS.

October 4: New Jersey government officials attend a ground-breaking ceremony in Newark for the nation's first Head Start center for children with AIDS.

October 6: A legal opinion issued by the U.S. Justice Department supports federal measures prohibiting discrimination against AIDS sufferers employed by the government or by institutions receiving federal monies.

October 8: Georgia prisoner Adam Brock, a carrier of the AIDS virus, is given a 15-year sentence for biting a prison guard who, it turns out, later tested negative for HIV.

October 13: The U.S. Congress passes compromise legislation outlining a comprehensive federal AIDS program. The omnibus bill funds various research, education and treatment efforts but leaves out a provision guaranteeing confidentiality for individuals testing positive for the AIDS virus.

October 19:
- Under increasing pressure from advocacy groups for AIDS victims, the FDA issues revamped procedures for approving AIDS drugs. Agency officials say the relaxed rules will speed the availability of new treatments to people with terminal diseases.
- Health officials report that the incidence of AIDS has reached an alarming level in Central America. WHO announces the start of an intensive public education campaign and blood-screening drive to stem the rapid spread of HIV throughout the area.

November 5: The CDC releases preliminary results of its study of 20 colleges showing that three of every 1,000 students are AIDS-virus carriers.

November 6: New York City health officials initiate a controversial hypodermic needle–exchange program for IV drug users. The effort is the centerpiece of an experiment to see whether such an exchange can limit the spread of AIDS. Only two drug users claim free needles on the program's first day. (Jan 29, 89)

November 19: In a ruling favorable to the insurance industry, the Massachusetts Supreme Court overturns regulations that would have prohibited HIV testing of applicants for health insurance and some life insurance coverage.

December 3: San Francisco's largest blood bank, subject of a civil suit, is found negligent for having given HIV-tainted blood to a patient who subsequently developed AIDS. The five-year-old victim is awarded $750,000 in damages and medical expenses. The case marks the nation's first successful AIDS-related negligence action against a blood bank.

December 25: Pope John Paul II, delivering his Christmas message from St. Peter's, calls for stepped-up scientific research efforts in the battle against AIDS.

1989

January 6: The Reagan administration reveals its proposed budget for the Department of HHS. AIDS funding requests amount to a 30% increase over current federal spending on the epidemic.

January 29: Disappointed by an extremely low turnout, New York City health officials shelve the needle-exchange program they speculated would cut the incidence of HIV infections among IV drug users. In the two months since the program kicked off, only 50 drug users enrolled. (Nov 6, 88)

February 6: The FDA announces it will expand availability of the experimental aerosol drug pentanidine to AIDS patients threatened with PCP, the most common immediate cause of death among AIDS patients.

February 9: The National Research Council, the research branch of the NAS, urges more extensive studies of sexual behavior and drug abuse to help slow the spread of HIV infection. The council calls on the federal government to endorse more open and aggressive programs aimed at changing the high-risk behavior associated with AIDS transmission.

February 15: A Los Angeles jury awards $14.5 million to Marc Christian, the one-time lover of Rock Hudson, who brought a suit against the late actor's estate. The jury finds that Hudson's concealment of his AIDS from his sexual partner was "reckless and outrageous." On February 17, Christian is awarded another $7.25 million in punitive damages.

March 9: Secretary of HHS Dr. Louis Sullivan endorses local needle-exchange programs directed at slowing the spread of HIV by drug users sharing contaminated syringes. The secretary emphasizes that he does not favor a similar effort at the federal level.

March 15: Researchers in San Francisco studying homosexual men report that only half had developed disease symptoms more than nine years after infection with HIV. This incubation period is two years longer than that previously estimated by experts.

April 7: A federal district judge orders the U.S. Immigration Service to release the imprisoned Hans Paul Verhoef, a Dutch visitor with AIDS. He is exempted from laws barring foreigners with communicable diseases so he may attend a Sans Francisco AIDS conference.

April 12: A top federal health expert declares that some Latin American and Caribbean countries may confront an AIDS epidemic on the order of that devastating parts of Africa. He estimates 2.5 million people in the Western Hemisphere are already HIV infected and that 500,000 will be diagnosed with AIDS by 1992.

May 22: Results of the first nationwide survey of HIV infection among college students, sponsored by the CDC, suggest that the threat of AIDS on campuses, while real, is not yet widespread. Researchers found that 2 in 1,000 students were infected with the virus, a rate called characteristic of groups seemingly not at notable risk of contracting the disease.

May 31: Findings of a study conducted by UCLA researchers show that some people may carry the AIDS virus for three years without its being detected by standard HIV tests. The results renew concerns about unintended transmission of the virus by people testing negative and about the safety of the nation's blood supply.

June 4: The Fifth International Conference on AIDS convenes in Montreal. Despite general predictions of a worsening epidemic in the 1990s and dim prospects for a vaccine breakthrough, some conferees are optimistic. Growing scientific evidence suggests early AIDS treatment can extend life expectancy and delay progression from HIV infection to symptomatic AIDS in many people.

June 26: The FDA gives limited approval to two new drugs for treating serious AIDS medical complications. Ganciclovir combats a viral infection causing blindness, and erythropoietin treats a severe form of anemia.

July 8: A report released by the CDC calls for a concerted national effort to locate and test the estimated 1 million Americans carrying the AIDS virus. It observes that treatments can prolong victims' lives in the initial stages of the disease.

July 27: Results of a major new study demonstrate that the experimental drug dideoxyinosine, or DDI, has benefited patients without causing toxic side effects. Researchers say they will conduct expanded and accelerated tests on DDI to compare it with AZT, the only drug approved for AIDS treatment.

August 2: President George Bush agrees to back civil rights legislation extending federal antidiscrimination protection of the disabled to people with AIDS and those carrying the AIDS virus.

August 3: A research team reports the first strong evidence that AZT can significantly delay the onset of AIDS in people with mild symptoms of immune system dysfunction.

August 15: The GMHC, in a major policy shift, endorses widespread voluntary testing for HIV. In explaining its switch on the issue, the organization cites enhanced protection of AIDS confidentiality and stronger antidiscrimination laws.

August 17: Experts release the conclusive findings of a study indicating the drug AZT can delay the onset of AIDS in people infected with HIV. Study subjects who took AZT were half as likely as the control group to develop AIDS symptoms. HHS Secretary Lewis Sullivan calls the results a turning point in the treatment of AIDS.

September 11: Illinois Governor James R. Thomas signs into law a measure repealing the nation's only mandatory premarital AIDS testing program.

September 18: The Burroughs Wellcome Co., maker of the AIDS treatment AZT, cuts the price of the drug 20% in the face of protests about its yearly cost of $8,000. Critics say the expense places AZT beyond the financial means of thousands of AIDS sufferers, thus shutting them off from the only established effective treatment.

October 7: Medical experts, disturbed by new data indicating that HIV is spreading rapidly among some teenage groups, urge a greater national effort against the epidemic. Recent studies find that equal numbers of teen boys and girls carry the virus and that HIV is being spread through heterosexual intercourse.

October 25: Federal health officials announce that AZT will be widely distributed to children even before it receives final FDA approval. The decision removes the delay, called inexcusable by critics, in offering AZT to AIDS children. Previous testing had demonstrated the drug could extend their lives and reverse mental deterioration.

November 8: The National Endowment of the Arts, citing a new federal law barring government funding of artwork deemed obscene, withdraws sponsorship of a New York City art show about AIDS. The show includes images of homosexuality and criticizes a number of conservative national political and religious figures. On November 16, under heavy pressure from artists' groups, the endowment reverses itself and agrees to restore the $10,000 grant to the New York gallery.

November 10: America's Roman Catholic bishops, days before the convening of the first Vatican's Conference on AIDS, issue a statement urging reliance on sexual abstinence outside of marriage to halt the spread of the disease.

November 30: WHO warns that the global AIDS epidemic is gaining momentum. Organization officials say the incidence of HIV infection in some parts of Africa and South America is as great among women as it is among men, raising concerns about possible patterns of heterosexual transmission.

December 1: Some 600 museums and galleries nationwide observe the event "A Day without Art" to focus attention on the devastating impact of AIDS on the arts community.

December 6: In a report to President Bush, the National Commission on AIDS faults the federal government for not taking the actions necessary to provide health care to people with AIDS. The commission describes a growing complacency about the epidemic and deplores the lack of a national plan for contending with the impact of AIDS on the health care system.

CHAPTER 3

COURT CASES

This chapter summarizes the court cases involving AIDS generally considered most significant. These cases concerned issues of broad relevance and addressed important questions of law. The widespread public attention they received contributed to the growing awareness of AIDS in the society at large. Each of these five cases is presented in the same format: Background, Legal Issues, Decision and Impact.

The first two cases dealt with the question of AIDS and education. In both instances, local communities sought to exclude children with AIDS from their public schools. In the third case, an avowedly gay male challenged the constitutionality of statues prohibiting homosexual sodomy. Many gay organizations believed that efforts to respond to the AIDS epidemic had been hindered by public attitudes about homosexuality; they saw this challenge as a key step in their attempts to achieve equal protection under the law. The final two cases were instrumental in resolving the issue of whether persons with AIDS were entitled to protection under the federal law barring discrimination against the handicapped.

The chapter concludes with a brief overview of other court cases pertinent to the AIDS epidemic. Although it is not yet possible to gauge the enduring legal significance of these cases, they clearly illustrate the central role the law has played in shaping American responses to the AIDS epidemic.

IN RE DISTRICT 27 COMMUNITY SCHOOL BOARD v. BOARD OF EDUCATION OF THE CITY OF NEW YORK

Background

New York City announced its policy governing the education of children with AIDS in September 1985. Based on guidelines recommended by the CDC, the policy called for case-by-case evaluations to determine whether these children should attend regular classes. City officials created a special panel to review the cases of those school-aged children already reported to have the disease. The city's action immediately became the subject of intense debate.

In Queens there was already a bitter dispute over the proposed placement of AIDS patients in a local nursing home. Two community school boards that had voted to bar students with AIDS from normal classes called on the city to postpone its new policy. Community school board members expressed concern that medical evidence about the transmission of AIDS was inconclusive and constantly changing. Two days before school reopened city health and education officials, acting on the recommendation of the special panel, said that one of four children known to have AIDS would be allowed to attend regular classes. The two community school boards went to court to contest the decision. A five-week trial in the state supreme court ensued.

Legal Issues

The local school boards contended that city officials had abused the broad discretionary powers afforded them under the city charter in failing to exclude children with AIDS from the public school. They argued that the city's policy placed healthy children at unacceptable risk and endangered the public's safety. City officials responded by saying the policy had been carefully formulated based on the best medical advice available. In an effort to precisely define the actual risk of AIDS transmission, the court heard testimony from a total of 11 medical experts.

Decision

Judge Harold Hyman spent almost four months reviewing the evidence. In February 1986 he upheld New York City's policy of not automatically excluding all children with AIDS from public school classrooms. Focusing on the risks posed by children with AIDS, the judge noted that medical experts unanimously agreed the disease was not spread by casual interpersonal contact. He concluded that city officials had properly exercised their discretionary authority in setting the policy.

The court went on to address the constitutional and federal statutory issues involved. The judge ruled that mandatory exclusion of schoolchildren with AIDS would violate their right to equal protection of the law under the Fourteenth Amendment. Because their infection did not normally result in any significant health hazard, there was no reason to single them out for different treatment under the law. Judge Hyman foreshadowed the Supreme Court's reasoning in *School Board of Nassau County v. Arline* when he held that the Federal Rehabilitation Act of 1973 prohibiting discrimination against the handicapped applied to children with AIDS.

Impact

The court's decision meant that children with AIDS and, by extension, children infected with HIV who are asymptomatic, are entitled to a case-by-case assessment of their ability to attend school. School districts seeking to restrict HIV-infected children have the responsibility of proving that such children present an unacceptable health risk to their classmates.

Although the court's ruling was legally binding only in the state of New York, the case had an impact across the nation. The news that Rock Hudson had AIDS, revealed the previous summer, had raised not only public awareness of the disease but also public fears about its contagiousness. School districts in New Jersey, Florida, Indiana and California were involved in similar well-publicized disputes over the admission of children with AIDS. Judge Hyman's opinion became part of a growing body of legal precedents to which other courts could refer. In *District 27 v. Board of Education*, the public was informed about the facts of AIDS transmission, and thus it helped assuage growing concerns about the disease's infectiousness.

RYAN WHITE

Background

In December 1984 Ryan White was forced to leave school in Howard County, Indiana, due to acute illness. Ryan, a hemophiliac, was diagnosed as having contracted AIDS through the transfusion of an infected blood product. As Ryan's condition improved, his mother met with school officials to discuss her teenage son's return to classes in the fall. When the superintendent of schools decided against Ryan's readmission, the family brought suit against the school board charging unlawful discrimination under the Education of the Handicapped Act.

The federal court dismissed Ryan White's action on the procedural grounds that the Education of the Handicapped Act required him first to take his case through state administrative channels before seeking legal relief. During the period his appeal was under review, Ryan participated in classes at home via telephonic hookup with his school. The state held extensive hearings on the questions of both Ryan White's right to "appropriate public education" under the federal statute and the ways in which AIDS can be transmitted. Indiana officials in February 1986 concluded that Ryan could attend school, and he was issued a health certificate securing his admission.

Believing that Ryan posed a risk to their children, a group of parents then asked the local county court to restrict him from public schools on the basis of a 1949 Indiana law concerning communicable diseases. The statute directs that "persons having custody of any child infected with a communicable disease shall not permit him to attend school or appear in public." Ryan had been back in school one day when the court issued a temporary injunction barring his return until such time as it could determine whether the statute covered AIDS. The case was subsequently moved to a neighboring jurisdiction because of the intense emotions and publicity involved.

Legal Issues

In arriving at their decision permitting Ryan to attend school, Indiana state officials relied on the expert medical advice of the public health community. There was a strong consensus among health professionals that children with AIDS posed no meaningful risk of infection to their classmates. The parents opposing Ryan's return were skeptical of recent medical findings that AIDS could not be transmitted by casual contact. They felt the state's decision sacrificed the rights of their children to a safe education. Their purpose in going to court was not to exclude Ryan White per se, but rather to protect their children from what they perceived as the real danger of infection with a mysterious, incurable and terminal disease.

Decision

In April 1986 the judge for the Clinton County Court reversed the temporary injunction, ruling there was no legal or medical reason to keep Ryan White from school. The judge held that Ryan's health certificate superseded the restrictions of the 1949 law in question. Ryan returned to classes without further interruption. The group of parents dropped their efforts to appeal the decision the following July.

Impact

The case of Ryan White gained nationwide attention. To many, Ryan was a more sympathetic figure than either the homosexual or intravenous drug user commonly associated with AIDS. People responded to the problems of a child who had contracted the disease through no cause of his own. It has been suggested that the case's impact and legacy stem from the role it played in helping to educate the public about AIDS. Opposition to Ryan's presence in a classroom diminished as his community came to better understand the limited ways in which AIDS can be spread. Few similarly protracted disputes have occurred since Ryan White's ordeal. An ever-greater number of states have enacted guidelines providing for the education of children suffering from HIV infection.

BOWERS v. HARDWICK

Background

In August 1982 an Atlanta police officer went to the home of Michael Hardwick to serve a warrant for his failure to pay a fine for public drunkenness. The man answering the door was not sure about Hardwick's whereabouts but told the police officer he was free to enter and look for himself. The officer walked down the hall to a bedroom where, through an open door, he saw Hardwick and another man engaged in oral sex. Both men were arrested and charged under Georgia's sodomy statute, which makes it a criminal offense to perform or submit "to any sexual act involving the sex organs of one person and the mouth or anus of another."

Although the local district attorney declined to prosecute in the absence of further evidence, Hardwick brought suit in a federal district court challenging the constitutionality of the statute. The district court sided with the state of Georgia in dismissing the suit on the procedural ground that, since there was no prosecution, it failed to state a claim. The case was appealed to the Court of Appeals for the Eleventh Circuit where, in May 1985, a three-judge panel held the antisodomy law unconstitutional. The state of Georgia, represented by its attorney general, Michael J. Bowers, then successfully petitioned the Supreme Court for review.

Legal Issues

Hardwick contended that the Georgia sodomy statute violated his constitutional right to privacy and asserted that, as a practicing homosexual, the law placed him in unwarranted constant danger of arrest. The court of appeals concurred with this claim. It held that Hardwick's homosexual activity was a private and intimate association beyond the reach of state regulation by reason of the Due Process Clause of the Fourteenth Amendment. In response, the state of Georgia argued that homosexual sodomy was an unnatural act and that the Constitution could not be read as bestowing on consenting adults a fundamental right to participate in any and all sexual activity.

Decision

The Supreme Court ruled in June 1986 that the Constitution and, specifically, the Due Process Clause of the Fourteenth Amendment, does not confer a fundamental right on homosexuals to engage in consensual sodomy. The court did not address the constitutionality of the statute as it pertains to heterosexual activity.

Impact

As Justice Byron R. White stressed in his majority opinion, the Supreme Court's decision did not involve a judgment about whether laws prohibiting homosexual sodomy are wise or desirable, but considered only the issue of their constitutionality. As a result of the ruling, a number of homosexual advocacy groups turned their focus from judicial to legislative action in an effort to repeal antisodomy statutes in the states where they were still in effect. More militant homosexual rights advocates saw the court's decision as a reflection of a new wave of homophobia sweeping the country in the wake of the AIDS epidemic. The general consensus in the homosexual community, with which many health professionals agreed, was that the ruling would make attempts to combat AIDS more difficult. They were concerned that gay men would be less willing to come forward for counseling and treatment out of fear of criminal action. This worry has subsided in light of the fact that antisodomy statutes have rarely, if ever, been enforced.

SCHOOL BOARD OF NASSAU COUNTY
v. ARLINE

Background

Gene H. Arline began teaching elementary school in Nassau County, Florida, in 1966. Almost 10 years earlier she had been briefly hospitalized for tuberculosis. In 1979, after suffering her third relapse in two years, she was released by the Nassau County School Board, who feared she might infect her students. After failing to win reinstatement through state administrative proceedings, Arline filed an action against the school board in federal court.

Arline alleged her dismissal violated Section 504 of the Rehabilitation Act of 1973. The act prohibits discrimination "solely on the basis of handicap" against any handicapped individual who is "otherwise qualified" on the part of any program or activity receiving federal monies. Arline maintained that her history of physical impairment resulting from tuberculosis made her a handicapped individual. She also argued that because the risk of her infecting her students was minimal, she was "otherwise qualified" for her job. The district court, while acknowledging Arline's physical handicap, denied her request for reinstatement. The court ruled that she had been dismissed on the basis of her contagiousness and that a contagious disease could not be construed as a handicap within the meaning of the Rehabilitation Act.

In reversing the judgment of the district court, the Court of Appeals for the Eleventh Circuit found that persons with contagious diseases were covered under Section 504. The appeals court referred to trial the question of whether Arline was "otherwise qualified" for a teaching position. The Supreme Court subsequently granted the Nassau County School Board's petition for review.

Legal Issues

Recognizing the potential applicability of the Supreme Court's decision to AIDS-related cases, numerous groups concerned with the AIDS epidemic filed legal briefs in support of both sides. The Justice Department, in a highly publicized and controversial brief, urged the court to rule that federal law did not prohibit discrimination, whether medically justified or not, "based on concern about contagiousness." Arline's counsel argued that discrimination against contagion could not be separated from discrimination against the underlying impairment. They contended that the Justice Department's narrow interpretation of the law would leave contagious persons without legal defense against the unreasonable fears of others.

Decision

In March 1987 the Supreme Court held that persons who were physically or mentally impaired by contagious diseases were protected against discrimination under the provisions of Section 504 of the 1973 Rehabilitation Act. Writing for the majority, Justice William H. Brennan Jr. noted that Arline's contagiousness and her physical impairment both resulted from the same underlying tubercular condition. He concluded that it would be unfair to allow employers to draw on the distinction between the effects of a disease on others and its effects on the patient in justifying discriminatory treatment. The court also affirmed the decision of the court of appeals to send the case back to district court for determination, based on competent medical judgment, about whether Arline was "otherwise qualified" to be a teacher.

Impact

Arline is generally considered the most significant court case bearing on AIDS. Although it specifically addressed the issue of tuberculosis, *Arline* established a precedent for extending federal safeguards against discrimination to persons with AIDS. In November of the same year a federal appeals court, in *Chalk v. U.S. District Court*, relied on *Arline* in holding AIDS to be a handicap under Section 504. Classification of AIDS as a handicap meant that individuals with AIDS were entitled to a case-by-case assessment of their infectiousness and its impact on their qualifications. Since current medical opinion views the risk of transmitting AIDS through casual contact as virtually nonexistent, it is believed that persons with AIDS will normally be found to be "otherwise qualified."

AIDS rights advocates see *Arline* as an important, but limited, victory. The *Arline* decision applies only to recipients of federal funds. It does not bar discrimination at the state or local level or in the private arena. Legal remedies in these areas are contingent on state and local laws and regulations.

Arline presented the Supreme Court with an instance of discrimination against someone who had an actual physical disability. The court's decision was not that Arline's contagiousness made her handicapped, but that her contagiousness did not change her handicapped status. In a footnote to the majority opinion, Justice Brennan explicitly declined to rule whether the Rehabilitation Act protects carriers of the AIDS virus who do not have disabling symptoms but are able to transmit the disease. His observation that "society's accumulated myths and fears about disability and disease are as handicapping as are the physical limitations that flow from actual impairment" seemed to provide interested lower courts with the basis for extending the law's reach. In June 1988 a federal court in California ruled that the 1973 act's protections, in fact, apply to AIDS virus carriers who are not yet ill.

CHALK v. U.S. DISTRICT COURT

Background

Vincent L. Chalk had taught classes for the hearing impaired for seven years in the Orange County, California, school system. In February 1987, following a period of hospitalization, he was diagnosed as having AIDS. When his doctor approved his return to work in April, the county turned to its director of epidemiology and disease control for medical advice on how to proceed. The director reported in May that Chalk's presence in a classroom would not pose a risk to his students. Chalk returned from leave in August to find the county had decided to transfer him from teaching to administrative duties. His new desk job involved developing an AIDS education program for students. Chalk filed suit in federal court alleging discrimination. He also asked the court to issue a preliminary injunction ordering his reinstatement to his teaching position.

The U.S. District Court, expressing doubts about the completeness of current AIDS knowledge, denied Chalk's request on the grounds it could not be absolutely certain his students were free from risk. The court discussed its obligation to balance Chalk's right to fair treatment against the potential risk of harm to the students. It noted that Chalk had not been dismissed. Rather, he had simply been moved to other duties entailing the same pay and benefits. Chalk appealed the district court's decision to the Court of Appeals for the Ninth Circuit.

Legal Issues

Chalk's suit hinged on his claim that he was handicapped by virtue of his AIDS condition, and thus, was entitled to specific legal safeguards contained in the 1973 Rehabilitation Act. Section 504 of the law bars recipients of federal financial assistance from arbitrary discrimination against handicapped persons. Chalk's counsel argued that the county was not medically justified in removing him from the classroom. He portrayed the county's action as discriminatory because it denied to Chalk the benefits of his chosen profession for the relatively short period he had left to live. The request for a preliminary injunction stemmed from the concern that Chalk's remaining time not be spent in protracted litigation.

Decision

The court of appeals granted the request for a preliminary injunction in November 1987. In directing Chalk's return to the classroom, the three-judge panel made reference to the consensus throughout the medical community that AIDS could not be spread by the casual contact to which students would be exposed. Underlining the importance of the preliminary ruling, the court said Chalk faced possible "irreparable harm" if he could not continue teaching for all the time remaining to him.

In February 1988 the court of appeals delivered its final decision in which it affirmed the reasoning of the preliminary injunction. In holding AIDS to be a handicap under Section 504, the court drew heavily on *School Board of Nassau County v. Arline* as precedent. In that March 1987 decision, the Supreme Court had ruled that "allowing discrimination based on the contagious effects of a physical impairment would be inconsistent with the basic purpose of Section 504." Citing the Supreme Court's recommendation to defer to the reasonable medical judgments of public health officials, the court of appeals found that Chalk was qualified to teach and determined he had suffered from job discrimination.

Impact

This is the first case in which AIDS was given the status of a handicap under federal law. Legal experts agree that the federal court's decision sends a clear message that it is improper, based on what is known about the disease, to discriminate against persons with AIDS. In practical terms, the ruling is important because of the widespread use of federal monies in all facets of American life. Its impact is nonetheless limited by the fact that the Rehabilitation Act does not pertain to instances of discrimination at the state and local level where federal monies are not involved or in the private sector. Current efforts to expand the rights of persons with AIDS are accordingly concentrated on enacting comprehensive national AIDS antidiscrimination legislation.

OTHER COURT CASES

Other important court cases have embraced a wide range of AIDS legal issues. These cases have addressed the rights of persons with AIDS to nondiscrimination under state laws; the rights of HIV-infected persons to confidentiality about their medical status; the liability of blood banks for HIV-contaminated blood; the prosecution of persons accused of attempting to spread the AIDS virus to others; and the authority of government officials to implement measures to control high-risk behavior.

The issue of whether state laws against discrimination pertain to persons with AIDS was confronted at approximately the same time in Florida and Massachusetts. In both states an employee with AIDS had been dismissed out of fear he would infect his co-workers. In Florida, the State Commission on Human Relations ruled in December 1985 that Broward County had violated the state's disability law when it released Todd Shuttleworth from his job as a budget policy analyst. Shuttleworth subsequently agreed to an out-of-court settlement with Broward County that included his full reinstatement. In October 1986, Paul F. Cronan returned to work as part of the settlement of his lawsuit against the New England Telephone Company. The previous August a Massachusetts state court had determined that AIDS was a disability under the state's handicapped discrimination law and concluded that Cronan's employment rights were consequently protected. These two cases, which set precedents for classifying AIDS as a handicap, directly influenced similar court actions in other states.

HIV-infected persons have been particularly sensitive about their right to confidentiality or privacy. They have contended that disclosure of their medical status could expose them to embarrassment, social condemnation and discrimination. The right was tested in South Florida Blood Service Inc. v. Rasmussen. Donald Rasmussen had died of AIDS allegedly contracted through blood transfusions he received in 1982 after he was struck by an automobile. His estate, as part of a lawsuit against the automobile driver, wanted the blood service to reveal the names of those donors whose blood had been given to Rasmussen. It was the plaintiff's intent to prove that Rasmussen's injuries were aggravated when he became infected with the AIDS virus. A Florida state court in January 1987 declined to order disclosure of the donors' names, ruling that the donors' rights to privacy regarding their medical status outweighed the plaintiff's need to know.

In the Rasmussen case the justices reasoned that society's interest in promoting an adequate blood supply would not be served by judicial inquiries into the private lives of donors. Whether the blood service was itself liable for AIDS-contaminated blood was not at issue. This question was raised by a woman who contracted AIDS through a tainted transfusion in 1983 and subsequently sued United Blood Services for damages. In June 1988 a Denver district court dismissed the lawsuit on the ground that since there was no screening test for the AIDS virus at the time of the transfusion, there was no basis for finding negligence. The

---

decision implied that blood services would be held liable for HIV-contaminated blood obtained after the development of the screening test.

The courts have held that those who attempt to infect others with the AIDS virus are subject to criminal prosecution. In a well-publicized case, a prison inmate with AIDS bit two guards at the Federal Medical Center in Rochester, Minnesota. James V. Moore was found guilty by a Minnesota court in June 1987 of assault with a deadly weapon, namely, his mouth and teeth. This innovative use of an existing statute illustrates how most jurisdictions, in the absence of specific offenses covering the deliberate transmission of the AIDS virus, are relying on current laws to prosecute these kinds of cases.

The right of local health authorities to close homosexual bathhouses to stop unsafe sexual acts that spread the AIDS virus was tested in court in both California and New York. Homosexual rights advocates unsuccessfully argued that closing the private establishments violated the constitutionally protected rights of individuals to engage in private activities. The courts in both states upheld the actions of the public health officials as a legal exercise of their authority to control the transmission of contagious diseases. In California certain bathhouses were permitted to reopen under tight restrictions prohibiting high-risk sexual behavior. In those instances where the restrictions were not followed, public authorities took action to shut down the noncomplying establishments.

The discovery of the AIDS virus has itself been a matter of litigation. In late 1985 the Pasteur Institute filed suit against the United States Government. The suit contended that U.S. federal researchers led by Dr. Robert C. Gallo had relied on materials and information provided by Dr. Luc Montagnier's research team at the Institute in its isolation of the AIDS virus. At stake were both the international prestige that would accompany credit for discovery of the virus and the right to patent the blood test developed to screen for its presence. President Reagan and Prime Minister Chirac of France jointly announced in March 1987 an agreement where researchers from the two countries would share recognition for the discovery of HIV. This was an unprecedented involvement of heads of state in a scientific dispute. The settlement stipulated that patent rights to the blood test derived from the discovery would also be shared, with the majority of the royalties going to a new AIDS research and education fund.

CHAPTER 4

BIOGRAPHICAL LISTING

This chapter contains brief biographical sketches on a cross-section of significant figures in the story of the AIDS epidemic. Entries share basic format. Individuals are identified by the position they held, or currently hold, relevant to AIDS. A description of the person's salient actions or involvement in the AIDS issue follows.

Dr. Arthur J. Ammann   Director of Pediatric Immunology, the University of California at San Francisco. A pioneering physician in the diagnosis and treatment of AIDS in infant children, he also was among the first medical experts to alert the nation in December 1982 to the threat of the AIDS virus in the blood supply.

Dr. Joseph R. Bove   Director, Blood Banks, Yale University Hospitals, New Haven, Connecticut. A leading spokesman for the blood industry, he was a key figure in the debate on blood-donation policies and procedures during the initial stages of the AIDS epidemic.

Dr. Otis R. Bowen   Secretary of the Department of Health and Human Services (HHS) between December 1985 and January 1989, he was active in the AIDS issue on several fronts. He led Reagan administration calls for expanded testing of randomly selected blood samples to chart the incidence of HIV infection among Americans. Addressing the worldwide implications of AIDS in a speech in early 1987, Dr. Bowen said the epidemic "will become so serious that it will dwarf such earlier medical disasters as smallpox and typhoid". As HHS secretary, he advocated further legal measures to protect individuals with AIDS against discrimination be enacted at the state rather than federal level.

AIDS

Dr. Edward N. Brandt Assistant Secretary of Health, Department of HHS, from 1981 to 1984. During his tenure he led efforts within the Reagan administration to gain increases in federal funding levels for AIDS. In May 1983 he declared AIDS the number-one priority of the U.S. Public Health Service. As the official responsible for coordinating and setting federal guidelines on the nation's blood supply, he mediated the debate over appropriate screening and donation policies that followed the implication of blood and blood products in the transmission of AIDS.

Dr. Jean-Claude Chermann French retrovirologist. He was part of the Pasteur Institute team that first isolated the AIDs virus in the spring of 1983. He also led in the development of the drug HPA-23 as an experimental AIDS treatment.

Dr. Marcus A. Conant A dermatologist with the University of California at San Francisco (UCSF). He was the founder and codirector of the nation's first Kaposi's sarcoma (KS) clinic, organized through UCSF and San Francisco General Hospital. He also helped organize the KS Education and Research Foundation.

Dr. Ellen C. Cooper A manager at the Food and Drug Administration (FDA), she emerged in the late 1980s as the agency's most important gatekeeper for AIDS drugs under review. Although credited for her role in speeding approval of AZI to deathly ill AIDS sufferers, Cooper has endured criticism for her strict adherence to scientific screening procedures. Detractors say she has needlessly denied terminally ill persons drugs that were still undergoing testing even though the patients were willing to try them.

Dr. Theodore Cooper Chairman and chief executive officer of the Upjohn Company. He served as chairman of the expert committee appointed by the National Academy of Sciences to assess the performance of the federal government in confronting the AIDS epidemic.

Dr. James W. Curran An epidemiologist, Curran is director of the division of HIV/AIDS at the CID. The first chairman of the Kaposi's Sarcoma and Opportunistic Infections (KSOI) Task Force, he became the administrative director of AIDS research efforts at the Centers for Disease Control (CDC).

Dr. Selma Dritz Assistant director of the Bureau of Communicable Disease Control at the San Francisco Department of Public Health during the initial years of the AIDS epidemic. She was the first public health official to draw a connection between the initial, random cases of AIDS in San Francisco. In October 1982, she assisted Dr. Arthur Ammann and Dr. Harold Jaffe in documenting the first case of AIDS acquired through a blood transfusion.

Dr. Peter H. Duesberg   Molecular biologist at the University of California at Berkeley. A controversial figure in AIDS research, he has challenged conventional scientific premises about the epidemic. Duesberg contends that HIV is not the exclusive cause of AIDS.

Gaetan Dugas   A French Canadian airline steward and AIDS victim who died in March 1984. He was linked sexually to 9 of the first 19 reported cases of the disease in Los Angeles by Centers for Disease Control (CDC) researchers, who dubbed him "Patient Zero." These links lent strong support to the theory that AIDS was transmitted by sexual contact.

Dr. Myron E. Essex   A retrovirologist with the Harvard University School of Public Health in Cambridge, Massachusetts. His research helped establish that HIV is a retrovirus. His work with monkey viruses has revealed important parallels to the AIDS virus. These efforts have contributed to developing theories on the natural history of the AIDS virus.

Dr. Bruce L. Evatt   Director of the Division of Immunological, Oncological and Hemotological Disease at the CDC and a former head of its Division of Host Factors. An expert on hemophilia, he followed the earliest cases of AIDS reported among hemophiliacs and hypothesized that whatever infectious agent was causing the disease had found its way into blood-clotting substances. He subsequently helped coordinate measures taken to protect the nation's blood supply from HIV contamination.

Dr. Anthony S. Fauci   Associate director for AIDS Research at the National Institutes of Health (NIH) and long-standing director of the National Institute of Allergy and Infectious Diseases (NIAID), he is the federal official in charge of testing of experimental AIDS drugs. Dr. Fauci has been near the center of the ongoing controversy over the pace and funding of federal efforts to develop AIDS treatment therapies. He has frequently appeared before congressional committees investigating the epidemic to outline the progress of NIAID AIDS research and to answer inquiries about the adequacy of presently allocated resources. In 1989 he urged the PHS to adopt a new system to allow AIDS patients far greater access to experimental drugs.

Dr. Donald P. Francis   As a retrovirologist and coordinator of laboratory research for the AIDS Activities Office of the CDC, he was involved in a range of important AIDS research and policy initiatives. He worked on the initial epidemiologial studies conducted by the CDC and was among the very first scientists anywhere in the Public Health Service (PHS) to advance the theory that AIDS was caused by a transmissible viral agent. He was an early advocate of taking decisive measures to protect the nation's blood supply from AIDS virus contamination. Francis is now a regional AIDS consultant to the CDC in San Francisco.

Dr. Robert C. Gallo A retrovirologist with the National Cancer Institute (NCI). Discoverer of the first recognized human retrovirus HTLV in 1980, he directed the NCI research that resulted in successful isolation of the AIDS virus in the spring of 1984. He initially called the virus HILV-III, but the name was later changed to HIV. Dr. Gallo is credited, with Dr. Luc Montagnier, as a codiscoverer of HIV.

Dr. Michael S. Gottlieb An immunologist with UCLA. He treated the first patients in Los Angeles afflicted with the opportunistic infection PCP, and collaborated with Dr. Wayne Shandera on pioneering studies of the epidemiology of AIDS in Los Angeles. He initially established the National AIDS Research Foundation with $250,000 bequeathed by the actor Rock Hudson, who had been his patient. In September 1985, Dr. Gottlieb joined efforts with Dr. Mathilde Krim, and merged the National AIDS Research Foundation with her AIDS Medical Foundation to form AmFAR.

Dr. William A. Haseltine A pathologist at the Dana-Farber Cancer Institute in Boston who has been active in AIDS-related research. He was the first to locate the TAT3 gene in HIV and describe its key role in the virus's ability to rapidly reproduce.

Margaret M. Heckler Secretary of the Department of HHS from early 1983 through the end of 1985. In a major speech in June 1983, she proclaimed AIDS as the number-one health priority of the HHS. This was the first official declaration of federal AIDS policy by a cabinet-level official. In May 1984 she made the public announcement of the discovery of the AIDS virus by Dr. Robert Gallo and his research team at the NCI.

Rock Hudson An American movie actor, he died of medical complications stemming from AIDS in the fall of 1985. His donation of $250,000, made prior to his death, helped launch the American Foundation for AIDS Research.

Dr. Harold W. Jaffe Deputy Director for Science at the CID, Jaffe formerly served as chief of the epidemiology section of the AIDS Activities Office. He conducted the CDC's first epidemiological study of AIDS in San Francisco beginning in August 1981. Jaffe also assisted Dr. Arthur Ammann in confirming the first cases of transmission of HIV through blood transfusions.

Dr. Stephen C. Joseph The vocal and high-profile New York City

Health Commissioner from 1986 to 1989, Joseph earned a nationwide reputation for leadership on AIDS issues. He won praise for alerting the public to the severe health crisis and for pushing the city government to expand services. Joseph's campaign to give drug addicts free hypodermic needles to curb the spread of AIDS and his expressed view that all people testing positive for HIV be confidentially reported to city health authorities drew strong opposition from homosexual rights groups and civil libertarians.

Dr. C. Everett Koop   Surgeon general of the United States from 1981 to 1989, he became the most visible and vocal spokesperson in the federal government on the public health dimensions of AIDS. His "Surgeon General's Report on AIDS," released in October 1986, was widely credited for having elevated the epidemic to the level of a mainstream public health issue.

Larry Kramer   Novelist, playwright and film producer. His article "1112 and Counting," published in March 1983, challenged the gay community to confront the dire implications of the growing AIDS epidemic. He authored *The Normal Heart*, a critically acclaimed play about the searing impact of AIDS. A leading gay activist, and frequent critic of governmental responses to the epidemic, he was one of the founders of the Gay Men's Health Crisis (GMHC) and the protest group ACT-UP (Aids Coalition to Unleash Power).

Dr. Mathilde G. Krim   Cofounder and executive director of the American Foundation for AIDS Research (AmFAR), a private national organization whose primary purpose is to raise money to fund AIDS scientific research. Dr. Krim first established the AIDS Medical Foundation in 1983. In September 1985 she merged this organization with Dr. Michael Gottlieb's National AIDS Research Foundation to form AmFAR.

Dr. Dale N. Lawrence   As a researcher with the Division of Host Factors of the CDC, he developed one of the earliest statistical models for the long incubation period of the AIDS virus; he also led the field research in 1982 and 1983 on the incidence of AIDS among hemophiliacs and blood transfusion recipients.

Dr. Jacques Leibowitch   French immunologist and AIDS researcher at the Rene Descartes University in Paris. He was an early proponent of the theory that AIDS was caused by a virus. His treatment of AIDS patients in Paris led him to speculate that the disease had emerged from Africa in the mid-1970s.

Dr. Jay A. Levy   A retrovirologist with the University of California School of Medicine. In August 1984, he isolated the AIDS virus and named it *ARV*. Subsequent studies showed the virus to be the same as that previously discovered by researchers at the NCI and the Pasteur Institute.

Dr. Joseph M. Mann   Director of the World Health Organization's Global Program on AIDS since 1986, he is credited with organizing the United Nations' worldwide battle against AIDS. Mann has spearheaded the drive to persuade many countries in the developing world to recognize the threat of AIDS and to take the measures necessary to curb its spread and treat its victims.

Robert Mapplethorpe   A photographer whose graphic work has been praised as art and reviled as pornography, he died of AIDS in March 1989. A retrospective exhibit of Mapplethorpe's photographs, some homoerotic and others chronicling his own AIDS struggle, set off fierce debate in Congress in the summer of 1989 over public funding of art that might be deemed offensive.

Dr. James O. Mason   A former Director of the CDC, he is the assistant secretary for health in the Bush administration. As head of the CDC, Mason had a hand in the range of important AIDS initiatives: scientific research, epidemiological studies, formulation of risk-reduction guidelines and preventive education. In his administrative capacity, Dr. Mason was a key participant in the battle over federal funding for AIDS programs.

Dr. W. Eugene Mayberry   Chief executive of the Mayo Clinic. In June 1987, he was appointed director of the newly established President's Commission on AIDS. He resigned the post in October 1987 after other commission members openly criticized his leadership performance.

Dr. Luc Montagnier   French retrovirologist with the Pasteur Institute in Paris. He directed the French team of researchers that first isolated the AIDS virus in the spring and summer of 1983. He is credited, with Dr. Robert Gallo, as a codiscoverer of HIV.

Dr. Kary Mullis   A research scientist with the Cetus Corporation in California. He originated the idea of *polymerase chain reaction* (PCR), the key component in a new AIDS virus test that detects the actual genetic material of the HIV in blood and tissue samples.

Paul Popham   A leading gay political activist and the first president of the GMHC in New York. He died from AIDS in May 1987.

Dr. Willy Rozenbaum   A French AIDS clinician at the Pitie-Salpetriere Hospital in Paris. He treated a small number of patients with immune disorders and opportunistic infections as early as 1978. In retrospect, it is thought that these persons were the first AIDS victims in France. With Dr. Jacques Leibowitch, he organized the earliest studies of the epidemiology of AIDS in France.

Dr. Jonas E. Salk   American medical research scientist who developed the first vaccine against polio. Since 1987 Salk, employing techniques used in his earlier polio research, has searched for a vaccine that would prevent people already infected with the AIDS virus from developing the deadly disease. According to his theory, such a vaccine would stimulate the body to destroy cells infected with HIV and stop its spread.

Dr. David J. Sencer   Health commissioner of New York City in the first years of the AIDS epidemic. During his tenure he helped formulate the city's guidelines for the admission of children with AIDS to school classrooms. He was involved in the November 1985 decision to close a number of gay bathhouses and other establishments in New York City on the ground they allowed high-risk sexual activity linked to the spread of AIDS.

Randy Shilts   A reporter with the *San Francisco Chronicle* who has covered the AIDS epidemic since 1982. He was the first journalist assigned full-time to report on the AIDS story. His book *And the Band Played On: Politics, People and the AIDS Epidemic*, published in 1987, is considered the preeminent study of the early years of the epidemic.

Dr. Mervyn F. Silverman   Director of the San Francisco Department of Public Health during the initial years of the AIDS epidemic, he was the official responsible for the controversial decision to close the city's gay bathhouses in October 1984. He is currently president and national chairman of AmFAR.

Dr. Louis W. Sullivan   Secretary of HHS since March 1989, he has acted as President George Bush's main spokesman on the administration's AIDS policy and related issues. Sullivan, in charge of the executive department that disperses most federal AIDS funding, has urged government's compassionate response to the AIDS epidemic and supported federal measures to bar discrimination against AIDS victims.

Elizabeth Taylor   American movie actress. She helped Dr. Mathilde Krim and Dr. Michael Gottlieb organize AmFAR, and has been director and national spokesperson for the organization since its inception.

Dr. Paul A. Volberding   Director of the AIDS Clinic at San Francisco General Hospital. As an AIDS researcher and clinician, he was involved in the treatment of the initial outbreak of KS in San Francisco in 1981. He served as a member of the expert panel appointed by the National Academy of Sciences (NAS) to study the AIDS issue and draft proposals for public and private sector responses to the epidemic.

Admiral James D. Watkins   A retired U.S. Navy admiral. In October 1987 he was appointed by President Reagan to succeed Dr. Eugene Mayberry as the chairman of the president's commission on AIDS. The commission submitted its final report on June 24, 1988. In January 1989 President Bush named Watkins as U.S. Energy Secretary.

Rep. Henry A. Waxman (D-CA)   Chairman of the House Subcommittee on Health and the Environment of the Committee on Energy and Commerce. Beginning with the first-ever congressional hearings on AIDS in the spring of 1982, his subcommittee has probed AIDS funding and policy responses at the federal level over the course of the epidemic.

Rep. Theodore S. Weiss (D-NY)   Chairman, House Subcommittee on Human Resources and Intergovernmental Relations of the Committee on Government Operations. Since 1983, his subcommittee has investigated federal spending on AIDS and monitored developments in government medical research on the epidemic.

Ryan White   A teenaged hemophiliac boy who contracted AIDS through blood transfusions, and died on April 8, 1990; his protracted and ultimately successful legal struggle to return to school in his home state of Indiana gained nationwide attention.

Dr. Frank E. Young   Commissioner of the FDA from May 1984 until his resignation in December 1989. As administrative head and coordinator of FDA policies, he was deeply involved in the debate over the long screening and approval process for potential AIDS drugs. Beginning in 1987, in response to increasingly harsh criticism, Young initiated a program to speed the approval of experimental treatments for terminally ill AIDS patients by modifying lengthy FDA testing requirements. He was under attack throughout his tenure for the agency's limited progress in approving drugs for AIDS. Young attributed the slow going to the fact that few AIDS drugs had proved sufficiently effective to warrant use in patients.

PART II

GUIDE TO FURTHER RESEARCH

CHAPTER 5

INFORMATION ON AIDS

The literature devoted to AIDS is vast and ever expanding. Audiovisual (AV) and other materials on the epidemic abound. This chapter is a brief primer on basic AIDS research. It discusses the principal reference tools now available to assist in finding information on AIDS, and then briefly profiles some of the primary sources on the subject.

Much of the information on AIDS normally sought by students and others interested in the topic is available at a standard municipal or school library. Within the library, several basic reference resources facilitate identifying and locating current AIDS materials.

Card Catalogs

The card catalog remains a key reference tool. It is a central inventory of a library's holdings, from books and periodicals, to AV materials and microforms. The catalog contains individual bibliographic citations on all items in the library. Rather than consolidating all holdings in a single catalog, some libraries maintain separate ones for AV materials, noncirculating reference works, government documents or special collections.

Most libraries use the traditional manual card catalog. Increasingly, though many facilities are converting to automated systems. The advent of automated catalogs have marked a parallel trend toward interlibrary networks. Computers allow libraries to cross-reference holdings more readily. With this capability, public and school facilities are joining in cooperative lending systems. A library that is part of such a network now has access to vastly enlarged resources.

AIDS

Automated Systems

Automated, or computer-based, information systems and services have emerged as major research tools. On-line and CD ROM systems offer quick access to numerous data bases encompassing a broad range of subjects. *On-line* means the library, as a subscriber, taps into a regional, national or international data base network over a phone line. CD ROM is a system of information storage on laser disks for use with microcomputers.

Most of these data bases furnish bibliographic citations and abstracts of articles, documents, books and reports. Some provide the full text of articles. With AIDS, which is so recent and so dynamic, computer-based systems are particularly helpful because they are updated frequently and therefore list the most current resources.

Several automated data bases and information systems are helpful guides to the large and growing store of books and periodical literature on AIDS. *InfoTrac*, which indexes mainstream and generally accessible periodical sources, is easy to use and widely available. It provides bibliographic records from more than 900 business, technical and general interest magazines and newspapers. *InfoTrac* covers the current year plus the three preceding years. *WILSONLINE* provides the full range of printed H. W. Wilson Co. indexes. Users have access to *Reader's Guide to Periodical Literature*, *Book Review Digest*, *General Science Index*, *Social Science Index* and the *Humanities Index*. These and the other indexes available on *WILSONLINE* are valuable guides to some of the most recent AIDS sources.

AIDSLINE provides bibliographic citations to scientific articles on current AIDS research, clinical aspects of the disease, epidemiology and health policy issues. References are drawn from the National Library of Medicine's *MEDLINE* data base and cover from 1980 to the present. The *Health Information Network* (HIN) is a full-text data base network that provides health care professionals with access to the most up-to-date information. The *AIDS Information Clearinghouse*, a part of HIN, includes news items, announcements of the key federal agencies involved in AIDS issues and data on conferences and important legal decisions.

Indexes

Indexes are an integral part of a library's reference complement. These guides compile citations on books, magazine literature, newspaper articles, scholarly tracts, government publications, film strips, audio recordings and historical materials. There is significant overlap of the book- and pamphlet-form indexes and the automated information systems. Some

---

guides appear both in the traditional printed form and in automation. Other indexes are converting from print to computer-based systems.

Book Review Index is a guide to book reviews published in over 300 magazines and newspapers. This bimonthly publication furnishes only the citation to reviews. The monthly *Book Review Digest* provides citations to reviews of current English-language fiction and nonfiction. In addition, the *Digest* prints excerpts from the reviews, which are drawn from some 90 selected periodicals and journals. A good source for annotated citations to AIDS reference books is Sheehy's *Guide to Reference Books*.

Several major city dailies have become excellent sources of information through steadily expanded coverage of AIDS. The *New York Times* has chronicled the legal, political, medical, social and cultural developments since the disease syndrome appeared in 1981. The *New York Times Index* is an essential research tool for anyone interested in AIDS. It gives summaries of all articles with exact reference to the dates, pages and columns on which they appeared. Back issues of the *New York Times* and some other major dailies are recorded on microfilm. The *Newspaper Index* is a monthly publication that indexes major newspapers such as the *Chicago Tribune*, the *Los Angeles Times*, the *Denver Post*, the *Detroit News* and the *San Francisco Chronicle*.

The periodical literature on AIDS is massive. Two useful sources of citations to articles in mainstream publications are the *Reader's Guide to Periodical Literature*, which indexes more than 200 general interest periodicals published in the United States; and the *Magazine Index*, which compiles citations to the approximately 370 popular magazines and professional journals. Other indexes track the periodical literature on subject areas in the hard sciences and liberal arts. *General Science Index*, *Social Science Index*, *Humanities Index* and *Education Index* cite AIDS articles from publications devoted to these disciplines.

The *Encyclopedia of Associations* is standard to any basic library reference collection. A guide to national and international organizations, it provides short explanatory abstracts on each entry. The *Encyclopedia of Associations: Regional, State and Local Organizations* is a seven-volume, geographically organized guide to more than 50,000 nonprofit organizations on the state, city or local level. Both of these indexes also are available on-line.

Government Documents

The federal government and state agencies issue a substantial volume of information on AIDS. The *Monthly Catalog of United States Government*

Publications has bibliographic entries for virtually all documents published by federal agencies, including books, reports, studies and serials. The *Monthly Catalog* also is on CD ROM. This automated version is called *GPO Silverplatter*. The *Index to U.S. Government Periodicals* covers periodicals of the federal government. *Congressional Information Service Index* (CIS), a directory to the publications of the U.S. Congress, is an excellent source. It is the primary tool for locating documents issued by the various committees of both houses of Congress: hearings, committee prints, reports, treaties and public laws. This source is issued in two parts: One volume is the index, and the other volume contains abstracts on the cited publications.

The methods for cataloging state documents vary. Generally, libraries will maintain a separate catalog for state government sources. Certain government documents may also be housed in the reference or general book collections, in which case they most likely are listed in the main card catalog.

Basic Sources

There are a number of basic resources on AIDS. Following is a discussion of some of the primary works on key aspects of the AIDS epidemic. Any one of these general texts would serve as a good starting point. *AIDS: Origins, Prevention and Cure*, is a comprehensive four-volume set on the history, prevention and treatment of the disease. *AIDS: The Facts*, by John Langone, reviews the major medical and social facets of the epidemic. The 20 articles in *AIDS: Principles, Practice, and Politics*, eds. Inge Corless and Mary Pitman-Lindeman, sketch an overview of AIDS epidemiology and the social and political responses to the epidemic. A solid basic word is *The Essential AIDS Fact Book: What You Need to Know to Protect Yourself, Your Family, All Your Loved Ones*, by Paul Harding Douglas and Laura Pinsky. For a global perspective, there is *AIDS: The Deadly Epidemic*, by Graham Hancock and Carim Enver.

For historical background, *The AIDS Reader*, eds. Loren K. Clarke and Malcolm Potts, provides a thorough and balanced account. This compilation of articles offers a documentary history of the epidemic through 1988. Two fine narrative historical treatments are *AIDS, from the Beginning*, by M. Cole and George D. Lundberg, and *The Truth about AIDS: Evolution of an Epidemic*, by Ann G. Fettner and William A. Check. *And the Band Played On: Politics, People, and the AIDS Epidemic*, by Randy Shilts, examines the political history of AIDS in the early and mid-1980s.

The literature on medical aspects of AIDS tends to be technical and therefore challenging for the general reading public. A good beginning book is *Questions and Answers on AIDS*, by Lyn Frumkin and John Leonard. Prepared by doctors with experience treating AIDS, this book provides comprehensive factual information on the disease in question-and-answer format. *AIDS and the Healer Within,* by Nick Bamforth, contains a discussion of alternative AIDS treatment methods. Periodicals that track statistics and current information on the medical dimensions of AIDS include the monthly newsletter *AIDS Alert,* Atlanta, American Health Consultants, and *AIDS Medical Update,* Los Angeles, UCLA AIDS Clinical Research Center.

Among personal narratives, three works are powerful accounts of the devastating impact of AIDS on individual lives. In *Surviving AIDS,* author Michael Cullen recounts his own struggle with the disease and relates stories of 25 long-term AIDS survivors. Emmanual Dreuilhe describes his battle with AIDS in *Mortal Embrace: Living with AIDS.* The award-winning *Borrowed Time: An AIDS Memoir,* by Paul Monette, is an emotional portrait of an AIDS sufferer, written by his partner.

For anyone interested in the legal dimensions of the epidemic, a good overview work is *AIDS and the Law,* by William Dornette. *AIDS and the Law: A Guide for the Public,* eds. Harlon Dalton and Scott Burris, offers a thorough analysis of AIDS-related legal issues. Its collection of essays examines the legal impact of AIDS in schools, housing, civil rights, insurance, the military and prisons. The periodical *AIDS Update,* from the Lambda Legal Defense and Education Fund, covers AIDS-related legal and legislative developments.

Probably the best easily accessible source on federal activities is the *Congressional Quarterly Almanac.* Published annually, it provides a thorough overview of political developments, legislative initiatives and activities of Congress, the White House and the Supreme Court.

Among federal agencies, the Department of Health and Human Services acts as a clearinghouse for AIDS informational and educational materials. *Facts About AIDS* is a short compendium of basic AIDS information for the general public. A series of *Information Packets* issued by the Centers for Disease Control's (CDC) Division of HIV/AIDS is quite useful. These topical collections of articles cover such areas as current AIDS medical research, treatment efforts, HIV transmission and economic impact.

Congress has monitored public policy responses to AIDS through hearings and studies. Three House panels have been particularly active in AIDS issues: the Energy and Commerce Committee; the Government Operations Committee; and the Budget Committee. The hearings and reports of the committees are published as government documents.

The Public Health Service has established a *National AIDS Information Clearinghouse* (NAIC). The *Clearinghouse* serves as a centralized source of in-depth information about available AIDS services, resources and statistics. Reference specialists are available to assist callers on NAIC's toll free number: (800) 458–5231. The California-based American Foundation for AIDS Research (AmFAR), (213) 273–5547, promotes AIDS education and awareness and welcomes inquiries from the general public. The American Red Cross, AIDS Education Office, (202) 639–3223, runs an extensive AIDS public awareness campaign, providing a broad range of information and materials. Project Inform is a private organization that maintains detailed, well-organized information on AIDS drug treatments. Located in San Francisco, its national hotline is (800) 822–7422. Informational materials on the whole range of legal issues related to AIDS are available from Lambda Legal Defense and Education Fund, (202) 995–8585.

Numerous public and private organizations at the state and local levels provide information, run educational programs and oversee outreach programs. The listing in Chapter 7 identifies agencies in each of the states.

The most up-to-date AIDS statistics on incidence, deaths, epidemiology and economic costs are available from the CDC at (404) 330–3020. Several CDC publications provide statistical information: *Morbidity and Mortality Weekly Report, CDC AIDS Weekly* and the annual *HIV/AIDS Surveillance Report*. International statistics can be obtained from the World Health Organization, (202) 861–4353.

CHAPTER 6

―――――■―――――

ANNOTATED
BIBLIOGRAPHY

This chapter provides information on AIDS sources drawn from a broad spectrum of print and other media. Separate listings are provided for bibliographies, books, encyclopedias, periodicals, articles, government documents and audiovisual materials. Each item is identified by a standard library citation. A brief annotation then describes the resource's contents and scope.

There is a wealth of information on AIDS. Two basic rules have guided the inclusion of materials in this bibliography: First, emphasis is on sources that are available in most medium-sized public or school libraries. Second, items have been selected for their usefulness to students and others doing general research on AIDS. Highly technical works on the subject have not been included. Readers desiring further specialized information should consult either the listing of bibliographies in this chapter or the discussion of reference sources in Chapter 5.

BIBLIOGRAPHIES

Abrams, E. J. *Acquired Immunodeficiency Syndrome (AIDS): Thirteenth Update*. Bethesda, Md.: U.S. Department of Health and Human Services, Public Health Service, National Institutes of Health, National Library of Medicine.

Updates and supplements Public Health Service AIDS literature from 1980 through 1986. Provides over 650 new citations on the clinical aspects, epidemiology and prevention of AIDS.

AIDS

AIDS Bibliography: Selected Resources for Church Educators. New York: National Council of Churches, Division of Education and Ministry, 1989.

Includes educational materials concerning AIDS: its prevention and transmission, pastoral care, spiritual support and concerns of minority populations.

"AIDS: A Multimedia Bibliography." *Booklist*, Vol. 84, Oct. 15, 1987, p. 365–368.

A bibliography of books and films on AIDS for young adults and the general public.

AIDS Prevention among Female Sex Partners of Intravenous Drug Users: Annotated Bibliography, Number 3, May 1989. Special Issue: AIDS and Prostitution. Bethesda, Md.: Nova Research Company, 1989.

Over 70 annotated citations from journals, popular magazines, newspapers, books and unpublished sources on the issues of AIDS and prostitution.

AIDS Prevention among Female Sexual Partners of Intravenous Drug Users. Annotated Bibliography for Project Staff and Clients. Bethesda, Md.: Nova Research Company, 1989.

Annotated bibliography on prevention of HIV and AIDS in female sexual partners of IV drug users and in children.

AIDS in Prison Bibliography, 1988. Washington, D.C.: National Prison Project, 1988.

Provides references to educational materials and articles on AIDS in correctional facilities; includes federal, state and local corrections policies on AIDS and cites litigation cases.

AIDS Resource Listing: Audio Visuals. Rockville, Md.: U.S. Department of Health and Human Services, Health Resources and Services Administration, Bureau of Maternal and Child Health Resources Development, Office of Special Projects, 1989.

Provides a listing of videotapes and films for AIDS education and prevention.

AIDS Resource Listing: Selected CDC Guidance. Rockville, Md.: U.S. Department of Health and Human Services, Health Resources and Services Administration, Bureau of Maternal and Child Health and Resources Development, Office of Special Projects, 1989.

Bibliography of selected recommendations, guidelines and information issued by the Centers for Disease Control concerning HIV.

Annotated Bibliography

AIDS in the Workplace Bibliography. Los Angeles: Human Interaction Research Institute, 1988.

Bibliography cites books, periodical articles and other documents on HIV and AIDS in the workplace, covering such issues as discrimination, insurance, health safety, employee assistance programs, etc.

AIDS in the Workplace: Publications, July 1989. Los Angeles: Human Interaction Research Institute. AIDS in the Workplace Initiative, 1989.

Lists publications pertaining to AIDS in the workplace, particularly in the entertainment industry.

Alcohol and AIDS. Rockville, Md.: U.S. Department of Health and Human Services; Public Health Service; Alcohol, Drug Abuse, and Mental Health Administration; Office for Substance Abuse Prevention; National Clearinghouse for Alcohol and Drug Information, 1987.

Annotated reading list of publications and articles focusing on the possible relationship between alcohol consumption and AIDS.

Davis, C. C., comp. *AIDS Resource Guide*. Los Angeles: National Organization of Black County Officials. AIDS Education Project.

Bibliography of print and nonprint educational materials on AIDS.

Evans, Joanna W. *Acquired Immune Deficiency Syndrome*. Washington, D.C.: Library of Congress, Science and Technology Div., Science Reference Section, 1985.

8-page bibliography on AIDS.

Garoogian, Rhoda. *AIDS, 1981–1983: An Annotated Bibliography*. Mineola, N.Y.: CompuBibs, 1984.

Annotated AIDS bibliography covering general sources.

Gays and Acquired Immune Deficiency Syndrome (AIDS): A Bibliography. Brooklyn, N.Y.: Revisionist Press, 1986.

Extensive listing of information sources on AIDS with emphasis on the disease and gays.

Halleron, Trish, and Janet Pisanechi. *AIDS Information Resources Directory*. New York: American Foundation for AIDS Research, 1988.

Lists over 1,000 educational and informational materials including the following: books, manuals, videos and films, brochures, pamphlets, posters, cards, inserts, public service campaigns and instructional programs.

Hanson, P., and K. L. Speck. *A Resource Library on AIDS*. Rensselaer-ville, N.Y.: Rensselaerville Institute, 1988.

Compilation of audiovisual aids, books and training guides with emphasis on education for the prevention of the spread of AIDS.

Helping Teens Wait. Seattle: Center for Health Training, 1987.

Lists available brochures, books and audiovisual materials on adolescent sexual abstinence.

Iffrig, W. A. *Acquired Immune Deficiency Syndrome: Reference List*. Callaway, Florida: William A. Iffrig, 1988.

Bibliography of information sources on AIDS and the social, legal and political concerns raised by the disease. Also includes selections of personal narratives, materials with AIDS as the theme and dramatic plays.

Iosco, R. C. *AIDS: Laws, Ethics, and Public Policy*. Washington, D.C.: Georgetown University, Kennedy Institute of Ethics, National Reference Center for Bioethics Literature, 1988.

Provides general information on the AIDS epidemic, a summary of ethical issues relating to AIDS and citations and abstracts of 47 journal articles and books on ethical issues.

Kenton, Charlotte, and Estelle J. Abrams. *Acquired Immunodeficiency Syndrome*. Bethesda, Md.: U.S. Department of Health and Human Services, Public Health Service, National Institutes of Health, 1983–.

Covers citations from 1980 and is updated quarterly. Focus is on epidemiology and preclinical, diagnostic and prevention areas.

Korda, Holly, et al., *An Annotated Bibliography of Scientific Articles on AIDS for Policymakers*. Washington, D.C.: Public Health Service, 1987.

Select annotated bibliography on AIDS research.

Kraft, R., and E. Randall-David, comps. *AIDS: A Virus That Doesn't Discriminate. A Resource Guide*. Gainesville, Florida: Florida Association of Pediatric Tumor Programs, 1987.

Bibliography includes list of social service organizations nationwide, brochures, posters, informational games and audiovisual materials.

Learning AIDS: An Information Resources Directory. 2nd ed. New York: American Foundation for AIDS Research, 1989.

Provides information on materials relating to HIV and AIDS, arranged by audience groups such as black community, gay and bisexual men, policymakers and lawyers, etc., and by format.

Annotated Bibliography

Leonard, Arthur S. "AIDS Legal Bibliography." *AIDS and Public Policy Journal*, Vol. 2, no. 2, Spring–Summer 1987, p. 54–61.

Bibliography covering legal issues surrounding AIDS.

Lingle, Virginia, and M. Sandra Wood. *How to Find Information about AIDS*. New York: Haworth Press, 1988.

A guide to key sources of information on AIDS. Includes books, periodicals, articles, state health departments, hotlines, on-line data bases and audiovisual producers.

Malinowsky, Robert, and Gerald Perry. *AIDS Information Sourcebook*. Phoenix: Oryx Press, 1988.

Consists of three sections: a chronology of the AIDS epidemic; a directory of U.S. organizations involved with AIDS; and a bibliography of books, periodicals, articles and audiovisual materials.

Malinowsky, Robert, and Gerald Perry, *AIDS Information Sourcebook*. Phoenix: Oryx Press, 1989.

Updated edition of over 2,000 entries. Includes in appendices statistical tables and AIDS medicines in development.

Mangan, B. F., *AIDS: Acquired Immune Deficiency Syndrome: Selected References*. Washington, D.C.: Library of Congress, Congressional Research Service, 1989.

Annotated bibliography covering major topics such as the epidemiology of AIDS and social, legal, political and ethical issues relating to the disease.

Nagasankara Rao, Dittakavi. *AIDS and Law: Selected Bibliography*. Monticello, Illinois: Vance Bibliographics, 1987.

List of resources on legal responses to the AIDS epidemic.

Reed, Robert D., *AIDS, A Bibliography*. Saratoga, Calif.: R and E Publishers, 1987.

List of general articles on AIDS from magazines, newspapers and books.

Tyckoson, David A. *AIDS (Acquired Immune Deficiency Syndrome)*. Phoenix: Oryx Press, 1985.

Annotated bibliography of over 200 articles from general periodicals from 1982–1985.

Tyckoson, David A. *AIDS 1986*. Phoenix: Oryx Press, 1986.

First in a series of annual and then semiannual annotated bibliographies on AIDS. Composed of over 500 references to general, readily available articles written at the college level. Volumes do not duplicate each other.

Tyckoson, David A. *AIDS 1987*. Phoenix: Oryx Press, 1988.

Tyckoson, David A. *AIDS 1988, Part 1*. Phoenix: Oryx Press, 1988.

Tyckoson, David A. *AIDS 1988, Part 2*. Phoenix: Oryx Press, 1989.

Tyckoson, David A. *AIDS 1989, Part 1*. Phoenix: Oryx Press, 1989.

Weber, M. A., and R. Young. *AIDS and Adolescents: Resources for Educators*, Vol. 2. Washington, D.C.: Center for Population Options, 1988.

Annotated bibliography of educational resources including curricula, books, brochures and audiovisual materials dealing with AIDS-related issues.

Weissberg, Nancy C. *AIDS Bibliography for Nineteen Eighty-One to Nineteen Eighty-Six*. Troy, N.Y.: Whitston Publishing Company, 1988.

Comprehensive compilation of about 4,000 citations on AIDS. Most of the references are to periodical articles, and range from technical to general.

"The Workplace and AIDS: A Guide to Services and Information." *Personnel Journal*, October 1987, p. 65–68.

Provides information on organizations, educational programs, consultants and articles concerned with AIDS in the workplace.

BOOKS

GENERAL

AIDS: Origins, Prevention and Cure. 4 vols. New York: Gordon Press, 1987.

Comprehensive 4-volume work on the history, prevention and treatment of AIDS.

Altman, Dennis. *AIDS in the Mind of America*. New York: Anchor Press, 1986.

Based on his thesis that an epidemic is shaped not just by an infectious organism but also by the historical setting, the author examines cultural, economic and political factors having an impact on AIDS.

Annotated Bibliography

Antonio, Gene. *AIDS Cover-Up? The Real and Alarming Facts about AIDS.* San Francisco: Ignatius Press, 1986.

Author presents controversial view of the AIDS epidemic, claiming that the real facts have been withheld from the public.

Bateson, Mary Catherine, and Richard Goldsby. *Thinking AIDS.* Reading, Mass.: Addison-Wesley, 1988.

Authors present philosophical as well as practical ways society could choose to deal with the AIDS epidemic. Suggestions range from legalizing gay marriage to providing cheap disposable hypodermic needles.

Bayer, Ronald. *Private Acts, Social Consequences: AIDS and the Politics of Public Health.* New York: Free Press, 1989.

Addresses the issues faced by health officials and policymakers dealing with the AIDS epidemic. Author traces the political history of AIDS and suggests some measures to combat the disease.

Cameron, Paul. *Exposing the AIDS Coverup: What You Don't Know Can Kill You.* Lafayette, Louisiana: Huntington House, 1988.

Author's controversial report and viewpoint on what information has been withheld from the American public.

Cantwell, Alan. *AIDS and the Doctors of Death: An Inquiry into the Origins of the AIDS Epidemic.* Los Angeles: Aries Rising Press, 1988.

Examines the cause and epidemiology of AIDS.

Check, William. *AIDS.* Edgemont, Pa.: Chelsea House, 1988.

Provides a basic overview of AIDS, written for teenagers up to high school level. Introduction by C. Everett Koop.

Clarke, Loren K., and Malcolm Potts, eds. *The AIDS Reader.* Boston: Branden Publishing, 1988.

This balanced selection of articles offers a documentary history of the AIDS epidemic from 1981–1987. Authors deal with past, present and future issues.

Cole, Helene M., and George D. Lundberg. *AIDS, From the Beginning.* Chicago: American Medical Association, 1986.

Historical account of the AIDS epidemic.

Colman, Warren. *Understanding and Preventing AIDS: A Guide for Young People.* Chicago: Children's Press, 1988.

General overview of the AIDS epidemic, its history, symptoms, prevention and treatment.

Corless, Inge, and Mary Pitman-Lindeman, eds. *AIDS: Principles, Practice and Politics*. New York: Hemisphere Publishing, 1988.

These 20 articles present an overview of the history of AIDS. The authors trace its epidemiology in different populations and describe health, social and political responses to the epidemic.

Douglas, Paul Harding, and Laura Pinsky. *The Essential AIDS Fact Book: What You Need to Know to Protect Yourself, Your Family, All Your Loved Ones*. New York: Pocket Books, 1987.

The facts about AIDS and how to avoid it, including advice to IV drug users.

Ethical Response to AIDS. New York: America Press, 1988.

Various writers discuss the ethical issues related to the AIDS epidemic.

Fee, Elizabeth, and Daniel Fox, eds. *AIDS: The Burdens of History*. Berkeley: University of California Press, 1988.

Collection of essays written by historians, public policy experts and social scientists in an effort to analyze social, cultural and historical issues as they relate to AIDS.

Feldman, Douglas, and Thomas M. Johnson. *The Social Dimensions of AIDS: Method and Theory*. Westport, Conn.: Praeger, 1986.

Academic discussion on the social dimensions of AIDS, using research theory and methodology as a framework.

Fettner, Ann Giudicu, and William A. Check. *The Truth About AIDS: Evolution of an Epidemic*. New York: Henry Holt and Co., 1986.

The history of AIDS from early isolated cases of the time it became an epidemic. Also touches on the research, treatment and sociopolitical concerns surrounding AIDS.

Flynn, Eileen P. *AIDS: A Catholic Call for Compassion*. Kansas City, Missouri: Sheed and Ward, 1985.

Discusses Catholic concerns and positions on AIDS and the role of the church.

Fortunato, John E. *AIDS: The Spiritual Dilemma*. New York: Harper and Row, 1987.

Focus is on the response of orthodox Christianity to gays and AIDS. The author urges the traditional churches to quicken their response.

Fromer, Margot. *A.I.D.S. Acquired Immune Deficiency Syndrome.* New York: J. Pinnacle Books, 1983.

Provides general information on AIDS. One of the first books on the disease.

Galea, Robert P., Benjamin F. Lewis and Lori Baker. *AIDS and IV Drug Abusers: Current Perspectives.* Owings Mills, Md.: National Health Publishing, 1988.

Describes how HIV is spread by intravenous drug abusers, and reports on incidence.

Gallagher, Joseph. *Voices of Strength and Hope for a Friend with AIDS.* Kansas City, Mo.: Sheed and Ward, 1987.

Gives general information about AIDS, and advice on how to be encouraging and supportive of friends and family who have AIDS.

Gong, Victor, and Norman Rudnick, *AIDS: Facts and Issues.* New Brunswick, N.J.: Rutgers University Press, 1986.

A comprehensive guide to the numerous problems surrounding AIDS. Examines a range of topics about the disease and presents studies on the key issues.

Haffner, Debra W. *AIDS and Adolescents: The Time for Prevention Is Now.* Washington, D.C.: Center for Population Options, 1987.

Provides recommendations for developing and implementing an effective AIDS prevention program for teenagers.

Hall, Lyn, and Thomas Modl, eds. *AIDS. Opposing Viewpoints Series.* San Diego: Greenhaven Press, 1987.

Collection of articles presenting controversial issues associated with AIDS.

Hancock, Graham, and Enver Carim. *AIDS: The Deadly Epidemic.* North Pomfret, Vt.: David and Charles, 1986.

General introduction to AIDS from a global perspective.

Hawkes, Nigel. *AIDS.* New York: Gloucester Press, 1987.

A general overview of AIDS intended to teach middle school children about the disease, including how it is spread, testing and preventive measures.

AIDS

Holleran, Andrew. *Ground Zero.* New York: Morrow, 1988.

A collection of essays examining the psychological and physical effects of AIDS, especially in the homosexual community.

Hunt, Morton. *Gay: What Teenagers Should Know about Homosexuality and the AIDS Crisis.* New York: Farrar, Straus and Giroux, 1987.

Discusses gay lifestyles, explains why AIDS has been linked to gay sexual behavior and presents guidelines for safe sex.

Hyde, Margaret O., and Elizabeth H. Forsyth. *AIDS: What Does It Mean to You?* Rev. ed. New York: Walker, 1987.

Presents information on the cause and transmission of AIDS; opportunistic infections; and the physical and emotional effects on persons with AIDS.

Keeling, Richard P. *AIDS on the College Campus: ACHA Special Report.* Rockville, Md.: American College Health Association, 1986.

Report on AIDS on college campuses and discussion of safe sex for college students.

Kramer, Larry. *Reports from the Holocaust: The Making of an AIDS Activist.* New York: St. Martin's Press, 1989.

A compilation of the author's letters, speeches and articles on his feelings about the gay community and AIDS, which he sees as the gay holocaust. Intended to provoke political action.

Kresden, Bradley. *Sex, Drugs, and AIDS.* New York: Bantam Books, 1987.

Covers the symptoms of AIDS; precautions for avoiding the disease; populations at risk; and transmission of AIDS by blood and semen. Adapted from an educational video of the same name.

Kubler-Ross, Elisabeth. *AIDS: The Ultimate Challenge.* New York: Macmillan, 1987.

Focuses on the suffering of AIDS patients, particularly in the final stages of their struggle with the syndrome. Includes case histories and discussions from public meetings.

Kuklin, Susan. *Fighting Back: What Some People Are Doing about AIDS.* New York: Putnam, 1989.

Recommended for teenagers, this book is about the author's experience working with volunteers from the Gay Men's Health Crisis organization in New York. Provides factual information about AIDS and portrays the physical and emotional strain caused by the illness.

Annotated Bibliography

Kurland, Morton L. *Coping With AIDS: Facts and Fears.* New York: Rosen Publishing Group, 1988.

Author argues that humankind, who has found means to contain such contagious diseases as smallpox, will be able to cope with AIDS provided some of the same methods are applied.

Langone, John. *AIDS: The Facts.* Boston: Little, Brown, 1988.

History and current status of the AIDS epidemic. The author describes the symptoms and clinical characteristics of the disease as well as the features of the HIV virus.

Lee, Robert E. *AIDS in America: Our Chances, Our Choices.* Troy, N.Y.: Whitston Publishing, 1987.

Review of how AIDS has affected American society and government.

Leukefeld, Carl G., and Manuel Fimbres. *Responding to AIDS: Psychosocial Initiatives.* Silver Spring, Md.: NASW Publications, 1987.

Eight papers presented at the National Association of Social Workers Conference, 1986. Covers current information on psychosocial profiles of persons with AIDS.

McKusick, Leon, ed. *What to Do about AIDS: Physicians and Mental Health Professionals Discuss the Issues.* Berkeley: University of California Press, 1986.

Twenty-eight health care professionals discuss such issues relating to AIDS as medical prognoses, victims' mental health and psychological counseling.

Martelli, Leonard J., et al. *When Someone You Know Has AIDS: A Practical Guide.* New York: Crown, 1987.

A guide on providing care and emotional support; coping with the crisis; and managing medical, legal and financial issues.

Masters, William H., et al. *Crisis: Heterosexual Behavior in the Age of AIDS.* New York: Grove Press, 1988.

This work contradicts many of the currently held beliefs on AIDS. It claims there is a higher rate of AIDS infection among heterosexuals than is being reported and that the blood supply is not HIV free.

Menitove, Jay E., and Jerry Kolins. *AIDS.* Arlington, Va.: American Association of Blood Banks, 1986.

Compilation of papers presented at a 1986 AIDS Technical Workshop in San Francisco. The papers cover history, incidence, clinical factors, immunology and testing.

Moffat, Betty Clare, et al. *AIDS: A Self-Care Manual.* Santa Monica: IBS Press, 1987.

A handbook on the psychological and physical care of persons with AIDS. Also gives advice on preventive and precautionary measures as well as dealing with the legal and business matters of patients.

Norwood, Chris. *Advice for Life: A Woman's Guide to AIDS Risks and Prevention.* New York: Pantheon Press, 1987.

The guidelines for women cover such topics as how to question dates about their sexual histories, how to use condoms correctly and how to tell children about AIDS.

Nungesser, Lon. *Epidemic of Courage: Facing AIDS in America.* New York: St. Martin's Press, 1988.

Discussion of the psychological impact of AIDS on the person with AIDS as well as the general public.

Quackenbush, Marcia, and Mary Nelson, eds. *The AIDS Challenge: Prevention Education for Young People.* Santa Cruz, Calif.: Network Publications, 1988.

A collection of essays providing comprehensive and accurate information on ways to educate young children and teenagers about AIDS.

Reed, Paul. *Serenity: Challenging the Fears of AIDS.* Berkeley, Calif.: Celestial Arts, 1987.

Personal reflections on changing sexual attitudes and lifestyles and the impact of AIDS on promiscuity.

Richardson, Diana. *Women and AIDS.* New York: Methuen, 1987.

An analysis of the social, economic and emotional impact of AIDS on various categories of women in the United Kingdom, United States and Africa.

Rieder, Ines, and Patricia Ruppelt, eds. *AIDS: The Women.* Pittsburgh: Cleis Press, 1988.

An anthology of essays written by a variety of women who have personal experience with the disease, either as patients, mothers, wives, siblings, lovers, nurses, doctors or counselors.

Sabatier, Renee. *AIDS and the Third World.* Philadelphia: New Society Publishers, 1988.

General overview of the AIDS epidemic in Third World countries, especially Africa.

Annotated Bibliography

Saint-Phalle, Niki De. *AIDS: You Can't Catch It Holding Hands.* San Francisco: Lapis Press, 1987.

The work teaches young adults the facts about AIDS. The author clarifies the ways in which the virus is transmitted.

Schinazi, Raymond F., and Andre J. Nahmias, eds. *AIDS in Children, Adolescents and Heterosexual Adults: An Interdisciplinary Approach to Prevention.* New York: Elsevier, 1988.

This book is the outcome of a conference held in Atlanta, Georgia, in February 1987 where AIDS in children, adolescents and heterosexuals was discussed from international and interdisciplinary perspectives.

Shelp, Earl E., and Ronald H. Sunderland. *AIDS and the Church.* Philadelphia: Westminster Press, 1987.

Discusses the role of the church in ministering to and counseling of persons with AIDS as well as Christian viewpoints on the disease.

Shilts, Randy. *And the Band Played On: Politics, People, and the AIDS Epidemic.* New York: St. Martin's, 1987.

Journalist Shilts chronicles the history of AIDS in the 1980s from a political standpoint. He reports on medical and governmental responses to the disease and profiles many of the key researchers and political leaders involved with the issue.

Shoutmatoff, Alex. *African Madness.* New York: Knopf, 1988.

Author recounts four trips he made to Africa and his observations on the spread of AIDS across that continent.

Silverstein, Alvin, and Virginia Silverstein. *AIDS: Deadly Threat.* Hillside, N.J.: Enslow, 1986.

Discusses the human, medical and ethical dilemmas of AIDS.

Sontag, Susan. *AIDS and Its Metaphors.* New York: Farrar, Straus and Giroux, 1988.

Presents the author's point of view that the metaphors applied to AIDS increase the suffering of patients and add to unnecessary anxiety.

Trager, Oliver, ed. *AIDS: Plague or Panic.* New York: Facts On File, 1988.

Composed of newspaper articles, including editorials on AIDS.

Ulene, Art. *Safe Sex in a Dangerous World: Understanding and Coping with the Threat of AIDS.* New York: Vintage, 1987.

Information on safe sex for young adults with an emphasis on abstinence as the only truly safe way.

Weiner, Roberta. *AIDS: Impact on Schools.* Saratoga, Calif.: A.I.D.S. International/Information Distribution Service, 1986.

Discusses the impact of AIDS on schools and makes recommendations for developing local school AIDS policies.

LEGAL

Actenberg, Roberta. *Sexual Orientation and the Law.* New York: Clark Boardman, 1985.

Addresses AIDS-related legal issues.

AIDS: Employer Rights and Responsibilities. Chicago: Commerce Clearing House, 1985.

Addresses how management should deal with AIDS in the workplace: testing, precautions, benefits and other legal issues.

Bakaly, Charles, and Saul Kramer. *AIDS and Drug Abuse in the Workplace: Resolving the Thorny Legal-Medical Issues.* New York: Harcourt Brace Jovanovich, 1986.

Discussion with some guidelines on resolving the legal problems in the workplace created by AIDS and drug abuse. Emphasizes labor laws and industrial hygiene legislation.

Banta, William F. *AIDS in the Workplace: Legal Questions and Practical Answers.* Lexington, Mass.: Lexington Books, 1988.

Written by an attorney, this book addresses a variety of legal questions relating to AIDS in the workplace. Includes U.S. government guidelines on AIDS, sample policy statements and sample legal documents.

Dalton, Harlon L., and Scott Buriss, eds. *AIDS and the Law: A Guide for the Public.* New Haven: Yale University Press, 1987.

This collection of essays outlines the legal mechanisms and processes currently in place to deal with policy disputes and social conflicts relating to AIDS.

Dornette, William H. L. *AIDS and the Law.* New York: John Wiley and Sons, 1987.

Explains the various legal issues raised by infection with HIV.

Gostin, Larry, and William J. Curran. *AIDS, Law and Policy.* Boston: American Society of Law and Medicine, 1987.

Discusses the legal issues affecting medical professionals and administrators involved in caring for persons with AIDS.

Harrington, Eugene. *AIDS, Minorities and the Law.* Frederick, Md.: University Publishing, 1988.

Reviews legal issues pertinent to minority persons, women and children with AIDS.

Pierce, Christine, and Donald VanDeVeer. *AIDS: Ethics and Public Policy.* Belmont, Calif.: Wadsworth, 1988.

Discusses ethical issues that affect the making of public policy concerning AIDS testing and treatment.

Schachter, Victor, and Susan Von Seeburg. *AIDS: A Manager's Guide.* New York: Executive Enterprises, 1986.

A guide to assist managers in dealing with legal issues surrounding AIDS in the workplace, with emphasis on those aspects pertaining to labor legislation.

Steins, Robert E. *The Settlement of AIDS Disputes: A Report for the National Center for Health Services Research.* Washington, D.C.: Environmental Mediation International, 1987.

Provides legal advice for people with AIDS.

Witt, Michael D. *AIDS and Patient Management: Legal, Ethical and Social Issues.* Owings Mills, Md.: National Health Publishers, 1986.

Includes papers on caring for AIDS patients that were presented at the "AIDS: The Ethical, Legal and Social Considerations" conference held by Public Responsibility in Medicine and Research.

MEDICAL

Bamforth, Nick. *AIDS and the Healer Within.* New York: Amethyst Books, 1988.

Explores alternate methods for treating AIDS.

Breitman, Patti. *How to Persuade Your Lover to Use a Condom . . . and Why You Should.* New York: St. Martin's Press, 1987.

Using the question-and-answer format, this guide provides information on the use of condoms to protect against the transmission of AIDS.

Coulter, Harris. *AIDS and Syphilis: The Hidden Link.* Berkeley, Calif.: North Atlantic Books, 1987.

Explores the theory that AIDS and syphilis are interrelated.

Friedlander, Mark P. Jr., and Terry M. Phillips. *Winning the War Within: Understanding, Protecting, and Building Your Body's Immunity*. Emmaus, Pa.: Rodale Press, 1986.

Provides general information on the body's immune system, how it works and ways of maintaining its health. Includes a chapter on AIDS.

Frumkin, Lyn, and John Leonard. *Questions and Answers on AIDS*. New York: Avon Books, 1987.

This book, in question-and-answer format, provides comprehensive factual information about AIDS. Prepared by medical doctors directly experienced with AIDS patients.

Gregory, Scott J. *Conquering AIDS Now: With Natural Treatment, a Non-Drug Approach*. New York: Warner Books, 1986.

Presents various alternative, unconventional approaches to treating AIDS.

Gregory, Scott, J., and Bianca Leonardo. *Conquering AIDS Now!*, 3rd ed. New York: Tree of Life, 1986.

Presents alternate approaches to treating AIDS.

Gregory, Scott J., and Bianca Leonardo. *They Conquered AIDS*. New York: Tree of Life, 1989.

Describes alternative treatments that have shown some success with AIDS patients.

Hay, Louise. *The AIDS Book: Creating a Positive Approach*. Santa Monica: Hay House, 1987.

Presents health care techniques using positive thinking for people with AIDS.

Kushi, Michio, and Martha C. Cottrell. *AIDS: Macrobiotics and Natural Immunity*. New York: Farrar, Straus and Giroux, 1989.

Discusses the causes of AIDS and immune deficiency; considers new ways of fighting the disease through a macrobiotic approach to diet and lifestyle.

Lauritsen, John, and Hank Wilson. *Death Rush: Poppers and AIDS*. New York: Pagan Press, 1986.

The author in his argument correlates the use of amyl nitrate and the occurrence of AIDS.

Nourse E. *AIDS.* New York: Watts, 1986.

Provides medical explanation of how HIV works on the human immune system. Written for teenagers.

Russell-Manning, Betsy. *Self-Treatment for AIDS: Oxygen Therapies.* Berkeley, Calif.: Celestial Arts, 1987.

Written for AIDS patients. Gives alternative therapies for AIDS treatment.

PERSONAL NARRATIVE

Callen, Michael. *Surviving AIDS.* New York: Harper and Row, 1990.

Founder of People with AIDS, the author tells his own story as well as the stories of more than 25 long-term AIDS survivors.

Dreuilhe, Emmanuel. *Mortal Embrace: Living with AIDS.* New York: Hill and Wang, 1988.

The author describes his struggle with AIDS, taking the metaphor of war to describe the disease's attack on its victims and his counterattack.

Hudson, Rock, and Sara Davidson. *Rock Hudson: His Own Story.* New York: William Morrow, 1986.

The famous movie star's life and experience with AIDS.

LeVert, Suzanne. *AIDS: In Search of a Killer.* Englewood Cliffs, N.J.: Messner, 1987.

Provides background information on AIDS virus as well as civil rights and economic issues through the personal stories of two persons with AIDS.

Moffatt, Betty Clare. *When Someone You Love Has AIDS: A Book of Hope for Family and Friends.* rev. ed. New York: NAL, 1987.

Story of author's son and other AIDS sufferers as well as her own story as a cancer victim. Offers inspiration to others living with disabling sickness.

Monette, Paul. *Borrowed Time: An AIDS Memoir.* San Diego: Harcourt, Brace and Jovanovich, 1988.

Personal account of Roger Horwitz an AIDS sufferer, written by his lover, Paul Monette.

Money, J. W. *To All The Girls I've Loved Before: An A.I.D.S. Diary.* Boston: Alyson, 1987.

Memoirs of a man dying of AIDS, reflecting on his life and illness.

AIDS

O'Connor, Tom, and Ahmed Gonzalez-Nunez. *Living with AIDS: Reaching Out.* San Francisco: Corwin Publishers, 1987.

The Author, who has lived with ARC for seven years, writes about the various conventional and other therapies he has investigated or experienced. These include drugs, nutrition, exercise, etc.

Whitmore, George. *Someone Was Here: Profiles in the AIDS Epidemic.* New York: NAL, 1988.

Author discusses the lives of three people with AIDS, including a child, and the people who love and care for them.

FICTION

Kerr, M. E. *Night Kites.* New York: Harper and Row, 1986.

Story of a young boy keeping his brother's AIDS a secret while trying to accept it himself.

Miklowitz, Gloria D. *Good-bye, Tomorrow.* New York: Delacorte, 1987.

The main character, a high school senior, contracts AIDS through a blood transfusion and experiences not only the physical trauma of the disease but the psychological and emotional stress of prejudices and misconceptions.

ENCYCLOPEDIAS

"Acquired Immune Deficiency Syndrome." In *The New Encyclopedia Britannica.* Vol. 1. Chicago: Encyclopedia Britannica, 1988, p67.

An overview of AIDS providing historical, medical and general information.

Considine, Douglas, and Glenn D. Considine, eds. "AIDS (Acquired Immune Deficiency Syndrome)" *Van Nostrand's Scientific Encyclopedia.* 7th ed. New York: Van Nostrand Reinhold, 1989, p57–58.

Gives historical background and scientific description of AIDS. Includes list of references.

Drofman, D. Peter. "AIDS." In *The World Book Encyclopedia.* Vol. 1. Chicago: World Book, 1990, p164–165.

General information on AIDS: its cause, symptoms, transmission, diagnosis and prevention. Discusses the social issues raised by the disease.

Glanze, Walter D., Kenneth n. Anderson and Lois E. Anderson, eds. "AIDS." *The Mosby Medical Encyclopedia.* New York: New American Library, 1985, p8.

Short medical definition of AIDS.

Haseltine, William. "AIDS." In *Encyclopedia Americana*. Vol. 1. Danbury, Conn.: Grolier, 1988, p365–366.

Brief description of the disease.

Hollander, Harry. "AIDS and Related Conditions." In *Current Medical Diagnosis and Treatment 1989*. Norwalk, Conn.: Appleton and Lange, 1989, p872–876.

Furnishes a general description of AIDS and then outlines the epidemiology, etiology and clinical findings related to the disease.

Kunz, Jeffrey R. M., and Asher J. Finkel, eds. "AIDS (Acquired Immunodeficiency Syndrome)". In *The American Medical Association Family Medical Guide*. Revised and updated. New York: Random House, 1987, p441.

Defines and describes the symptoms, transmission and treatment of AIDS.

Macher, Abe M. "Acquired Immune Deficiency Syndrome (AIDS)." In *McGraw-Hill Encyclopedia of Science and Technology*. Vol. 1. 6th ed. New York: McGraw-Hill, 1987, p89–90.

Defines and describes the disease with cross-reference to "Cellular Immunology." Gives brief description of opportunistic infections common in AIDS patients.

Siegal, Frederick, and Marta Siegal. "Acquired Immune Deficiency Syndrome (AIDS)." In *Collier's Encyclopedia*. Vol. 1. New York: Macmillan, 1989, p87–88.

Defines what AIDS is, gives a brief epidemiology and describes the signs, symptoms, diagnosis, treatment and transmission of the disease.

Tapby, Donald F., et al., eds. "Acquired Immune Deficiency Syndrome (AIDS)." In *The Columbia University College of Physicians and Surgeons Complete Home Medical Guide*. New York: Crown Publishers, 1985, p446.

General definition and description of the disease. Provides cross-references to opportunistic infections that result from having the AIDS virus.

PERIODICALS

AIDS Action Update. Washington, D.C.: AIDS Action Council (monthly).

Newsletter with information on legislation related to AIDS.

AIDS Alert. Atlanta: American Health Consultants (monthly).

Medical newsletter on AIDS.

AIDS and Public Policy Journal. Frederick, Md.: University Publishing Group (quarterly).

Journal addressing social, political, ethical and legal issues in public health policy that relate to AIDS.

AIDS Education and Prevention. New York: Guilford Publications (quarterly).

An interdisciplinary journal providing information on the prevention of AIDS, especially for those in the health care profession.

AIDS Forum: Diverse Views about Acquired Immune Deficiency Syndrome. New York: Significant Other, Inc. (minimum 6 times annually).

Presents and discusses AIDS ethical and scientific issues.

AIDS Information Exchange. Washington, D.C.: U.S. Conference of Mayors (monthly).

National newsletter reporting on AIDS research, programs and grants.

AIDS Law and Litigation Reporter. Frederick, Md.: University Publishing Group (annual).

Provides complete coverage of all AIDS court cases, synopses of proposed and enacted statutes and legislation, and analysis of developments in AIDS law and litigation.

AIDS Letter. London: Royal Society of Medicine (bimonthly).

Provides information on AIDS collected from around the world.

AIDS Medical Update. Los Angeles: UCLA AIDS Clinical Research Center (monthly).

Newsletter provides updated statistics and current information on AIDS.

AIDS Patient Care. New York: Mary Ann Liebert, Inc. (bimonthly).

Journal for health professionals on patient care.

AIDS Policy and Law. Washington, D.C.: Buraff Publications (biweekly).

Newsletter on legislation, regulation and litigation concerning AIDS.

AIDS Research and Human Retroviruses. New York: Mary Ann Liebert, Inc. (bimonthly).

Covers research on AIDS, HIV and other retroviruses.

Annotated Bibliography

AIDS Treatment News. San Francisco: John S. James (biweekly).

Newsletter giving current information on alternative treatments for infection.

AIDS Update (New York). New York: Lambda Legal Defense and Educational Fund (11 times annually).

Covers AIDS-related legal and legislative developments.

CDC AIDS Weekly. Atlanta: Charles Henderson (weekly).

Gives national and international news on AIDS, abstracts of articles on the disease and an up-to-date list of AIDS meetings and conferences around the world.

Focus: A Review of AIDS Research. San Francisco: UCSF AIDS Health Project (monthly).

Gives reports and articles on AIDS research.

Health Letter. New York: Gay Men's Health Crisis (bimonthly).

Information about AIDS and its prevention. Discusses safe sex practices.

Hemophilia World. Los Angeles: World Hemophilia AIDS Center (quarterly).

Newsletter giving information and statistics on AIDS and hemophilia.

Lifeline. Houston: AIDS Foundation Houston (monthly).

Monthly newsletter on AIDS giving local and national information.

Morbidity and Mortality Weekly Report. Atlanta: Centers for Disease Control (weekly).

Newsletter carries weekly AIDS report and statistics as well as brief articles on the disease.

NAN News. Washington, D.C.: National AIDS Network (quarterly).

Newsletter providing an overview of AIDS topics and issues.

Progress Report. Phoenix: Arizona AIDS Project (bimonthly).

Local and national AIDS news and information.

Spotlight on AIDS. Westport, Conn: Odyssey Institute Corp., Concerned Physicians Network (monthly).

Formerly the *Odyssey Institute Journal, Spotlight on AIDS* focuses on medical care and research.

Reports on AIDS frequently appear in the following journals:

American Journal of Public Health   *New England Journal of Medicine*
Annals of Internal Medicine   *Public Health Reports*
Journal of the American Medical As-   *Science*
  sociation   *Scientific American*
Nature

ARTICLES

GENERAL

Adams, Reed. "The Role of Prostitution in AIDS and Other STDs." *Medical Aspects of Human Sexuality*, vol. 21, Aug. 1987, p27–33.

Examines the role of prostitutes in the spread of AIDS and other sexually transmitted diseases.

"Africa Does Not Belong to Another Planet." *New Scientist*, vol. 116, Oct. 15, 1987, p26.

Article addresses the need for African nations to be involved in the global fight against AIDS.

"Aggressive Marketers Will Pay Price in AIDS Claims." *National Underwriter* (Life, Health, and Financial Services Edition), vol. 91, Aug. 17, 1987, p3.

The insurance industry projects that AIDS-related death claims could cost the companies $50 billion by the year 2000.

"AIDS Is Here to Stay." *World Health*, Mar. 1988, p27.

Researchers look to the future of AIDS and identify areas requiring further attention.

"AIDS Ranked 5th Leading Killer of Black Women." *Jet*, vol. 77, Dec. 4, 1989, p36.

Brief article on the impact of AIDS on the health and survival of black women.

"AIDS: Will It Spread in China?" *Beijing Review*, vol. 30, Aug. 10, 1987, p7.

Report on prevention measures being taken by the government of China after the identification of several AIDS cases there.

Altman, Lawrence K. "Spread of AIDS Virus Found Slowing among Drug Users in 3 Cities." *New York Times*, June 16, 1988, pA25.

Reviews studies showing that in New York, San Francisco and Stockholm the proportion of IV drug users carrying the AIDS virus has stayed more or less constant from 1986 to 1988.

Amer-Hirsch, Wendy. "Educating Youth about AIDS: A Model Program." *Children Today*, vol. 18, Sept.–Oct. 1989, p16ff.

Reports on a new educational program for teaching children about AIDS.

Andrulis, Dennis P., et al. "The Provision and Financing of Medical Care for AIDS Patients in U.S. Public and Private Teaching Hospitals." *JAMA*, vol. 258, Sep. 11, 1987, p1343–1346.

Reports on the high cost of hospital care for AIDS patients.

Arno, Peter S. "The Economic Impact of AIDS." *JAMA*, vol. 258, Sep. 11, 1987, p1376–1377.

The escalating cost of health care for AIDS patients has an impact not only on insurance companies but also on the federal government.

"Arresting the Epidemic: What Will It Take?" *Psychology Today*, vol. 22, May 1988, p58.

Review of proposed methods to stop the AIDS epidemic: free needles to addicts, quarantine of AIDS patients, mandatory testing and behavior modification.

Baker, James N. "Needing a Place to Die." *Newsweek*, vol. 111, Apr. 4, 1988, p24–25.

Addresses the increasing problem of AIDS and the homeless.

Barnes, Deborah M. "AIDS: Statistics but Few Answers." *Science*, vol. 236, June 12, 1987, p1423–1425.

Furnishes statistics and analysis of the global spread of AIDS.

Barnes, Deborah M. "Meeting on AIDS Drugs Turns into Open Forum." *Science*, vol. 237, Sep. 11, 1987, p1287–1288.

Critical analysis of the adequacy of federally funded AIDS programs.

Bass, Thomas A. "California Fever." *Omni*, vol. 10, Nov. 1987, p43.

Describes how fear of the spread of AIDS across national boundaries has given rise to hostility toward foreigners in many countries.

Bass, Thomas A. "Luc Montagnier." *Omni*, vol. 11, Dec. 1988, p102–104.

Interview with the French scientist who first isolated HIV in early 1983.

Batchelor, Walter F. "AIDS 1988." *American Psychologist*, vol. 43, Nov. 1988, p853–858.

Assessment of the various responses to the AIDS epidemic by the end of 1988.

Bazell, Robert. "AIDS Again." *New Republic*, vol. 199, July 18, 1988, p15–16.

The rate at which AIDS is spreading apparently is slowing, but the number of new cases is still rising.

Bazell, Robert. "The Plague." *New Republic*, vol. 196, June 1, 1987, p14–15.

Gives projections of the devastating effect AIDS will have in Africa and other Third World regions. Author contends there is an immediate need for financial and technical assistance to deal with the emerging epidemic.

Beck, Melinda. "1989: AIDS." *Newsweek*, vol. 114, July 3, 1989, p57.

Discusses the impact of the disease on the homosexual liberation movement and reviews advances in AIDS treatment.

Benditt, John. "Report from Stockholm." *Scientific American*, vol. 259, Aug. 1988, p14–15.

Report on the Fourth International Conference on AIDS.

Bennett, Joanne. "Nurses Talk about the Challenge of AIDS." *American Journal of Nursing*, vol. 87, Sep. 1987, p1150–1155.

Discussion of the stress nurses experience in dealing with the deterioration and death of AIDS patients.

Black, David. "An Era of Indifference: AIDS and the Death of Passion." *American Health*, vol. 7, Oct. 1988, p87–88.

Explores the impact of AIDS on sexual attitudes and practices. The author weighs people's fears against the statistical evidence.

Bloom, David, and Geoffrey Carliner. "The Economic Impact of AIDS in the United States." *Science*, vol. 239, Feb. 5, 1988, p604–610.

Summarizes several studies on the projected economic burden of AIDS on American society. Looks also at how society will share in the cost of dealing with the epidemic.

Annotated Bibliography

Boffey, Philip. "Expert Panel Sees Poor Leadership in U.S. AIDS Battle." *New York Times,* June 2, 1988, pA1.

A panel of experts appointed by the National Academy of Sciences criticizes the absence of strong federal leadership in the fight against AIDS. The committee points out serious deficiencies in programs for controlling drug abuse related to AIDS.

Booth, William. "AIDS and Insects." *Science,* vol. 237, July 24, 1987, p355–356.

Data show transmission of AIDS virus is not by mosquitos or other insects but through sexual contact, shared needles and blood transfusions.

Booth, William. "Experts Fault Leadership on AIDS." *Science,* vol. 237, Aug. 21, 1987, p838.

Report of the General Accounting Office criticizing government for inadequate funding of AIDS research and education programs.

"Britain Blocks European AIDS Research." *New Scientist,* vol. 114, May 14, 1987, p29.

Describes how AIDS research in Europe has been slowed by lack of British support for collaborative scientific efforts.

Burda, David. "Hospital Not Liable for AIDS from Blood Transfusion." *Hospitals,* vol. 61, Sep. 5, 1987, p60.

A critical analysis of the AIDS epidemic as a disease and the fear surrounding it. Looks at moral, ethical and legal aspects of blood testing.

Byrne, Gregory. "AIDS Panel Urges New Focus." *Science,* vol. 243, Feb. 17, 1989, p887.

An expert panel of the National Research Council has called for initiatives to halt the spread of AIDS.

Chen, Lincoln C. "The AIDS Pandemic: An Internationalist Approach to Disease Control." *Daedalus,* vol. 116, Spring 1987, p181–195.

Overview of the global concerns about the AIDS epidemic. Outlines suggestions for stemming the spread of the disease.

Chin, James. "Understanding the Figures." *World Health,* Oct. 1989, p8.

Analyzes current AIDS statistics and forecasts their implications for future epidemiological patterns.

Clark, Matt. "Plagues, Man, and History." *Newsweek*, vol. 111, May 9, 1988, p65–66.

Compares AIDS to past epidemics.

Coles, Peter. "NCI and Pasteur Reveal Details of AIDS Foundations." *Nature*, vol. 330, Dec. 10, 1987, p507.

Reports on the establishment by the National Cancer Institute and the French Pasteur Institute of two international AIDS foundations. The foundations are the result of a compromise resolution to the patent lawsuit over the AIDS virus.

"The Columbus of AIDS." *National Review*, vol. 39, Nov. 6, 1987, p19.

Piece on Gaetan Dugas, a French Canadian airline steward who is alleged to be the first man to bring AIDS to the American continent.

Conant, Jennet. "The Fashionable Charity." *Newsweek*, vol. 110, Dec. 28, 1987, p54–55.

Discusses AIDS fund-raising and charity events sponsored by celebrities.

Conway, George A., et al. "Underreporting of AIDS Cases in South Carolina, 1986 and 1987." *JAMA*, vol. 262, Nov. 24, 1989, p2859ff.

Discusses patterns of underreporting of AIDS cases in hospitals.

Corliss, Richard. "How Artists Respond to AIDS." *Time*, vol. 130, July 27, 1987, p62–63.

Reports on how the American arts community deals with the epidemic through creative expression and by raising money for research.

DeMantini, Rodney J. "AIDS and Catholic Education: Proclamation or Phobia?" *Momentum*, vol. 18, Sep. 1987, p29–33.

Deals with the dilemma Catholic educators face in teaching about AIDS in parochial schools. Some behaviors associated with the disease are in conflict with doctrines of the church.

Dentzer, Susan. "The Network of Life and Death." *U.S. News & World Report*, vol. 106, June 19, 1989, p42–44.

Article describes the work of the Dallas AIDS ARMS network.

DiBlase, Donna. "AIDS Claims Hard to Track for Insurers." *Business Insurance*, vol. 21, Sep. 7, 1987, p22–23.

Some insurance experts say why it is difficult to give an accurate cost of AIDS claims as the cases are not always listed as AIDS related; also the claims seem no higher than those for any other catastrophic illness.

Donahue, Richard J. "Health Care Cost of AIDS Called Trivial." *National Underwriter* (Property, Casualty and Employee Benefits Edition), vol. 91, Sep. 14, 1987, p80.

Explains that current cost of AIDS is small compared to the total national health care expenditures, amounting to no more than 2%. Claims that this amount should not overburden the insurance industry.

Dunkel, Joan, and Shellie Hatfield. "Countertransference Issues in Working with Persons with AIDS." *Social Work*, Mar.–Apr. 1986, p114–117.

Authors highlight eight countertransference issues that social workers typically confront when working with persons diagnosed with AIDS and their friends and families.

"Earmarked Money Starts to Flow." *New Scientist*, vol. 114, May 14, 1987, p28.

British Medical Research Council has appropriated funding for AIDS vaccine and antiviral therapies research.

Edwards, Diane D. "Pessimistic Outlook in AIDS Reports." *Science News*, vol. 133, June 11, 1988, p372.

Researchers analyze the future of the AIDS epidemic, projecting 450,000 cases by 1993.

Ember, Lois. "Physicians Issue Ethics Guidelines for AIDS." *Chemical and Engineering News*, vol. 65, Nov. 30, 1987, p22.

The American Medical Association's ethical guidelines for the care and treatment of AIDS.

"Facing the AIDS Crisis." *Newsweek*, vol. 109, June 8, 1987, p16–18.

President Reagan, in a speech at a fund-raiser for AIDS, discusses issues to be addressed at the presidential level.

"Fear and Loving and AIDS." *Film Comment*, vol. 22, Mar.–Apr. 1986, p44–50.

Critical analysis of the media and its presentation of gays, gay lifestyles and the spread of AIDS.

"The Federal Avant-garde." *National Review*, vol. 41, Dec. 31, 1989, p14.

Discusses public opinion on federal funding of the arts, especially of projects dealing with homosexuality and AIDS.

Feldschuh, Joseph. "AIDS and Ostriches: Business Is Not Facing Up to the Scourge." *Barron's*, vol. 69, Dec. 18, 1989, p16ff.

Analyzes the impact of AIDS in the workplace and discusses economic ramifications of the AIDS epidemic.

Findlay, Steven. "The Emerging Strategy to Contain AIDS." *U.S. News & World Report*, vol. 106, June 19, 1989, p46.

Discusses the further spread of AIDS, research efforts and new ways to treat patients with AIDS.

Fineberg, Harvey V. "Education to Prevent AIDS: Prospects and Obstacles." *Science*, vol. 239, Feb. 5, 1988, p592–596.

Identifies obstacles standing in the way of effective AIDS-prevention education in the United States. Calls for a comprehensive nationwide education program aimed at changing behaviors.

Fineberg, Harvey V. "The Social Dimensions of AIDS." *Scientific American*, vol. 259, Oct. 1988, p128–134.

Explores the social impact of AIDS and what nonmedical measures can be taken to prevent the spread of AIDS. Also looks at social ways of caring for people with AIDS.

Francis, Donald P., et al. "Targeting AIDS Prevention and Treatment Toward HIV-I Infected Persons: The Concept of Early Intervention." *JAMA*, vol. 262, Nov. 10, 1989, p2572ff.

Examines approaches to care and treatment of persons identified as HIV-positive.

"Future Costs of AZT Worry Health Authorities." *New Scientist*, vol. 116, Oct. 1, 1987, p28–29.

Analysis of the increasing cost of AIDS and how this will affect the insurance industry as well as the government's ability to cover the bill.

Gadsby, Patricia. "Mapping the Epidemic: Geography as Destiny." *Discover*, vol. 9, Apr. 1988, p28–31.

Analysis of how geographical location is a factor in the risk of contracting AIDS.

Gallo, Robert C., and Luc Montagnier. "Letters" (discussion of Oct 1988 article, "AIDS in 1988"), *Scientific American*, vol. 260, June 1989, p10–11.

Letter refutes previous article's claim that AIDS originated in Africa. Authors of article defend their assertion in response.

Gallup, George H. Jr., and Alex Gallup. "AIDS: We Worry about the Wrong Things." *American Health*, vol. 7, June 1988, p50–52.

Results of an international poll on AIDS indicate awareness is high but changes in behavior are slow to occur.

Garagusi, Vincent F. "AIDS Patients in Private Practice." *American Family Physician*, vol. 35, June 1987, p82–84.

Raises some of the problems family physicians will face as the numbers of AIDS patients in their care increase.

Garvey, John. "A Fact of Life." *Commonweal*, vol. 114, Dec. 4, 1987, p694–695.

A look at AIDS from the conservative perspective. Author objects to explicit AIDS education for moral reasons.

Gevisser, Mark. "More Gay-Bashing." *Nation*, vol. 245, Oct. 31, 1987, p473.

Reviews amendment passed by Congress prohibiting the use of federal funds for any AIDS education materials that encourage homosexuality.

Goldsmith, Marsha F. "December 1 Designated World AIDS Day: Message Is Join the Worldwide Effort." *JAMA*, vol. 260, Nov. 25, 1988, p2969–2970.

Discusses the designation of December 1, 1988, as World AIDS Day by the World Health Organization.

Goldsmith, Marsha F. "Inescapable Problem: AIDS in Prison." *JAMA*, vol. 258, Dec. 11, 1987, p3215.

Addresses the broad spectrum of concerns on AIDS in correctional facilities. Problems include identifying infected persons, cost of treatment, testing and confidentiality.

Goldsmith, Marsha F. "Small Scientific Steps Important in Gigantic AIDS Control Mission." *JAMA*, vol. 260, Aug. 19, 1988, p893–894.

Reviews estimates that 200,000 cases of AIDS have occurred worldwide and upwards of 10 million people may be infected.

Goode, Erica E. "Telling '80s Kids about Sex." *U.S. News & World Report*, vol. 103, Nov. 16, 1987, p83–84.

Article focuses on parents' role in providing children with accurate and balanced information about AIDS.

Gooding, Judson. "Pasteur's Progress." *Omni*, vol. 10, Apr. 1988, p22.

Article marking the 100th anniversary of the Pasteur Institute and its work on AIDS.

Goodman, Simon. "The Joy of Chastity." *New Scientist*, vol. 116, Oct. 15, 1987, p62.

An analysis of popular music as an advocate of multiple sexual partners at a time when AIDS education and safe sex are being promoted.

Grady, Denise. "The Shaky Case for an AIDS-Syphilis Connection." *Discovery*, vol. 9, Dec. 1988, p24–25.

Reviews the highly disputed claim that syphilis is the cause of AIDS or a major contributing factor.

Grant, Daniel. "Health Insurance for Artists: The AIDS Stigma." *American Artist*, vol. 52, July 1988, p10ff.

Insurance companies consider artists to be a high-risk group for AIDS. As a result, artists and their associations are having problems locating affordable health coverage.

Green, Jesse. "More Questions than Answers: A Gay Man Takes the AIDS Test." *Gentleman's Quarterly*, vol. 59, Dec. 1989, p152ff.

A personal account of taking the test for HIV detection.

Greenberg, Eric Rolfe. "Workplace Testing: Results of a New AMA Survey." *Personnel*, vol. 65, Apr. 1988, p36–44.

Report on an American Management Association survey on drugs, polygraph, competency and AIDS virus testing of employees.

Halcrow, Allan. "AIDS: The Corporate Response." *Personnel Journal*, Aug. 1986, p123–127.

Describes the creation of educational materials and programs for employees by seven major corporations with the assistance of the San Francisco AIDS Foundation.

Harris, Richard F. "AIDS Meeting Suggests Basic Research Gaps." *Science News*, vol. 133, June 25, 1988, p405.

Article reviews the direction of AIDS research and the development of vaccines and other drug therapy.

Healy, Rita. "The AIDS Tracers." *Life*, vol. 10, Oct. 1987, p52–55.

Profiles the activities of a program in Colorado that requires the reporting of all blood test results positive for AIDS and the tracing of sexual partners of AIDS victims.

Henry, W. A. "The Appalling Saga of Patient Zero." *Time*, vol. 130, Oct. 19, 1987, p40–45.

Story of Gaetan Dugas, the person identified as primarily responsible for the spread of the AIDS virus in America. Dugas is linked sexually to 40 of the first 248 confirmed cases of the syndrome.

Heyward, William L., and James W. Curran. "The Epidemiology of AIDS in the U.S." *Scientific American*, vol. 259, Oct. 1988, p72–81.

Statistical report and analysis of the spread of AIDS in the United States. Identifies risk groups and behavior patterns that increase the chance of contracting AIDS and suggests ways of controlling further spread of the disease.

Hoffman, Paul. "A New Realism." *Discover*, vol. 9, Apr. 1988, p4.

Discusses how the death of Rock Hudson brought the severity of the AIDS problem to the attention of the American people.

Hollenbach, David M. "AIDS Education: The Moral Substance." *America*, vol. 157, Dec. 26, 1987, p493–494.

Covers the controversy within the Catholic Church about the section on the use of condoms included in the bishops' recent pastoral statement on AIDS.

Hopkins, Donald R. "AIDS in Minority Populations in the United States." *Public Health Reports*, vol. 102, Nov.–Dec. 1987, p677–681.

Statistical and analytical report on the incidence of AIDS among minorities.

Horgan, John. "Affirmative Action: AIDS Researchers Seek to Enroll More Minorities in Clinical Trials." *Scientific American*, vol. 261, Dec. 1989, p34.

Describes the efforts of AIDS researchers to get more minorities into drug-testing programs and clinical research.

Horn, Miriam. "The Artists' Diagnosis." *U.S. News & World Report*, vol. 106, Mar. 27, 1989, p62–63ff.

Discusses how the arts community is trying to change society's response to the AIDS epidemic.

Iglehart, John K. "Financing the Struggle against AIDS." *New England Journal of Medicine*, vol. 317, July 16, 1987, p180–184.

Author argues that government must balance funding for AIDS research between caring for the victims and protecting the public.

"Is AIDS Underreported?" *Newsweek*, vol. 113, June 19, 1989, p71.

Reports on a new study indicating that AIDS statistics compiled by the Centers for Disease Control may seriously underrepresent the number of white Americans who have the disease.

Johnson, George. "Dr. Krim's Crusade." *New York Times Magazine*, Feb. 14, 1988, p30–34.

Story of Dr. Mathilde Krim's efforts in collaboration with the American Foundation for AIDS Research to raise millions of dollars for AIDS research.

Jones, David C. "AIDS Costs Threaten HMOs, Health Insurers." *National Underwriter* (Property, Casualty and Employee Benefits Edition), vol. 91, July 13, 1987, p2ff. Also in *National Underwriter* (Life, Health, and Financial Services Edition), vol. 91, July 13, 1987, p6ff.

HMOs face serious financial difficulties as the costs of AIDS treatment continue to increase.

Jones, David C. "Perspective on AIDS: Ethical, Socioeconomic and Political Aspects." *Vital Speeches of the Day*, vol. 54, Jan. 1, 1988, p176–179.

Speaker discusses public policy issues framed by the AIDS crisis. He recommends bioethical approaches that would help resolve many of these issues.

Kaufman, David. "AIDS: The Creative Response." *Horizon*, vol. 30, Nov. 1987, p2, 13–20.

Author relates that how artists deal with AIDS—raising money and treating the disease as a creative subject—helps contribute to a more humane response to the epidemic.

Kerr, Peter. "Syphilis Surge with Crack Use Raises Fears on Spread of AIDS." *New York Times*, June 29, 1988, pB1.

Reports on the increasing concern that crack use in poor neighborhoods may be accelerating the spread of AIDS.

Kirp, David L., and Steven Epstein. "AIDS in America's Schoolhouses: Learning the Hard Lessons." *Phi Delta Kappan 2*, vol. 70, Apr. 1989, p578, 584–593.

Discusses the moral, ethical, legal and practical problems associated with children who have AIDS attending school.

Kolata, Gina. "Children and AIDS: Drug Tests Raise Hope and Ethical Concerns." *New York Times*, May 24, 1988, p.C3.

Discusses plans by some doctors to begin antiviral treatment for babies who may carry the AIDS virus.

Kolata, Gina. "Women and AIDS: What You Must Know Now." *Ladies Home Journal*, vol. 106, Nov. 1989, p98ff.

Explores women's concerns about AIDS generally and the transmission of the virus in particular.

Krim, Mathilde. "How Not to Control the AIDS Epidemic." *Humanist*, vol. 47, Nov./Dec. 1987, p14–16.

Author opposes quarantining of AIDS patients and mandatory testing for exposure to the virus. She argues these steps would violate privacy and civil rights.

Langone, John. "How to Block a Killer's Path." *Time*, vol. 133, Jan. 30, 1989, p60–62.

Discusses high-risk behaviors associated with AIDS and the segments of society hit hardest by the epidemic.

Laver, Ross. "Uniting Against AIDS." *MacLeans's*, vol. 101, Feb. 8, 1988, p34.

Reports on the meeting of health officials from 146 countries as they unite in the fight against AIDS.

Lawton, Kim. "Citizens Join Government in Addressing the AIDS Crisis." *Christianity Today*, vol. 31, Oct. 16, 1987, p38–39.

Critical overview of policy recommendations of the president's commission on AIDS. A new group, Americans for a Sound AIDS Policy, seeks to get all sides to work together.

Lenaghan, Donna D., and Michael J. Lenaghan. "AIDS and Education: The Frontline of Prevention." *Futurist*, vol. 21, Nov./Dec. 1987, p17–19.

Stresses the role of early education as the most effective weapon against the spread of AIDS.

Lord, Lewis J. "The Staggering Price of AIDS." *U.S. News & World Report*, vol. 102, June 15, 1987, p16–18.

AIDS

Insurance companies jarred by the overwhelming cost of the AIDS
epidemic seek to control costs by testing applicants for antibodies to
the AIDS virus.

Lutgen, Lorraine. "AIDS in the Workplace: Fighting Fear with Facts
and Policy." *Personnel*, vol. 64, Nov. 1987, p53–57.

Discusses guidelines for an employment policy on AIDS-related issues
in the workplace.

Luzzatto, Donald. "MONY, with Its AIDS Grants, Calls Others to Follow Suit." *National Underwriter*, vol. 91, June 15, 1987, p1ff.

MONY financial services company donates $80,000 to four organiza-
tions providing care for AIDS patients and urges other insurers to do
the same.

McAuliffe, Kathleen. "Misplaced Fears over New AIDS Cases." *U.S.
News & World Report*, vol. 102, June 1, 1987, p58.

The incidence of three health care workers who contracted AIDS has
raised new fears that AIDS can be spread through the skin.

McGrath, Tom, and Franklin McMahon. "Forty Hours." *U.S. Catholic*,
vol. 54, Nov. 1989, p20ff.

Discusses comparative religious attitudes toward the AIDS epidemic.

Mann, Jonathan M. "Global AIDS into the 1990's." *World Health*, Oct.
1989, p6–7.

Covers the international impact of AIDS and the World Health Organization's plans to deal with the disease.

Mann, Jonathan M., et al. "The International Epidemiology of AIDS."
Scientific American, vol. 259, Oct. 1988, p82–89.

Report on the spread of AIDS worldwide as the disease reaches an
almost pandemic level.

Marsa, Linda. "Phoenix Rising." *Omni*, vol. 12, Dec. 1989, p50ff.

Assesses social aspects of AIDS. Also discusses the powers and responsibilities of the Food and Drug Administration to approve AIDS
drugs.

Marwick, Charles. "Is Institute of Medicine the Agency to Lead Science's Attack on AIDS?" *JAMA*, vol. 258, Oct. 2, 1987, p1699.

Author says AIDS research can be accelerated by cooperation and
sharing among private industries, academic researchers and the National Institutes of Health.

"Media and the Message." *Commonweal*, vol. 114, Nov. 6, 1987, p612–613.

The federal government has distributed several television public service announcements on AIDS. Some stations have not aired these announcements because of the open discussion of sexuality.

Merina, Anita. "AIDS Prevention . . . through Education. Is Your School Ready for AIDS?" *NEA Today*, vol. 8, Dec. 1989, p10–11.

Guide for teaching AIDS prevention, including a short quiz and list of resources.

Micheli, Robin. "When AIDS Hits Home." *Money*, vol. 16, Nov. 1987, p137–150.

Overview of the cost of AIDS. Some financial planning possibilities are presented for AIDS patients.

Miles, Donna. "On the Front Lines against AIDS." *Soldiers*, May 1988, p4–11.

Describes the U.S. Army's treatment program for HIV-infected soldiers.

Miller, Holly G. "Surgeon General Koop Asks for More Voluntary AIDS Testing." *Saturday Evening Post*, vol. 259, Nov. 1987, p58–61.

Profile of U.S. Surgeon General Koop and his proactive involvement in the AIDS issue.

"The Missionary Doctor." *Time*, vol. 129, June 8, 1987, p22.

Details Surgeon General Koop's advocacy of sex education and the use of condoms as effective methods of stopping the spread of AIDS.

Monmaney, Terrence. "More Facts, Less Hope." *Newsweek*, vol. 111, June 27, 1988, p46–47.

Outlook on the future of the AIDS epidemic as cases continue to escalate with no scientific breakthrough in sight.

Morgan, Thomas. "Mainstream Strategy for AIDS Group." *New York Times*, July 22, 1988, pB1.

Profiles protest group ACT-UP, which has been highly critical of the response of the government and medical establishment to the AIDS crisis.

Moseley, Charles J. "AIDS Update." *Editorial Research Reports*, vol. 2, Dec. 16, 1988, p630–643.

Examines the current status of the AIDS epidemic: statistics, therapies, vaccines, and economic and political aspects.

Nakajima, Hiroshi. "A Vital Role for WHO." *World Health*, Oct. 1989, p3.

Outlines AIDS educational programs being promoted by the World Health Organization.

Nelson, Sara. "AIDS: An Up-to-the-Minute Report." *Seventeen*, vol. 47, Mar. 1988, p244–245ff.

Article clarifies the methods of AIDS transmission.

"New Database for AIDS Research." *Science*, vol. 236, Feb. 5, 1987, p634.

Article on data base being established at Los Alamos National Laboratory in New Mexico.

"New Study Sees Lower Cost for AIDS Care." *New York Times*, May 26, 1988, pB17.

A government health economist predicts lower costs for providing health care to AIDS patients despite the high price of the drug AZT.

Newmark, Peter. "New Areas in AIDS Research." *Nature*, vol. 333, June 1988, p697.

Article calls for more research in the areas of virology, sexual behavior, STD and the search for an animal model of AIDS.

Ostling, Richard N. "The Bishops Split on Aids." *Time*, vol. 130, Dec. 28, 1987, p64.

Reports on the split among the Catholic bishops on the issue of educating people to use condoms to stop the spread of AIDS.

Palca, Joseph. "Lab Worker Infected with AIDS Virus." *Nature*, vol. 329, Sep. 10, 1987, p92.

Reports on the incident of a laboratory worker who reportedly contracted AIDS on the job.

Piot, Peter, et al. "AIDS: An International Perspective." *Science*, vol. 239, Feb. 5, 1988, p573–579.

Reviews AIDS and infection with HIV as a worldwide public health problem. Although in America transmission is mostly among homosexual men and IV drug users, in Africa the virus is mainly heterosexually acquired.

"Poverty Spreads AIDS." *New Scientist,* vol. 118, June 23, 1988, p26.

Reports show that the spread of AIDS has been correlated with social class and disproportionally affects the poor, who are more likely to be IV drug users.

"The President Talks about AIDS." *America,* vol. 156, June 20, 1987, p493–494.

In his first speech on AIDS, President Reagan calls for mandatory testing of certain groups of people and for AIDS education in the schools.

Prince, Alfred M., et al. "Chimpanzees and AIDS Research." *Nature,* vol. 333, June 9, 1988, p513.

Reports on the use of chimpanzees in the testing of AIDS drugs and vaccines before they are tested in humans.

"Questions about AIDS." *Consumer Reports,* vol. 54, Mar. 1989, p142.

Answers to commonly asked questions about AIDS, such as the numbers of people infected with the virus, the symptoms of infection, the groups of people at greatest risk and the ways the virus is transmitted.

Reininger, Alon. "AIDS: Another Sad Year for the Sick, a Frightening Future for the Country." *Life,* vol. 11, Jan. 1988, p42–48.

Review of AIDS epidemic in 1987.

"Report of the Second Public Health Service AIDS Prevention and Control Conference." *Public Health Reports,* vol. 103, suppl. 1, 1988, p1–109.

Discusses the annual PHS Conference on AIDS. Issues addressed included: epidemiology; prevention; treatment; and AIDS among drug users, women, children and minorities.

Richland, Jordan H. "Role of State Health Agencies in Responding to AIDS." *Public Health Reports,* vol. 103, May/June 1988, p267–272.

Overview of the work done by state health agencies in the fight against AIDS.

Rist, Darrell Yates. "The Deadly Costs of an Obsession." *The Nation,* vol. 248, Feb. 13, 1989, p181ff.

The concern with the AIDS epidemic has diverted the campaign for gay rights.

Ritter, Anne. "AIDS and the Medicinal Power of Work." *Personnel,* vol. 66, Nov. 1989, p36–39.

Reports the efforts of Multitasking Systems, a nonprofit business to provide jobs for persons suffering from AIDS and HIV infections.

Rock, Andrea. "What We Must Do." *Money*, vol. 16, Nov. 1987, p153.

Outlines several strategies that can be implemented to cope with the financial burden of AIDS.

Rosellini, Lynn. "Rebel with a Cause—Koop." *U.S. News & World Report*, vol. 105, May 30, 1988, p55–63.

Biographical profile on Surgeon General Dr. C. Everett Koop, with emphasis on his impact in helping shape federal policy on AIDS.

Rossett, Jane, and Gypsy Ray. "Facing AIDS." *Ms.*, vol. 16, Sep. 1987, p65–69.

Personal accounts of women and their experiences with AIDS—as patients, family members of victims, caretakers and protestors.

Saholz, Eloise. "Acting Up to Fight AIDS." *Newsweek*, vol. 111, June 6, 1988, p42.

Covers the group ACT-UP and its measures taken to convince the government to do more in the fight against AIDS.

Schaeffer, Charles. "Talking to Kids about AIDS." *Changing Times*, vol. 41, Dec. 1987, p23–27.

Advice on educating children on the facts of AIDS, with special reference to teenagers who tend to ignore the realities of the disease.

Schmeck, Harold. "Family Tree of AIDS Viruses is Viewed as 37 to 80 Years Old." *New York Times*, June 9, 1988, pA32.

Provides results of a study suggesting that the origin of HIV in its current form could be as recent as 40 years ago.

Schwartz, William A. "Drug Addicts with Dirty Needles." *Nation*, vol. 244, June 20, 1988, p843–846.

Addresses the problem of the rapid spread of AIDS among intravenous drug users, the need for effective education campaigns and the policy option of providing sterile needles to drug users.

Seibert, Gary. "A Plague, Not a War." *America*, vol. 157, Oct. 24, 1987, p260–261.

Author urges religious writers to confront the issue of AIDS even though their views may be controversial.

Seligmann, Jean. "Checking Up on a Killer." *Newsweek*, vol. 113, June 12, 1989, p59–60.

Reports on the Fifth Annual International Conference on AIDS. Conferees predict a significant increase in reported AIDS cases in the future and call for increased prevention programs.

Seligmann, Jean. "The Mystery of Silent AIDS Infections." *Newsweek*, vol. 113, June 12, 1989, p59.

Describes studies showing that people take different amounts of time to produce antibodies after exposure to the AIDS virus. This fact could have serious implications for accuracy of blood testing for the virus.

Seligmann, Jean. "The Push for Prevention." *Newsweek*, vol. 113, June 19, 1989, p71.

Reviews a new set of AIDS-treatment guidelines for physicians issued by the Centers for Disease Control.

Sheff, David. "Just Say Know." *Rolling Stone*, Aug. 10, 1989, p58–59ff.

Interview with artist Keith Haring, who discusses his own battle with AIDS and the impact of the epidemic on the arts community.

Smith, Lee. "Throwing Money at AIDS." *Fortune*, vol. 116, Aug. 31, 1987, p64–67.

Author argues that money allocated for AIDS education should be directed at high-risk groups rather than middle-class heterosexuals.

Stein, M. L. "Using AIDS in Obituaries." *Editor and Publisher*, vol. 120, May 23, 1987, p38.

Newspaper industry must face the question of whether or not to mention AIDS as the cause of death in obituaries.

Steinem, Gloria. "Small Steps in Fighting AIDS." *Newsweek*, vol. 111, June 27, 1988, p8.

Addresses efforts that can be made by individuals such as drug abusers, teenagers, prostitutes and minorities to reduce the spread of AIDS.

Swenson, Robert M. "Plagues, History and AIDS." *American Scholar*, vol. 57, Spring 1988, p183–200.

Historical look at plagues and how AIDS fits into the context.

"The Surprising Death of Robert R." *U.S. News & World Report*, vol. 103, Nov. 9, 1987, p16.

Article on the mysterious death of a teenage boy in 1969. Researchers speculate he may have died from AIDS.

Taravella, Steve. "Insurers Promoting AIDS Service Efforts." *Business Insurance*, vol. 21, Sep. 7, 1987, p42–43.

Describes the financial support being provided by insurers for AIDS research and education programs.

"This Is What You Thought: 98 Percent Say It Should Be a Crime to Knowingly Spread AIDS." *Glamour*, vol. 85, Dec. 1987, p81.

Results of reader survey show that respondents are now less trusting of their sexual partners.

Thompson, Larry. "AIDS Diary." *Discover*, vol. 9, Jan. 1988, p36–38.

Summarizes activities related to the AIDS crisis in 1987.

Tierney, John. "Straight Talk—AIDS and Heterosexuals." *Rolling Stone*, Nov. 17, 1988, p122–137.

Disputes the prediction that AIDS increasingly will afflict heterosexuals.

Toufexis, Anastasia. "Cracking Down on the Victims." *Time*, vol. 130, July 6, 1987, p82–83.

Discusses how, as fear of AIDS spreads, some states are considering bills that could make it illegal to intentionally transmit the AIDS virus.

Treichler, Paula A. "Seduced and Terrorized." *ArtForum*, vol. 28, Oct. 1989, p147–153.

Critical analysis of the AIDS epidemic as it is presented by network television in movies, special reports, news, etc.

Voboril, Mary. "The Castaways: Fears about AIDS Drive Three Boys from Home." *Life*, vol. 10, Oct. 1987, p98–100.

Story of three hemophiliac boys who contracted AIDS through blood transfusions and were forced to leave their home because of discrimination and physical abuse.

Walters, LeRoy. "Ethical Issues in the Prevention and Treatment of HIV Infection and AIDS." *Science*, vol. 239, Feb. 5, 1988, p597–603.

Addresses the key question of how society can control the AIDS epidemic without at the same time infringing on individual liberties.

Annotated Bibliography

Weiss, Robin. "A National Strategy on AIDS." *Issues in Science and Technology*, vol. 5, Spring 1989, p52.

Discusses actions that can be taken by the Bush administration to slow the spread of AIDS and its damaging effects.

Wertz, Dorothy C., et al. "Knowledge and Attitudes of AIDS Health Care Providers Before and After Education Programs." *Public Health Reports*, vol. 102, May/June 1987, p248–254.

Survey indicates that health care workers' knowledge levels and attitudes significantly improved following AIDS education programs.

"What Science Knows about AIDS." *Scientific American*, vol. 259, Oct. 1988, p40–48ff.

Discusses origins and biology of AIDS virus and reviews state of current research. Part of a special issue on AIDS.

White, Edmund. "The Artist and AIDS." *Harper's*, vol. 274, May 1987, p22ff.

Reflects on how the AIDS epidemic has changed artists' and homosexuals' views of their lives and work.

Whitman, David. "A Fall from Grace on the Right." *U.S. News & World Report*, vol. 102, May 25, 1987, p27–28.

Describes how one-time supporters now criticize Surgeon General Koop for his views on AIDS education.

"WHO and the Global AIDS Strategy." *World Health*, Oct. 1989, p4.

Discusses the aims and objectives of the World Health Organization regarding control of the spread of AIDS worldwide.

Wober, Mallory. "Perceived Risk of Disease and Alcohol, Asbestos and AIDS: Links with Television Viewing?" *Health Education Research*, vol. 2, Sep. 1987, p175–184.

Discusses research on the link between perceptions of the likelihood of contracting AIDS and amounts of TV watched.

"The Workplace and AIDS: A Guide to Services and Information, Part II." *Personnel Journal*, Feb. 1988, p101–112.

A guide to AIDS information sources such as newsletters, magazines, videotapes, organizations, etc. Continuation of article first appearing in October 1987 issue.

Zyllke, Jody W. "Interest Heightens in Defining, Preventing AIDS in High-Risk Adolescent Population." *JAMA*, vol. 262, Oct. 27, 1989, p2197.

Reviews the status of AIDS among teenagers, with emphasis on risk factors, number of cases and the influence of drug abuse.

LEGAL

Aberth, John. "AIDS: The Human Element." *Personnel Journal*, Aug. 1986, p119–123.

Focuses on the feelings and experiences of people with AIDS who have confronted difficulties on the job. Recommends written policies for companies.

Boffey, Philip. "AIDS Panel's Chief Urges Ban on Bias against Infected." *New York Times*, June 3, 1988, pA1.

Summarizes the president's AIDS commission report recommending strong new federal laws to prevent discrimination against people with the AIDS virus.

Brennan, T.A. "The Acquired Immunodeficiency Syndrome as an Occupational Disease." *Annals of Internal Medicine*, vol. 107, Oct. 1987, p581–583.

Article addresses some of the legal and ethical questions raised by health care workers who, because of the risk of the transmission of AIDS, need a system of supplementary insurance benefits similar to worker's compensation.

Dickens, Bernard M. "Legal Rights and Duties in the AIDS Epidemic." *Science*, vol. 239, Feb. 5, 1988, p580–586.

Provides an overview of major legal concerns pertaining to AIDS, such as the rights of HIV-infected persons to confidential testing and treatment, and issues of nondiscrimination in housing and employment.

"Excerpts from Report by AIDS Panel Chairman." *New York Times*, June 3, 1988, pA16.

Excerpts from the "Legal and Ethical Issues" section of the Chairman's draft recommendations for the final report of the Presidential Commission on the HIV Epidemic.

Hoerr, John, et al. "Privacy: Companies Are Delving Further into Employees' Personal Lives—and Workers Are Fighting Harder for the Right to Be Let Alone." *Business Week*, Mar. 28, 1988, p61–66.

Recounts experiences of employees with discrimination and breach of privacy on the job.

Howard, Lisa S. "Health Groups File Lawsuit over N.Y. Dept.'s AIDS Regulation." *National Underwriter* (Property, Casualty and Employee Benefits Edition), vol. 91, Aug. 24, 1987, p3ff.

The insurance industry contests a New York State regulation prohibiting AIDS testing of insurance applicants.

Jenks, James M. "Protecting Privacy Rights." *Personnel Journal*, Sep. 1988, p123–126.

Addresses the problem of an employee's right to privacy and the employer's need to find workers who will perform jobs safely, honestly and well. Emphasizes the need for legal counsel and written policies.

Lewis, Hilary E. "Aquired Immunodeficiency Syndrome: State Legislative Activity." *JAMA*, vol. 258, Nov. 6, 1987, p2410–2414.

Overview of some of the more than 450 different bills on AIDS that have been introduced into state legislatures.

Libbin, Anne E., et al. "Employee Medical and Honesty Testing." *Personnel*, vol. 65, Nov. 1988, p38–47.

Addresses legal problems employers could face from extensive AIDS testing of job applicants and employees.

Masi, Dale A. "AIDS in the Workplace: What Can Be Done?" *Personnel*, vol. 64, July 1987, p57–60.

Survey showed that most employers did not have a plan for dealing with AIDS in the workplace. Includes recommendations for resolving the issues, such as developing policies and educational programs.

Monmaney, Terence, et al. "AIDS: Who Should Be Tested?" *Newsweek*, vol. 109, May 11, 1987, p64–65.

Discusses the controversy within the Reagan administration over which groups of people should be required to undergo testing for the AIDS virus.

Pear, Robert. "States' AIDS Discrimination Laws Reject Justice Department's Stand." *New York Times*, Sep. 17, 1986, pA20.

Reviews how a majority of states have adopted laws barring discrimination against persons with AIDS.

Press, Aric. "The Charge: AIDS Assault." *Newsweek*, vol. 109, June 22, 1987, p24.

Reports on one of the first cases in which AIDS has been labeled as a deadly weapon. A soldier in the Army was charged with aggravated assault for knowingly having sex while carrying the AIDS virus.

Redeker, James R., and Jonathan S. Segal. "Avoiding AIDS-related Liability." *Personnel*, vol. 66, Aug. 1989, p46–48.

Recommends several steps companies can take to reduce their liabilities relating to AIDS.

Smith, Andrew V. "AIDS: A Corporate Attitude." *Vital Speeches of the Day*, vol. 54, Dec. 1, 1987, p113–115.

Provides practical examples of how Pacific Northwestern Bell Telephone Co. is dealing with the problem of AIDS in the workplace.

Waldo, William. "A Practical Guide for Dealing with AIDS at Work." *Personnel Journal*, Aug. 1987, p135–138.

Sets out eight common problems employers face when dealing with applicants or employees who have AIDS or who have been exposed to the virus. Describes the employer's legal obligations.

Wing, David L. "AIDS: The Legal Debate." *Personnel Journal*, Aug. 1986, p114–119.

Addresses the guidelines provided by the Centers for Disease Control to employers on dealing with AIDS in the workplace.

MEDICAL

Altman, Lawrence. "Poor Nations Plagued with AIDS Posing Haunting Ethical Questions." *New York Times*, June 28, 1988, pC3.

Addresses the plight of those with AIDS in developing countries owing to lack of effective health care systems and funds.

American Medical Association, Board of Trustees. "Prevention and Control of A-I-D-S: an interim report." *JAMA*, vol. 258, Oct. 16, 1987, p2097.

Outlines recommendations of the AMA for a national policy to control AIDS. These include public education, counseling of victims, blood testing, and protection against discrimination.

"AZT May Protect Health Workers after Accidents." *New Scientist*, vol. 116, Oct. 29, 1987, p33.

Research with animals shows that it may be possible to prevent infection from AIDS with contaminated blood following accidents by administering AZT to the victim.

Annotated Bibliography

Boffey, Philip. "Official Blames Shortage of Staff for Delay in Testing AIDS Drugs." *New York Times*, Apr. 30, 1988, pA1.

Reports the contention of the director of the National Institute of Allergy and Infectious Diseases that clinical trials of some promising drugs were delayed because of insufficient staff to guide each treatment through the testing process.

Buckingham, Stephan, and Wilfred Van Gorp. "Essential Knowledge about AIDS Dementia." *Social Work*, Mar.–Apr. 1988. p112–115.

Reviews the research on dementia in AIDS patients. The social, emotional and legal issues stemming from this factor are identified.

"CDC Guidelines to Prevent AIDS in Health Care Workers." *American Family Physician*, vol. 36, Oct, 1987, p357–358.

Explains guidelines from the Centers for Disease Control for health care workers for preventing exposure to the AIDS virus.

Cherfas, Jeremy. "Hope for AIDS Vaccines." *Science*, vol. 246, Oct. 6, 1989, p23–24.

Background information on research and development efforts for an AIDS vaccine.

Culliton, Barbara J. "AIDS Drugs Remain Unavailable for Kids." *Science*, vol. 246, Oct. 6, 1989, p22.

Covers the special problem of the unavailability of drugs for children with AIDS.

Culliton, Barbara J. "AZT Reverses AIDS Dementia in Children." *Science*, vol. 246, Oct. 6, 1989, p21ff.

Discusses effectiveness of AZT in treating AIDS dementia in children.

Curran, James W., et al. "Epidemiology of HIV Infection and AIDS in the United States." *Science*, vol. 239, Feb. 5, 1988, p610–616.

An analysis of the incidence of AIDS among different population groups by race, sex and age.

"Doctors Fear AIDS, Too." *Newsweek*, vol. 109, Aug. 3, 1987, p58–59.

Some physicians, especially surgeons, are reluctant to treat patients who test positive for AIDS.

Droste, Therese. "Koop: AIDS Poses Ethical Dilemmas for Physicians." *Hospitals*, vol. 61, Dec. 5, 1987, p61ff.

Surgeon General Koop's opinion on problems physicians have dealing with AIDS.

Essex, Max, and Phyllis J. Kanki. "The Origins of the AIDS Virus." *Scientific American*, vol. 259, Oct. 1988, p64–71.

An inquiry into the family history of the AIDS virus, and how the related viruses interact with human beings and monkeys.

Ezzell, Carol. "Hospital Workers Have AIDS Virus." *Nature*, vol. 327, May 28, 1987, p261.

Report on three health care workers who tested positive for antibodies after accidental exposure to the blood of AIDS patients.

Fillit, Howard, et al. "AIDS in the Elderly: A Case and Its Implications." *Geriatrics*, vol. 144, July 1989, p65–70.

A case study of a 90-year-old man with AIDS and its implications for care of the elderly with HIV infection.

Gallo, Robert C., and Luc Montagnier. "AIDS in 1988." *Scientific American*, vol. 259, Oct. 1988, p40–48.

The authors, codiscoverers of the human immunodeficiency virus (HIV), recount the discovery and offer prospects for a vaccine and for therapy.

Gallo, Robert C., et al. "Isolation of Human T-cell Leukemia Virus in Acquired Immune Deficiency Syndrome." *Science*, vol. 220, May 20, 1983, p865–867.

Early research on isolation and characterization of a variety of human T-cell leukemia viruses in AIDS.

Gorman, Christine. "Strange Trip Back to the Future." *Time*, vol. 130, Nov. 9, 1987, p83.

Describes how medical researchers determined that a boy who died in 1969 was a victim of AIDS. Their discovery followed testing of frozen tissue samples saved after the boy's mysterious death.

Haseltine, William A., and Flossie Wong-Staal. "The Molecular Biology of the AIDS Virus." *Scientific American*, vol. 259, Oct. 1988, p52–62.

Authors describe the genetic complexity of HIV and how this information explains the behavior of the virus.

"Health Care Workers Told to Take Care." *New Scientist*, vol. 114, June 25, 1987, p37.

Health care workers are advised to follow strict AIDS guidelines to avoid contracting the disease.

Hilgartner, Margaret W. "AIDS and Hemophilia." *New England Journal of Medicine*, vol. 317, Oct. 29, 1987, p1153–1154.

Updates what is being done to detect HIV in the blood supply. Recounts the devastating impact of AIDS on hemophiliacs.

Hopkins, Donald R. "Public Health Measures for Prevention and Control of AIDS." *Public Health Reports*, vol. 102, Sep./Oct. 1987, p463–467.

Author claims prevention and control of AIDS must be pursued through methods similar to those used in eradicating smallpox.

Kelly, Jeffrey A., et al. "Stigmatization of AIDS Patients by Physicians." *American Journal of Public Health*, vol. 77, July 1987, p789–791.

A study indicates that physicians have a more negative reaction to AIDS patients and homosexuals than to patients with leukemia who are heterosexual.

Kolata, Gina. "The Evolving Biology of AIDS: Scavenger Cell Looms Large." *New York Times*, June 7, 1988, pC1.

Report on scientific findings suggesting that macrophages, a form of white blood cells, may play a key part in the spread of the AIDS virus in the human body.

Koop, C. Everett. "Physician Leadership in Preventing AIDS." *JAMA*, vol. 258, Oct. 16, 1987, p2111.

Outlines how physicians, by educating patients, can help in preventing the spread of AIDS.

Kramer, Linda. "AIDS Commissioner Belinda Mason Speaks with Ringing Authority about the Disease: She Has It." *People Weekly*, vol. 32, Dec. 11, 1989, p147ff.

Biographical sketch of the commissioner of the Presidential Commission on the Human Immunodeficiency Virus Epidemic, herself an AIDS victim.

Landers, Robert K. "AIDS Is Spotlighting Medical Debate over Experimental Drugs and Whether Patients Should Be Able to Gamble Their Lives on Unproven Remedies." *Editorial Research Reports*, vol. 2, Jan. 23, 1987, p30–39.

Focus is on FDA policy regarding approval of experimental drugs and its impact on AIDS victims.

Larder, Brendan A., et al. "HIV with Reduced Sensitivity to Zidovudine Isolated During Prolonged Therapy." *Science*, vol. 243, Mar. 31, 1989, p1731–1734.

Reviews a study showing that prolonged treatment with AZT is effective against HIV in vitro and improves the quality and length of life of patients with AIDS.

Leishman, Katie. "AIDS and Syphilis." *Atlantic*, vol. 261, Jan. 1988, p17–26.

Reviews the hypotheses of U.S. and German researchers concerning a connection between AIDS and syphilis.

Lewis, Charles E., et al. "AIDS-Related Competence of California's Primary Care Physicians." *American Journal of Public Health*, vol. 77, July 1987, p795–799.

Reports on a telephone survey of physicians in southern California about AIDS revealing that the majority lacked the knowledge and skill to effectively deal with AIDS.

McIver, Mary. "Dentistry and AIDS." *Macleans'*, vol. 100, Nov. 16, 1987, p66.

Dentists fear contracting AIDS through contact with blood and saliva and are referring known AIDS carriers to clinics that observe more rigid safety guidelines.

McKenzie, A. "An AIDS-Associated Microbe Unmasked." *Science News*, vol. 136, Dec. 2, 1989, p356.

Outlines recent research findings on the physiological aspects of a microbe linked to AIDS.

Marx, Jean L. "Drug-resistant Strains of AIDS Virus Found." *Science*, vol. 243, Mar. 24, 1989, p1551–1552.

Describes a study revealing that AZT, the only approved drug for AIDS treatment, can lead to the emergence of resistant strains of the virus.

Matthews, Thomas J., and Dani P. Bolognesi. "AIDS Vaccines." *Scientific American*, vol. 259, Oct. 1988, p120–127.

Focuses on the obstacles scientists face in their search for a vaccine against AIDS.

Annotated Bibliography

Moss, Robert J., and Steven H. Miles. "AIDS and the Geriatrician." *Journal of the American Geriatrics Society*, vol. 35, May 1987, p460–464.

Provides history, statistics and epidemiology of AIDS among the elderly and discusses how geriatricians need to address the problem.

Murphey-Corb, Michael, et al. "A Formalin-Inactivated Whole SIV Vaccine Confers Protection in Macaques." *Science*, vol. 246, Dec. 8, 1989, p1293ff.

Summarizes current vaccine research on the simian immunodeficiency virus.

"Number of Sex Partners and Potential Risk of Sexual Exposure to Human Immunodeficiency Virus." *JAMA*, vol. 260, Oct. 14, 1988, p2020–2021.

Reports on a survey completed by the National Opinion Research Center drawing a profile of the statistical risk of sexual exposure to HIV-1 and sexually transmitted diseases in the United States.

"One Step Closer to an AIDS Vaccine." *Newsweek*, vol. 114, Dec. 18, 1989, p66.

Reports on current status of AIDS vaccine research.

Palca, Joseph. "AIDS Drug Trials Enter New Age." *Science*, vol. 246, Oct. 6, 1989, p19.

Reviews the status of development and testing of new AIDS drugs.

Palca, Joseph. "A New Antiviral Drug: Promising or Problematic?" *Science*, vol. 246, Oct. 6, 1989, p20.

Discusses the assorted side effects of dideoxyinosine, an antiviral drug in the treatment of AIDS.

Pekkanen, John. "Are We Closing in on AIDS?" *Reader's Digest*, vol. 135, Dec. 1989, p79ff.

Reports on the effectiveness, in limited trials, of the experimental drug AZT to combat the effects of AIDS.

Pellegrino, Edmund D. "Altruism, Self-Interest, and Medical Ethics." *JAMA*, vol. 258, Oct. 9, 1987, p1939–1940.

Focus is on the dilemma of physicians regarding their option to select patients, thus excluding those with AIDS, and their moral and ethical obligations to society.

163

Pence, David. "The AIDS Epidemic: Paradox and Purpose in Public Health Policy." *Vital Speeches of the Day*, vol. 54, Feb. 1, 1988, p252–256.

The author argues that while AIDS is a new phenomenon, certain traditional methods formulated centuries ago to combat the spread of infectious diseases could help curb transmission of the AIDS virus.

Poli, Guido, et al. "Inteferon—but Not AZT—Suppresses HIV Expression in Chronically Infected Cell Lines." *Science*, vol. 244, May 5, 1989, p575–577.

Reviews the study showing that AZT prevented HIV infection of susceptible cells, but did not suppress HIV expression in infected cells.

Price, Richard W., et al. "The Brain in AIDS: Central Nervous System HIV-1 Infection and AIDS Dementia Complex." *Science*, vol. 239, Feb. 5, 1988, p586–592.

Discusses the neurological disorder associated with HIV infection. This complex is a common cause of death for patients in the advanced stages of AIDS.

"Promising Monkey Puzzles." *Economist*, vol. 313, Dec. 23, 1989, p96–97.

Describes simian research that could hold the key to development of an AIDS vaccine.

Redfield, Robert R., and Donald S. Burke. "HIV Infection: The Clinical Picture." *Scientific American*, vol. 259, Oct. 1988, p90–98.

Article focuses on early diagnosis and treatment of HIV infection before it progresses to full-blown AIDS.

Schnittman, Steven, et al. "Direct Polyclonal Activation of Human B Lymphocytes by the AIDS Virus." *Science*, vol. 233, Sep. 5, 1986, p1084–1086.

Reports the findings of laboratory research on the effect of the AIDS retrovirus on B lymphocytes.

Seligmann, Jean, and Mary Hager. "A New Worry for Health-Care Workers." *Newsweek*, vol. 109, June 1, 1987, p55.

Reports on the anxiety of health care workers about contracting AIDS from their patients.

Shaw, George M., et al. "Molecular Characterization of Human T-cell Leukemia Virus Type III in AIDS." *Science*, vol. 226, Dec. 7, 1984, p1165–1171.

Describes common biological and physiochemical characteristics of human T-cell leukemia virus type III and human retrovirus in AIDS.

Siwolop, Sana, et al. "A Tough Old Soldier Joins the Fight Against AIDS." *Business Week*, July 27, 1987, p69–70.

Describes how Jonas Salk, who pioneered the polio vaccine, has joined in the search for an AIDS vaccine. Salk recommends inoculation after the victim of HIV is infected rather than before.

"Study Suggests AIDS Virus Didn't Come from Monkeys." *New York Times*, June 2, 1988, pB13.

Reports on research findings suggesting that the AIDS virus probably did not jump from monkeys to humans. Rather, it may have infected the common ancestors of humans and monkeys.

Taravella, Steve. "Coping with AIDS: Employers Tout Case Management." *Business Insurance*, vol. 21, Sep. 7, 1987, p1ff.

Discusses options of home and hospice care for AIDS patients as a means of cutting medical expenses.

Thomas, Lewis. "AIDS: An Unknown Distance Still to Go," *Scientific American*, vol. 259, Oct. 1988, p152.

Outlines efforts to develop safe antiviral drugs, an AIDS vaccine and ways to preserve the human immune system.

Thompson, Roger. "AIDS: Spreading Mystery Disease." *Editorial Research Reports*, vol. 2, Aug. 9, 1985, p599–615.

Article covers two aspects of the spread of AIDS: how to protect the public; how society copes with such an epidemic.

Weber, Jonathan N., and Robin A. Weiss. "HIV Infection: The Cellular Picture." *Scientific American*, vol. 259, Oct. 1988, p100–109.

Discusses findings of AIDS research showing that infection begins when HIV binds to a CD4 molecule and describes how this information can help in developing vaccines or other treatments.

Weiss, R. "Clues to Stimulating AIDS Immunity." *Science News*, vol. 136, Dec. 9, 1989, p372.

Reviews research on developing a vaccine against the AIDS virus.

Yarchoan, Robert, et al. "AIDS Therapies." *Scientific American*, vol. 259, Oct. 1988, p110–119.

Describes how understanding of the HIV life cycle makes it possible to design drugs that attack specific pathogenic targets.

Young, Frank. "New Information Available about AIDS Treatments." *FDA Consumer*, vol. 23, Nov. 1989, p6ff.

Provides updated information on clinical research on the care and treatment of AIDS patients.

Zuger, Abigail, and Steven H. Miles. "Physicians, AIDS, and Occupational Risk." *JAMA*, vol. 258, Oct. 9, 1987, p1924–1928.

Looks at how doctors have responded to patients with contagious diseases and compares the attitude to the present reluctance to treat people with AIDS.

GOVERNMENT DOCUMENTS

AIDS: Are Children at Risk? Washington, D.C.: Office of Educational Research and Improvement, 1986, GPO Item No.: 466-A-3.

Pamphlet outlining how to curb the spread of AIDS among children through counseling and education.

AIDS Clinical Trials: Talking It Over. Bethesda, Md.: National Institute of Allergy and Infectious Diseases, 1989, GPO item no.: 505-A-1.

Discussion of clinical testing of experimental drugs to combat the human immunodeficiency virus.

An Act to Provide for the Awarding of Grants for the Purchase of Drugs Used in the Treatment of AIDS. Washington, D.C.: GPO, 1988, GPO item no.: 575.

One page reprint of the public law that provides funding for the purchase of AIDS drug treatments.

Anderson, Linda. *NCI's AIDS Research Program.* Bethesda, Md.: National Cancer Institute, Office of Cancer Communications, 1987, GPO item no.: 507-G-37.

Informational pamphlet on the AIDS research program at the National Cancer Institute.

Anderson, Linda. *Progress on the Treatment of AIDS.* Bethesda, Md.: National Cancer Institute, Office of Cancer Communications, 1987, GPO item no.: 507-G-37.

Fact sheet on progress made in the treatment of AIDS.

Anderson, Linda. *Research on Development of an AIDS Vaccine.* Bethesda, Md.: National Cancer Institute, Office of Cancer Communications, 1987, GPO item no.: 507-G-37.

Informational pamphlet on the research and development of an AIDS vaccine.

Center for Prevention Services, Division of Sexually Transmitted Diseases, Program Services Branch. *Guidelines for AIDS Prevention Program Operations.* Atlanta: Centers for Disease Control, 1987, GPO item no.: 494-K-4.

Manual for implementing and running an AIDS prevention program.

Centers for Disease Control. *Guidelines for AIDS Prevention Program Operations.* Washington, D.C.: GPO, 1987, GPO item no.: 504.

Provides goals and procedures for AIDS-education programs for the public, school-aged children, persons at increased risk of exposure to the AIDS virus and health care workers.

Centers for Disease Control. *Quarterly Report to the Domestic Policy Council on the Prevalence and Rate of Spread of HIV and AIDS in the United States.* Atlanta: Centers for Disease Control, 1988, GPO item no.: 508-A-5.

Quarterly report on number of cases and rate of spread of HIV and AIDS in the U.S.

Centers for Disease Control. *What You Should Know About AIDS.* Washington, D.C.: GPO, 1987, GPO item no.: 504.

This public awareness booklet discusses the transmission of AIDS and how to prevent the spread of the virus.

Dawson, Deborah A. *AIDS Knowledge and Attitudes.* Hyattsville, Md.: National Center for Health Statistics, 1988, GPO item no.: 500-E.

Statistics and information on public knowledge of and attitudes toward AIDS. Report appears monthly.

Dawson, Deborah A., and Ann M. Hardy. *AIDS Knowledge and Attitudes of Black Americans: Provisional Data from the 1988 National Health Interview Survey.* Hyattsville, Md.: Centers for Disease Control, 1989, GPO item no.: 500-E.

Report of the findings of a survey on black Americans' knowledge of and attitudes toward AIDS.

Dawson, Deborah A., and Ann M. Hardy. *AIDS Knowledge and Attitudes of Hispanic Americans: Provisional Data from the 1988 National Health Interview Survey.* Hyattsville, Md.: Centers for Disease Control, 1989, GPO item No.: 500-E.

Report of the results of a study of Hispanic Americans' knowledge of and attitudes toward AIDS.

Des Jarlais, Don, and Dana E. Hunt, *AIDS and Intravenous Drug Use.* Washington, D.C.: National Institute of Justice, 1988, GPO item no.: 718-A-18.

General information bulletin on AIDS transmission among intravenous drug users and how to prevent it.

Eden, Jill, et al. *AIDS and Health Insurance: An OTA Survey.* Washington, D.C.: Office of Technology Assessment, 1988, GPO item no.: 1070-M.

Office of Technology survey on the issue of AIDS and its effect on health insurance.

Employee Counseling Service Program, Health Resources and Services Administration. *AIDS Resource Guide.* Rockville, Md.: Public Health Service, 1986, GPO item no.: 486-A.

Pamphlet on where to obtain assistance and information on AIDS.

Francis, Donald P., and James Chin. *The Prevention of Acquired Immunodeficiency Syndrome in the United States: An Objective Strategy for Medicine, Public Health, Business, and the Community.* Rockville, Md.: Public Health Service, 1987.

Outlines strategy for the prevention of AIDS in the United States.

Goedert, James J. *Rate of Heterosexual HIV Transmission and Associated Risk with HIV-Antigen.* Bethesda, Md.: National Cancer Institute, 1988, GPO item no.: 507-G-37.

Research report on the rate of transmission of AIDS among heterosexuals.

Graves, Edmund. *Utilization of Short-Stay Hospitals by Patients with AIDS: United States, 1984–86.* Hyattsville, Md.: National Center for Health Statistics, 1988, GPO item no.: 500-E.

Statistical report on AIDS-patient hospitalization and the advantages of short-stay facilities.

Graves, Edmund, and Mary Moien. *Hospitalization for AIDS: United States, 1984–85.* Hyattsville, Md.: National Center for Health Statistics, 1987, GPO item no.: 508.

Statistics and analysis of AIDS patients hospitalized between 1984 and 1985.

Hall, Thomas L. *Protocol 6: HIV-related Training Needs, Programs, and Costs.* Rockville, Md.: National Center for Health Services Research and Technology Assessment, 1989, GPO item no.: 491-B-13.

Covers the cost of health care programs for AIDS-infected persons.

Hammett, Theodore M. *AIDS and the Law Enforcement Officer.* Washington, D.C.: National Institute of Justice, 1987, GPO item no.: 968-H-10.

National Institute of Justice guidelines for protecting police from contracting or spreading AIDS.

Hammett, Theodore M. *AIDS and the Law Enforcement Officer: Concerns and Policy Responses.* Washington, D.C.: Office of Communication and Research Utilization, 1987, GPO item no.: 718-A-7.

Examines the challenges confronted by the law enforcement community in dealing with AIDS.

Hammett, Theodore M. *HIV Antibody Testing: Procedures, Interpretation, and Reliability of Results.* Washington, D.C.: National Institute of Justice, 1988, GPO item no.: 718-A-18.

Pamphlet on procedures for HIV testing, with emphasis on the interpretation and reliability of results.

Hammett, Theodore M., and Saira Moini. *AIDS in Correctional Facilities: Issues and Options.* 3rd ed. Washington, D.C.: National Institute of Justice, 1988, GPO item no.: 718-A-7.

Covers the issues, practices and possible options of dealing with AIDS in the prisons.

Hammett, Theodore M., et al. *AIDS in Correctional Facilities.* Washington, D.C.: National Institute of Justice, 1989, GPO item no.: 718-A-7.

General overview of the state of aids in correctional facilities.

Hammett, Theodore M., et al. *The Cause, Transmission and Incidence of AIDS.* Washington, D.C.: National Institute of Justice, 1987, GPO item no.: 718-A-18.

Three-page bulletin giving general information on the course, transmission and incidence of AIDS.

Hardy, Ann M., et al. *The Economic Impact of the First 10,000 Cases of Acquired Immunodeficiency Syndrome in the United States.* Atlanta: Centers for Disease Control, 1986.

Deals with the medical and other costs of the first 10,000 AIDS cases.

Health Resources and Services Administration. *AIDS Activities*. Washington, D.C.: Health Resources and Services Administration, 1989, GPO item no.: 507-H-17.

A directory-type monograph on the range of AIDS activities of the Health Resources and Services Administration.

Hellinger, Fred J. *Forecasting the Personal Medical Care Costs of AIDS from 1988 through 1991*. Washington, D.C.: National Center for Health Services Research and Health Care Technology Assessment, 1988, GPO item no.: 507-I-1.

Economic analysis of the cost of AIDS-patient care to the year 1991.

Henrichsen, Colleen. *NIH Study Finds That Hospital Workers' Risk of Acquiring AIDS from Patients Is Very Low*. Bethesda, Md.: National Institutes of Health, 1987, GPO item no.: 506-H.

Leaflet summarizes findings of a study indicating that the risk of health care workers contracting AIDS from their patients is very low.

Joint Resolution to Designate the Month of October 1988 as "National AIDS Awareness and Prevention Month." Washington, D.C.: GPO, 1988, GPO item no.: 575.

Pamphlet about National AIDS Awareness Month and what it means to the public.

Kapantais, Gloria H. *Characteristics of Persons Dying from AIDS: Preliminary Data from the 1986 National Mortality Followback Survey*. Hyattsville, Md.: National Center for Health Statistics, 1989, GPO item no.: 500-E.

Statistical profile of the characteristics of persons dying from AIDS.

Knickman, James, et al. *Protocol 3: Comparisons of the Cost Effectiveness of Alternative Models for Organizing Services for Persons with AIDS*. Rockville, Md.: National Center for Health Services Research and Health Care Technology Assessment, 1989, GPO item no.: 491-B-13.

A comparative analysis of the cost-effectiveness of services and medical care for AIDS patients.

Moini, Saira, and Susan McWhan. *AIDS in Probation and Parole*. Washington, D.C.: National Institute of Justice, 1989, GPO item no.: 718-A-7.

Reports on AIDS among ex-prisoners on probation or parole.

Annotated Bibliography

National Cancer Institute, Office of Cancer Communications. *AIDS Drug Development Program at NCI.* Bethesda, Md.: National Cancer Institute, 1988, GPO item no.: 507-G-37.

Fact sheet on the National Cancer Institute's program for the development of AIDS drugs.

National Cancer Institute, Office of Cancer Communications. *Viruses in Cancer and AIDS.* Bethesda, Md.: National Cancer Institute, 1988, GPO item no.: 507-G-37.

Informational pamphlet on viruses that cause cancer and AIDS.

National Center for Health Services Research and Health Care Technology Assessment. *AIDS Health Services Research.* Rockville, Md.: Public Health Service, 1988, GPO item no.: 491-B-13.

Pamphlet on the research done in the area of health services for AIDS patients.

National Center for Health Services Research and Health Care Technology Assessment. *Health Services Research on HIV-related Illnesses.* Rockville, Md.: Public Health Service, 1989, GPO item no.: 491-B-13.

Report on research funding and research on AIDS.

National Center for Health Services Research and Health Care Technology Assessment. *A Severity Classification System for AIDS Hospitalizations.* Rockville, Md.: Public Health Service, 1989, GPO item no.: 491-B-13.

System to differentiate AIDS patients who are hospitalized by severity of condition.

National Institutes of Health, Office of Medical Applications of Research. *The Impact of Routine HTLV-III Testing on Public Health.* Bethesda, Md.: Public Health Service, 1986, GPO item no.: 507-A-36.

A report on how testing for the AIDS virus has affected public health.

Paringer, Lynn, et al. *Estimating the Demand, Supply, and National Costs of HIV Testing.* Rockville, Md.: National Center for Health Services Research and Health Care Technology Assessment, 1989, GPO item no.: 491-B-13.

Projections of the need for HIV testing nationwide and what such an undertaking will cost.

Peterman, Thomas A., and James W. Curran. *Sexual Transmission of Human Immunodeficiency Virus*. Atlanta: Centers for Disease Control, 1986.

Article on exactly how the AIDS virus is sexually transmitted.

Rowe, Mona, and Caitlin Ryan. *AIDS, a Public Health Challenge: State Issues, Policies and Programs*. Washington, D.C.: Public Health Service, 1987, GPO item no.: 485.

A three-volume work on AIDS: assessing the problem; managing and financing the problem; and providing resource guidance for services.

Scitovsky, Anne A. *Estimating the Use and Costs of Medical, Social, and Support Services for Persons with AIDS and ARC*. Rockville, Md.: National Center for Health Services Research and Health Care Technology Assessment, 1989, GPO item no.: 491-B-13.

Estimate of use and cost of medical, social and support services for persons with AIDS.

Scott, James. *Communicable Diseases in the Schools*. Eugene, Oregon: ERIC Clearinghouse on Educational Management, 1986, GPO item no.: 466-A-3.

Pamphlet describes dangers of communicable diseases, such as AIDS, in primary schools.

Segal, Marian. *Defrauding the Desperate: Quackery and AIDS*. Rockville, Md.: Food and Drug Administration, 1988, GPO item no.: 475-H-1.

Covers the claims made by health professionals and others concerning various drugs and methods used to cure AIDS.

U.S. Bureau of Health Care Delivery and Assistance, Division of Maternal and Child Health, Children's Hospital of Philadelphia. *Report of the Surgeon General's Workshop on Children with HIV Infection and Their Families: AIDS*. Rockville, Md.: Public Health Service, 1987, GPO item no.: 532-E-10.

Conference paper presented (April 6–9, 1987) on problems faced by children with AIDS and their families.

U.S. Congress, House Committee on Armed Services, Military Personnel and Compensation Subcommittee. *DOD Policy on AIDS: Hearing before the Military Personnel and Compensation Subcommittee of the Committee on Armed Services*. House of Representatives, 100th Congress, 1st sess., September 16, 1987. Washington, D.C.: GPO, 1988, GPO item no.: 1012-A, 1012-B.

Report on the Department of Defense policy on AIDS in the military services.

U.S. Congress, House, Committee on the Budget, Ad Hoc Task Force on AIDS. *AIDS Crisis as Related to the Federal Budget: Hearing before the Ad Hoc Task Force on AIDS of the Committee on the Budget.* House of Representatives, 100th Congress, 1st sess., October 8, 1987. Washington, D.C.: GPO, 1987, GPO item no.: 1035-B-1.

Complete text of testimony on the impact the AIDS epidemic will have on the federal budget.

U.S. Congress, House, Committee on the Budget, Task Force on Human Resources. *Health Care Issues for Fiscal Year 1990: Hearing before the Task Force on Human Resources of the Committee on the Budget.* House of Representatives, 101st Congress, 1st sess., March 7, 1989. Washington, D.C.: GPO, 1989, GPO item no.: 1035-B-1.

Report on the cost of medical care and treatment of AIDS patients.

U.S. Congress, House, Committee on Education and Labor. *Oversight Hearing on Education on Acquired Immune Deficiency Syndrome (AIDS) in Elementary and Secondary Schools: Hearing before the Committee on Education and Labor.* House of Representatives, 100th Congress, 2nd sess., hearing held in Washington, D.C., February 3, 1988. Washington, D.C.: GPO, 1988, GPO item no.: 1015-A, 1015-B.

Congressional hearing on AIDS education in elementary and secondary schools.

U.S. Congress, House, Committee on Energy and Commerce. *Abandoned Infants Assistance Act of 1988.* Washington, D.C.: GPO, 1988, GPO item no.: 1008-C, 1008-D.

A report on how abandoned children with AIDS can benefit from the Abandoned Infants Assistance Act of 1988.

U.S. Congress, House, Committee on Energy and Commerce. *AIDS Counseling and Testing Act of 1988: Report Together with Additional Views.* Washington, D.C.: GPO, 1988, GPO item no.: 1008-C, 1008-D.

Report and discussion of the provisions of the AIDS Counseling and Testing Act of 1988.

U.S. Congress, House, Committee on Energy and Commerce. *AIDS Research Act of 1988: Report Together with Dissenting Views.* Washington, D.C.: GPO, 1988, GPO item no.: 1008-C, 1008-D.

Discussion on the various aspects of the AIDS Research Act of 1988.

U.S. Congress, House, Committee on Energy and Commerce. *AIDS Issues: Hearings before the Subcommittee on Health and the Environment.* Subcommittee on Health and the Environment. 101st Congress, 1st sess. Washington, D.C.: GPO, 1989, GPO item no.: 1019-A, 1019-B.

Hearings on the current status of federal research on AIDS; testimony on needle-exchange programs as a means of slowing the spread of AIDS.

U.S. Congress, House, Committee on Energy and Commerce. Subcommittee on Health and the Environment. *AIDS Issues: Hearings before a Subcommittee of the Committee on Energy and Commerce.* House of Representatives, 100th Congress, 1st sess. Washington, D.C.: GPO, 1988, GPO item on.: 1019-A, 1019-B.

Testimony covers AIDS-related issues of counseling, testing, confidentiality and discrimination.

U.S. Congress, House, Committee on Energy and Commerce, Subcommittee on Health and the Environment. *AIDS Issues: Hearings before the Subcommittee on Health and the Environment.* 99th Congress, 1st sess., on *Research and Treatment for Acquired Immune Deficiency Syndrome,* July 22, 1985; *Protection of Confidentiality of Records of Research Subjects and Blood Donors,* July 29, 1985; *Cost of AIDS Care and Who Is Going to Pay,* November 1, 1985. Washington, D.C.: GPO, 1986, GPO item no.: 1019-A, 1019-B.

Congressional hearings on AIDS research and treatment, shielding of confidential records of research subjects, and the cost and funding of AIDS care.

U.S. Congress, House, Committee on Energy and Commerce, Subcommittee on Health and the Environment. *Condom Advertising and AIDS; Hearing before a Subcommittee of the Committee on Energy and Commerce.* House of Representatives, 100th Congress, 1st sess., February 10, 1987. Washington, D.C.: GPO, 1987, GPO item no.: 1019-A, 1019-B.

Hearing on the program for condom advertising to control the spread of AIDS.

U.S. Congress, House, Committee on Energy and Commerce, Subcommittee on Health and the Environment. *Nonhospital Care for AIDS Victims: Hearing before a Subcommittee of the Committee on Energy and Commerce.* House of Representatives, 99th Congress, 2nd sess., March 5, 1986. Washington, D.C.: GPO, 1987, GPO item no.: 1019-A, 1019-B.

Hearing on alternative care for AIDS patients: the possibilities and costs.

U.S. Congress, House, Committee on Government Operations. *AIDS Drugs: Where Are They?* Washington, D.C.: GPO, 1988, GPO item no.: 1008-C, 1008-D.

Report on the drugs being developed for treatment and prevention of AIDS; reviews the role of the FDA in testing and approving drugs.

U.S. Congress, House, Committee on Government Operations. *Children and HIV Infection: Hearings before the Human Resources and Intergovernmental Relations Subcommittee.* 101st Congress, 1st sess., Washington, D.C.: GPO, 1989, GPO item no.: 1016-A, 1016-B.

Comprehensive report on children with AIDS: statistics, care and treatment, prevention, etc.

U.S. Congress, House, Committee on Government Operations, Human Resources and Intergovernmental Relations Subcommittee. *The Federal Response to the AIDS Epidemic: Information and Public Education: Hearing before a Subcommittee of the Committee on Government Operations.* House of Representatives, 100th Congress, 1st sess., March 16, 1987. Washington, D.C.: GPO, 1987, GPO item no.: 1016-A, 1016-B.

Congressional report on federally sponsored public education programs on AIDS.

U.S. Congress, House, Committee on Government Operations, Human Resources and Intergovernmental Relations Subcommittee. *Therapeutic Drugs for AIDS: Development, Testing, and Availability.* Washington, D.C.: GPO, 1989, GPO item no.: 1016-A, 1016-B.

Report on hearings conducted on research and availability of drugs to treat AIDS.

U.S. Congress, House, Committee on Government Operations, Intergovernmental Relations and Human Resources Subcommittee. *AIDS Drug Development: Hearing before a Subcommittee of the Committee on Government Operations.* 99th Congress, 2nd sess., July 1, 1986. Washington, D.C.: GPO, 1986, GPO item no.: 1016-A, 1016-B.

Hearing covers government policy on AIDS research and development of AIDS drugs.

U.S. Congress, House, Committee on Government Operations, Intergovernmental Relations and Human Resources Subcommittee. *Federal and Local Government's Response to the AIDS Epidemic: Hearings before a Subcommittee of the Committee on Government Operations.* 99th Congress, 1st session, July 3; September 13; and December 2, 1985. Washington, D.C.: GPO, 1986, GPO item no.: 1016-A, 1016-B.

Testimony on the pros and cons of federal and local government policies for dealing with AIDS.

U.S. Congress, House, Committee on the Judiciary. *AIDS and the Administration of Justice: Hearing before the Subcommittee on Courts, Civil Liberties, and the Administration of Justice.* 100th Congress, 1st sess., October 29, 1987. Washington, D.C.: GPO, 1987, GPO item no.: 1020-A, 1020-B.

An account of hearings on the control, treatment and prevention of AIDS in correctional facilities.

U.S. Congress, House, Committee on Science, Space, and Technology. Subcommittee on Natural Resources, Agriculture Research, and Environment. *Opportunities for International Scientific Cooperation to Control AIDS: Hearing before a Subcommittee of the Committee on Science, Space, and Technology.* 100th Congress, 1st sess., September 17, 1987. Washington, D.C.: GPO, 1988, GPO item no.: 1025-A-1.

Report and discussion on promoting international scientific cooperation to control AIDS.

U.S. Congress, House, Committee on Small Business. *Risks and Implications of AIDS-HIV Testing in Nontraditional Laboratories and in the Home: Hearing before the Subcommittee on Regulation, Business Opportunities, and Energy.* 101st Congress, 1st sess., March 23, 1989. Washington, D.C.: GPO, 1989.

Hearing covers the risk of diagnostic testing of AIDS virus in a nontraditional setting.

U.S. Congress, House, Committee on Small Business, Subcommittee on Regulation and Business Opportunities. *Quality AIDS Testing: Hearing before a Subcommittee of the Committee on Small Business.* 100th Congress, 1st sess., October 19, 1987. Washington, D.C.: GPO, 1988, GPO item no.: 1031-A, 1031-B.

Report to Congress on policy guidelines to ensure quality AIDS testing.

U.S. Congress, House, Committee on Veterans Affairs. *National Commission on Acquired Immune Deficiency Syndrome Act: Report Referred Jointly to the Committee on Energy and Commerce and the Committee on Veterans Affairs.* Washington, D.C.: GPO, 1987, GPO item no.: 1008-C, 1008-D.

A report on government AIDS policy including cost estimates for education, research and treatment.

Annotated Bibliography

U.S. Congress, House, Committee on Veterans Affairs, Subcommittee on Hospitals and Health Care. *Acquired Immune Deficiency Syndrome (AIDS) and the Veterans Administration: Hearing before a Subcommittee of the Committee on Veterans Affairs.* House of Representatives, 100th Congress, 1st sess., June 17, 1987. Washington, D.C.: GPO, 1987, GPO item no.: 1027-A, 1027-B.

Hearing on medical care of veterans with AIDS at the Veterans Administration hospitals.

U.S. Congress, House, Committee on Veterans Affairs, Subcommittee on Hospitals and Health Care. *Operational Aspects of AIDS Research and Medical Care within the Veterans Administration: Hearing before the Subcommittee on Hospitals and Health Care of the Committee on Veterans Affairs.* House of Representatives, 100th Congress, 1st sess., August 21, 1987. Washington, D.C.: GPO, 1987, GPO item no.: 1027-A, 1027-B.

Report on operation of AIDS research and medical care at the Veterans Administration hospitals.

U.S. Congress, House, Committee on Veterans Affairs, Subcommittee on Hospitals and Health Care. *Operational Aspects of AIDS Research and Medical Care within the Veterans Administration: Hearing before the Subcommittee on Hospitals and Health Care of the Committee on Veterans Affairs.* House of Representatives, 100th Congress, 1st sess., October 30, 1987. Washington, D.C.: GPO, 1988, GPO item no.: 1027-A, 1027-B.

Report on AIDS research and medical care of veterans with AIDS by the Veterans Administration.

U.S. Congress, House, Select Committee on Children, Youth and Families. *AIDS and Young Children: Emerging Issues; Hearing before the Select Committee on Children, Youth and Families.* House of Representatives, 100th Congress, 1st sess., hearing held in Berkeley, CA, February 21, 1987. Washington, D.C.: GPO, 1987, GPO item no.: 1009-B-10, 1009-C-10.

Hearing on issues concerning young children with AIDS.

U.S. Congress, House, Select Committee on Children, Youth and Families. *Continuing Jeopardy: Children and AIDS: A Staff Report of the Select Committee on Children, Youth and Families.* 100th Congress, 2nd sess., Washington, D.C.: GPO, 1988, GPO item no.: 1009-B-10, 1009-C-10.

A report on children and their exposure to AIDS.

U.S. Congress, House, Select Committee on Children, Youth and Families. *A Generation in Jeopardy: Children and AIDS: a Report of the Select Committee on Children, Youth and Families Together with Additional Views*

177

and Dissenting Minority Views. 100th Congress, 2nd sess., Washington, D.C.: GPO, 1988, GPO item no.: 1008-C, 1008-D.

Congressional hearing and discussion on the growing problem of AIDS and children.

U.S. Congress, House, Select Committee on Narcotics Abuse and Control. *Intravenous Drug Use and AIDS: The Impact on the Black Community: Hearing before the Select Committee on Narcotics Abuse and Control.* House of Representatives, 100th Congress, 1st sess., September 25, 1987. Washington, D.C.: GPO, 1988, GPO item no.: 1009-B-8, 1009-C-8.

Hearing before the House on the effect of drug abuse and AIDS on the black population.

U.S. Congress, House, Select Committee on Narcotics Abuse and Control. *Pediatric AIDS Hearing: Hearing before the Select Committee on Narcotics Abuse and Control.* House of Representatives, 100th Congress, 1st sess., July 27, 1987. Washington, D.C.: GPO, 1988, GPO item no.: 1009-B-8, 1009-C-8.

Another in a series of hearings on medical care and treatment of children with AIDS.

U.S. Congress, Office of Technology Assessment, Health Program. *How Effective Is AIDS Education?* Washington, D.C.: Health Program, Office of Technology Assessment, 1988, GPO item no.: 1070-M.

Report assesses the effectiveness of AIDS education programs in decreasing the spread of AIDS.

U.S. Congress, Office of Technology Assessment. *Medical Testing and Health Insurance: Summary.* Washington, D.C.: Office of Technology Assessment, 1988, GPO item no.: 1070-M.

Synopsis of the issues behind the health insurance industry's call for medical testing for the presence of the AIDS virus in applicants.

U.S. Congress, Senate, Committee on Appropriations, Subcommittee on Defense. *Acquired Immune Deficiency Syndrome (AIDS): Hearing before a Subcommittee of the Committee on Appropriations.* 99th Congress, 2nd sess., Washington, D.C.: GPO, 1986, GPO item no.: 1033, 1033-A.

Hearings on prevention programs and funding for AIDS education in the military.

U.S. Congress, Senate, Committee on Finance, Subcommittee on Social Security and Family Policy. *Social Security Benefits for AIDS Victims: Hearing before a Subcommittee of the Committee on Finance.* U.S. Senate,

100th Congress, 1st sess., September 10, 1987. Washington, D.C.: GPO, 1988, GPO item no.: 1038-A, 1038-B.

Hearing explores benefits for which AIDS patients and their surviving dependents are eligible.

U.S. Congress, Senate, Committee on Foreign Relations. *U.S. Role in International Efforts to Control and Prevent the Global Spread of the AIDS Epidemic.* Washington, D.C.: GPO, 1989, GPO item no.: 1039-A, 1039-B.

Account of hearings on U.S. cooperation in the global struggle against AIDS. Discussion of the impact of U.S. involvement on its foreign policy.

U.S. Congress, Senate, Committee on Governmental Affairs. *Federal Advisory Committee Act and the President's AIDS Commission: Hearing before the Committee on Governmental Affairs.* U.S. Senate, 100th Congress, 1st sess., December 3, 1987. Washington, D.C.: GPO, 1988, GPO item no.: 1037-B, 1037-C.

Comprehensive report by the president's AIDS commission on government policies relating to AIDS.

U.S. Congress, Senate, Committee on Labor and Human Resources. *Acquired Immunodeficiency Syndrome Research and Information Act of 1987: Report (to accompany S. 1220).* Washington, D.C.: GPO, 1987, GPO item no.: 1008-C, 1008-D.

Report and discussion of the AIDS Research and Information Act of 1987.

U.S. Congress, Senate, Committee on Labor and Human Resources. *AIDS Education, Care and Drug Development: Hearing before the Committee on Labor and Human Resources.* U.S. Senate, 101th Congress, 1st sess., on examining the adequacy of the federal government efforts to combat AIDS, with regard to education, care, and drug development. February 7, 1989. Washington, D.C.: GPO, 1989, GPO item no.: 1043-A, 1043-B.

Congressional hearing on government policy on AIDS education, care of people with AIDS, and development of AIDS drug therapies.

U.S. Congress, Senate, Committee on Labor and Human Resources. *AIDS Epidemic: Hearing before the Committee on Labor and Human Resources.* U.S. Senate, 100th Congress, 1st sess., January 16, 1987. Washington, D.C.: GPO, 1987, GPO item no.: 1043-A, 1043-B.

Hearing on the funding of AIDS research and prevention.

U.S. Congress, Senate, Committee on Labor and Human Resources. *AIDS Federal Policy Act of 1987: Hearings before the Committee on Labor and Human Resources.* U.S. Senate, 100th Congress, 1st sess., on S. 1575, September 11 and November 18, 1987. Washington, D.C.: GPO, 1988, GPO item no.: 1043-A, 1043-B.

Congressional hearings on AIDS Federal Policy Act of 1987.

U.S. Congress, Senate, Committee on Labor and Human Resources. *AIDS: Hearing before the Committee on Labor and Human Resources.* 99th Congress, 2nd sess., April 16, 1986. Washington, D.C.: GPO, 1986, GPO item no.: 1043-A, 1043-B.

Hearing explores what can or should be done to prevent the spread of AIDS.

U.S. Congress, Senate, Committee on Labor and Human Resources. *AIDS Research: Hearing before the Committee on Labor and Human Resources.* U.S. Senate, 100th Congress, 1st sess., May 15, 1987. Washington, D.C.: GPO, 1987, GPO item no.: 1043-A, 1043-B.

Hearing on progress, developments and problems in AIDS research.

U.S. Congress, Senate, Committee on Labor and Human Resources. *AIDS Treatment Research and Approval: Hearing before the Committee on Labor and Human Resources.* 100th Congress, 2nd sess., July 13, 1988. Washington, D.C.: GPO, 1988, GPO item no.: 1043-A, 1043-B.

Report presents recent findings in AIDS-treatment research.

U.S. Congress, Senate, Committee on Labor and Human Resources. *National Commission on Acquired Immune Deficiency Syndrome Act: Report Together with Additional Views.* Washington, D.C.: GPO, 1988, GPO item no.: 1008-C, 1008-D.

Report and discussion on proposed Acquired Immune Deficiency Syndrome Act.

U.S. Congress, Senate, Committee on Veterans Affairs. *AIDS and the Veterans Administration: Hearing before the Committee on Veterans Affairs.* U.S. Senate, 100th Congress, 1st sess., June 24, 1987. Washington, D.C.: GPO, 1988, GPO item no.: 1046-A-1.

Hearing on the Veterans Administration's work with veterans and AIDS.

U.S. Department of the Army. *AIDS Is a Woman's Health Issue.* Washington, D.C.: 1989, GPO item no.: 325.

Pamphlet for women on how to prevent contracting or spreading the disease.

U.S. Department of Education. *AIDS and the Education of Our Children: A Guide for Parents and Teachers*. Washington, D.C.: Department of Education, 1988, GPO item no.: 461-B-1.

A guide for parents and teachers for educating children about AIDS.

U.S. Department of Health and Human Services. *Final Report: Secretary's Work Group on Pediatric HIV Infection and Disease*. Washington, D.C.: GPO, 1988, GPO item no.: 445.

Report on HIV infection in children.

U.S. Department of Health and Human Services, World Health Organization. *3rd International Conference on AIDS*. Washington, D.C.: GPO, 1987, GPO item no.: 445.

Summary of the activities of the Third International Conference on AIDS.

U.S. Department of Labor. *Job Corps, AIDS, and Mental Health Counseling Guide*. Washington, D.C.: Department of Labor, 1988, GPO item no.: 745-A.

An employee counseling guide on AIDS and mental health.

U.S. Department of Labor. *Job Corps, AIDS and the Workplace: Employee's Guide*. Washington, D.C.: Department of Labor, 1988, GPO item no.: 745-A.

Employee's guide to AIDS prevention in the workplace.

U.S. Department of State. *Foreign Policy Implications of AIDS*. Washington, D.C.: Department of State, Bureau of Public Affairs, 1988, GPO item no.: 877-C.

Analysis of the effect the AIDS crisis has on the U.S. relationship with foreign countries, especially in regard to travel restrictions.

U.S. Department of State. *The U.S.S.R.'s AIDS Disinformation Campaign*. Washington, D.C.: Department of State, 1987, GPO item no.: 869-B-1.

A Foreign Affairs note outlining the Soviet Union's efforts to suppress information on the incidence of AIDS in the USSR.

U.S. Food and Drug Administration, Office of Public Affairs. *Tips on Preventing AIDS*. Rockville, Md.: Public Health Service, 1988, GPO item no.: 475-H-1.

Pamphlet outlining steps the public can take to prevent contracting AIDS.

U.S. Health Resources and Services Administration, Bureau of Health Professions. *HIV/AIDS Activities*. Rockville, Md.: Bureau of Health Professions, 1989, GPO item no.: 507-J-1.

Pamphlet providing general information on AIDS.

U.S. Marine Corps. *What You Should Know about HTLV-III and AIDS*. Washington, D.C.: GPO, 1986, GPO item no.: 383.

Informational booklet on the AIDS virus.

U.S. National Institute of Justice. *NIJ AIDS Clearinghouse Helps You Respond to the AIDS Challenge*. Washington, D.C.: National Institute of Justice, 1988, GPO item no.: 717-J-1.

Pamphlet issued by the National Institute of Justice on its AIDS information and resources programs.

U.S. President Ronald Reagan. *AIDS Initiatives: Message from the President of the United States Transmitting a 10-Point Action Plan to Respond to the Public Health Threat Posed by the Human Immunodeficiency Virus*. Washington, D.C.: GPO, 1988, GPO item no.: 996-A, 996-B.

A message from President Ronald Reagan outlining the action plan to be initiated by the government against the AIDS epidemic.

U.S. Presidential Commission on the Human Immunodeficiency Virus Epidemic. *Report of the Presidential Commission on the Human Immunodeficiency Virus Epidemic: Submitted to the President of the United States*. Washington, D.C.: The Commission, 1988, GPO item no.: 851-J-4.

An extensive report by the presidential committee on AIDS on formulation of government policy on preventing the spread of the disease.

U.S. President's Committee on Employment of the Handicapped, Medical Advisory Committee. *The Medical Advisory Committee of the President's Committee on Employment of the Handicapped Presents AIDS and Employment: Facts and Myths: A Special Report of the Proceedings of a Seminar Held at the Annual Meeting of the President's Committee on Employment of the Handicapped, April 30, 1986, Washington, D.C.* Washington, D.C.: President's Committee on Employment of the Handicapped, 1986, GPO item no.: 766-C-11.

Special report on the treatment of AIDS patients in the workplace and how government policies can protect them from discrimination.

U.S. Public Health Service. *AIDS among Blacks and Hispanics in the United States*. Bethesda, Md.: Public Health Service, 1986, GPO item no.: 508-A.

Statistics and analysis of the incidence of AIDS among blacks and Hispanics.

U.S. Public Health Service. *AIDS Information/Education Plan to Prevent and Control AIDS in the United States*. Rockville, Md.: Public Health Service, 1987, GPO item no.: 485.

Includes government policy and plans for AIDS-information campaign to prevent and control AIDS.

U.S. Public Health Service. *Facts about AIDS*. Rockville, Md.: Public Health Service, 1987, GPO item no.: 485.

General informational booklet on AIDS.

U.S. Public Health Service, Office of the Surgeon General. *Surgeon General's Report on Acquired Immune Deficiency Syndrome*. Washington, D.C.: Public Health Service, 1986, GPO item no.: 485.

Surgeon General's report on AIDS, issued by C. Everett Koop.

U.S. Veterans Administration, Building Management Service. *Technical Advisory: AIDS*. Washington, D.C.: Veterans Administration, 1986, GPO item no.: 986-A.

Informational bulletin on safety measures for nurses and other hospital personnel.

Westler, Jean A. *Drugs and AIDS: Getting the Message Out: A Program Guide*. Rockville, Md.: National Institute on Drug Abuse, 1988, GPO item no.: 467-A-2.

Addresses AIDS transmission through intravenous drug abuse. Designed to accompany videotape of the same name.

Zimmerman, Michael. *Issues Concerning CDC's AIDS Education Programs: Statement of Michael Zimmerman, Senior Associate Director, Human Resources Division, before the Committee on Governmental Affairs, United States Senate*. Washington, D.C.: GPO, 1988, GPO item no.: 546-D-1.

Statement from the CDC concerning its AIDS-education program.

AUDIOVISUAL MATERIALS

About A.I.D.S. Rosenthal, Ralph, and Russell Kightley. Santa Monica: Pyramid Film and Video, 1986, 18 min, video or 16-mm.

Provides general information about AIDS: the virus, symptoms, transmission, care and prevention.

Acquired Immune Deficiency Syndrome. Department of Pediatrics, Emory University School of Medicine. Atlanta: A. W. Calhoun Medical Library, 1983, 48 min, video.

Presentation on AIDS in general and AIDS in children in particular.

Acquired Immune Deficiency Syndrome. Klein, Robert S. New York: Network for Continuing Medical Education, 1985, 47 min, video with booklet.

Course on medical information and care of AIDS patients.

Acquired Immune Deficiency Syndrome. Taff, Mark L., and Frederick P. Siegal. Garden Grove, Calif.: Medcom Inc., 1983, 60 min, 54 slides with 2 audio-cassettes.

A teaching module on AIDS for health care workers.

Acquired Immune Deficiency Syndrome: A New, Mysterious, and Fatal Disorder. Hill, Harry R. Salt Lake City: University of Utah, School of Medicine, Continuing Medical Education, 1983, 45 min, video.

Medical information on AIDS—how the virus works in destroying the immune system, leading to other disorders.

Acquired Immune Deficiency Syndrome: Current Status and Concerns. Thorup, Oscar A. Charlottesville: University of Virginia Medical Center, 1983, 60 min, video.

General overview on AIDS: history, epidemiology, research, medical and social issues.

Acquired Immune Deficiency Syndrome (AIDS): Information and Precautions for Laboratory Personnel. Lipscomb, Helen L. Omaha: University of Nebraska Medical Center, 1984, 35 min, audio cassette.

Information for laboratory personnel on guidelines for avoiding infection by the AIDS virus.

AIDS. Armstrong, Donald, and J.J. Head. Burlington, N.C.: Carolina Biological Supply Co., 1986, 17min, 53 frame filmstrip and audiocassette.

Written for the general audience, the filmstrip explains the medical and biological theory needed to understand AIDS.

AIDS. Greenwood, J. R. Garden Grove, Calif.: Medcom Inc., 1986, slides with audiotape.

A two-part teaching program on AIDS.

Annotated Bibliography

AIDS. Hicks, Mary Jane, et al. Tucson: University of Arizona Biomedical Communications, 1984, 180 min, video.

Provides general information on AIDS with special focus on epidemiological and clinical aspects of the disease.

AIDS: A Model for Care. Contra Costa County Hospice. Martinez, Calif.: Contra Costa County Hospice, 1984, 60 min, video.

Designed to teach understanding and sensitivity in caring for people with AIDS.

AIDS: A Practical Approach to Prevention. IBT Video. 1988, 20 min, video.

Mainly on prevention, it also gives information about the disease, its history, evolution and method of attack.

AIDS: A Story. Mierendorf, Michael. Minneapolis: WCOO Television, 1986, 60 min, video.

Discussion of AIDS based on the life of Fabian Calvin Bridges.

AIDS—After the Fear. Ontario Ministry of Health. Toronto: Instructional Media Services, 1984, 20 min, video.

Doctors discuss the nature of AIDS and offer ways to lessen the risk of transmission. They also address blood donations and risks to hemophiliacs.

AIDS Alert. Creative Media Group, Charlottesville, Va.: Medical Electronic Educational Services, 1986, 23 min, video.

Educational film on AIDS and how to guard against contracting or spreading the virus.

AIDS Alert. Thompson, Chic. San Francisco: MultiFocus, 1986, 23 min, video.

Factual discussion of the AIDS epidemic for young people, using cartoons to illustrate such information as the cause of AIDS and how to avoid getting the disease.

AIDS: An ABC News Special Assignment. New York: ABC Video Enterprises, 1986, 12 min, video.

ABC award-winning documentary features discussion on AIDS with medical experts and people with AIDS.

AIDS: An Old or New Acquaintance? Emory Medical Television Network. Atlanta: Emory University School of Medicine, A. W. Calhoun Medical Library, 1985, 42 min, video.

Discussion of AIDS in an historical setting, comparing the epidemic with other previous ones.

AIDS and Ethics. Burck, Russell. Chicago: Rush Presbyterian St. Luke's Medical Center, Biomedical Communications, 1984, 216 min, video.

Program presents all aspects of AIDS: medical, social, legal and economic from an ethical point of view.

AIDS and Hepatitis-B Precautions. Criss, Elizabeth A. Tucson: MedFilms, Inc., 1986, 8 min, video.

Discussion of AIDS and hepatitis-B and the relationship between the two.

AIDS and the Arts. Princeton, N.J.: Films for the Humanities and Sciences, Inc., 1987, 20 min, video.

Documentary film on the impact of AIDS on the arts in America, featuring Elizabeth Taylor and Harvey Fierstein.

AIDS and the Health Care Provider. Advanced Imaging, Inc. Westlake, Ohio: Carevideo Productions, 1986, 22 min, video.

Presentation on how health care providers, whether family, friend or professional, are affected physically, mentally and emotionally by AIDS patients.

AIDS and the Health Care Worker. Deerfield, Illinois: Coronet/MTI Film and Video, 1985, 27 min, video.

The film addresses the physical risks and emotional trauma of dealing with AIDS victims with the hope of allaying the fears of case workers.

AIDS and the Immune System. Los Angeles: Churchill Films, 1986, 12 min, video.

Animated film for children describing how the AIDS virus weakens the immune system.

AIDS and the Law. University of Pennsylvania Law School. Philadelphia: American Law Institute, American Bar Association Committee on Continuing Professional Education, 1986, 2 videos.

Presents an update of the legal issues pertaining to AIDS.

Annotated Bibliography

AIDS and Your Job: What Everyone Should Know about AIDS. Centers for Disease Control. Capitol Heights, Md.: National Audiovisual Center, 1984, 20 min, video.

Describes work procedures designed to reduce the risk of exposure to AIDS.

AIDS: Answers for Everyone. American Medical Video. 1988, 55 min, video.

A comprehensive overview of information and issues surrounding AIDS and its impact on its victims and society. Includes statistics, symptoms, prevention and current research.

AIDS Anxiety. Truax, A. Brad. Chicago: Abbot Laboratories, 1985, 45 min, video.

Program covers psychological and social issues, especially the anxiety surrounding AIDS.

AIDS: Care beyond the Hospital. Schietinger, Helen, and Bobby Reynolds. San Francisco: San Francisco AIDS Foundation, 1984, 42 min, video.

The program details techniques for the home care of AIDS patients.

AIDS: Chapter One. New York: Ambrose Video, 1985, 57 min, video.

Describes the origins and effects of AIDS. Scientists' efforts to understand and cure the syndrome are reviewed.

AIDS Epidemic and the HTLV-III Antibody Test. Polk, B. Frank. Baltimore: John Hopkins University School of Medicine, 1986, 184 min, 4 audiocassettes.

Covers the diagnosis, prevention and control of AIDS, in particular the human T-cell leukemia virus and C-type virus as they relate to HTLV-III antibody test.

AIDS: Face to Face. Donahue, Phil. Princeton, N.J.: Films for the Humanities and Sciences, 1987, 30 min, video.

The message of AIDS being everyone's problem is presented through Phil Donahue's conversations with AIDS patients at St. Clare's Hospital in New York.

AIDS: Facts over Fears. Walters, Barbara. New York: ABC Video Enterprises, 1985, 10 min, 16-mm or video.

Barbara Walters and a physician discuss AIDS and how it is transmitted. New symptoms and ongoing research are described.

AIDS: Fears and Facts. Public Health Service. Capitol Heights, Md.: National Audiovisual Center, 1986, video.

Provides information about AIDS: what causes it, how it is transmitted, risk reduction and finding a cure.

AIDS: In Search of a Miracle. Columbia University Seminars on Media and Society. New York: Columbia University School of Journalism 1986, 60 min, video.

Debate by a panel of observers on controversial medical, legal and social AIDS-related issues.

AIDS in the Pediatric Age Group. Oleske, James M. Atlanta, Ga.: Emory University School of Medicine Production Co. 1986, 44 min, video.

Program covers AIDS in children.

AIDS in the Workplace. San Francisco: San Francisco AIDS Foundation, 1986, 180 min, video.

Reviews questions about the presence of AIDS in the workplace, workers' fears about the disease and how these concerns can be alleviated.

AIDS in Your School. Palo Alto, Calif.: Peregrine Productions, 1987, 23 min, video.

Program features teen hosts interviewing AIDS patients and health care experts about the facts of the disease.

AIDS: Issues for Health Care Workers. Clover, Thomas. Los Angeles: Churchill Films, 1988, 20 min, video.

Provides information for health care workers on AIDS and how to guard against being infected on the job.

AIDS: Medical Education for the Community. Palance, Jack. Tucson: Medical Electronic Educational Services, 1986, 30 min, video.

A documentary on AIDS providing medical information for the general public and health care professionals.

AIDS Movie. Durrin, Ginny. Wayne, N.J.: New Day Films, 1986, 26 min, video.

Provides information on AIDS for high school students. Case histories of AIDS patients illustrate the facts.

AIDS: Our Worst Fears. Princeton, N.J.: Films for the Humanities and Sciences, 1987, 60 min, video.

Documentary film on information about AIDS: who is most susceptible and most at risk, and what preventive actions and precautions can be taken.

Annotated Bibliography

AIDS Overview/Infection Control. Fairview General AV. Cleveland: Fairview General Hospital, 1985, 14 min, video.

Precautions for health workers treating AIDS patients are outlined in this program.

AIDS: Profile of an Epidemic. WNET New York. Bloomington: Indiana University AV Center, 1986, 58 min, video.

Patients who contracted AIDS in a variety of ways are profiled here to illustrate the high-risk behaviors linked to the spread of the disease.

AIDS: Profile of an Epidemic Update. WNET New York. Bloomington: Indiana University AV Center, 1986, 60 min, video.

Host Ed Asner recounts recent information and discoveries about AIDS: its causes, spread, treatment and effects. Earlier fears, rumors and misinformation are discussed.

AIDS: Public Health and Public Policy. Finberg, Robert, et al. Cambridge, Mass.: John F. Kennedy School of Government, Harvard University 1984, 120 min, 2 videos.

A discussion of public health and policy as it relates to AIDS. Program is intended for public health administrators and workers.

The AIDS Show: Artists Involved with Death and Survival. Los Angeles, Direct Cinema, 1986, 58 min, video.

Excerpts from a theatrical production highlighting the emotional experiences of people with AIDS, their friends, family and lovers.

AIDS: Social Response to a Medical Crisis. Bayer, Ronald. Syracuse: State University of New York, Upstate Medical Center, 1984, 48 min, video.

Program deals with many of the social problems associated with AIDS.

AIDS: The Classroom Conflict. Princeton, N.J.: Films for the Humanities and Sciences, 1987, 28 min, video.

AIDS-education program covering such conflicts as why, when and how children should be taught about AIDS.

AIDS: The Disease and What We Know. Sunburst. 1986, 13 min, video.

Presents information on AIDS and how it is transmitted. The program is designed to reduce anxiety about the disease.

AIDS: Tracking the Mystery. Public Health Service. Capitol Heights, Md.: National Audiovisual Center, 1984, 20 min, video.

Describes efforts to find the cause of AIDS. Also addresses public fear of the disease.

AIDS Update. Bartlett, John G. Baltimore: Johns Hopkins University School of Medicine, Office of Continuing Education, 1985, 136 min, 4 audiocassettes.

Presentation on the progress of AIDS research.

AIDS Ward. Princeton, N.J.: Films for the Humanities and Sciences, 1988, 56 min, video.

AIDS patients, medical personnel and other experts talk about the grim realities of caring for AIDS patients.

AIDS: What Are the Risks? Burlington, N.C.: Carolina Biological Supply, 1986, 2 filmstrips with audiocassettes and teacher's guide.

A two-part program providing a step-by-step explanation of AIDS and the methods of transmission, intended for people with AIDS and family and friends.

AIDS: What Every Kid Should Know. Irwindale, Calif.: Barr Films, 1987, 15 min, video or 16-mm.

For young adults. Presents general information on AIDS and ways to avoid the disease including safe sexual practices. The messages are presented in segments so that different portions can be skipped depending on community values.

AIDS: What Everyone Needs to Know. Renan, Sheldon. Los Angeles: Churchill Films, 1986, 18 min, 16-mm or video.

Discusses the nature and transmission of AIDS. Covers high-risk groups, effects of the disease on its victims and the outlook for treatment.

AIDS: What Is it? Southfield, Mich.: Health and Life, 1985, video.

General discussion on AIDS.

AIDS: What Is Practical to Rule Out. Weiss, Geoffrey R. San Antonio: University of Texas Health Science Center, 1986, 60 min, audiocassette.

Provides information on transmission of AIDS especially emphasizing the methods by which the disease cannot be spread.

Ally and AIDS. Sheedy, Ally. Burbank, Calif.: Walt Disney Educational Media, 1986, 18 min, video or 16-mm.

Program for teenagers explaining how AIDS is and is not transmitted and precautions to prevent spreading the disease.

Babies with AIDS. Princeton, N.J.: Films for the Humanities and Sciences, 1987, 28 min, video.

In a special adaptation of a Phil Donahue show medical specialists and care providers offer information and counseling about babies with AIDS.

Battle Against AIDS: Testing for HTLV-III. Considine, Bob and Howard Gingold. New York: Lifetime Medical Television, 1985, 120 min, 2 videos.

Describes the human T-cell leukemia virus and the testing program.

Beyond Fear. St. Petersburg, Florida: Modern Talking Picture Service, 1986, 60 min, video.

Provides background information on AIDS in three parts: the virus, the individual and the community.

Black People Get AIDS, Too. Pounds, Cedrick. San Francisco: Multicultural Prevention Resource Center, 1987, 22 min, video.

Presentation and discussion of the impact of AIDS on the black community. Includes information on high-risk behavior, AIDS testing and preventive methods.

The Burks Have AIDS. New York: Phoenix/BFA Films and Video, 1985, 17 min, video.

The story of the first mainstream American family reported to have AIDS.

Can AIDS Be Stopped? Dugan, David, and Max Whitby. Deerfield, Illinois: Coronet Film and Video, 1986, 58 min, video.

A PBS "Nova" documentary on AIDS. Uses personal experiences, scientific observation and research to provide factual information on AIDS.

Condom Education in Grade School. Princeton, N.J.: Films for the Humanities and Sciences, 1987, 28 min, video.

Special adaptation of Phil Donahue's show examines both sides of the issue of teaching fourth graders about the use of condoms to prevent AIDS.

Donor Notification. Tomasulo, Peter. Chicago: Abbot Laboratories, 1985, 60 min, video.

Program addressing AIDS and blood donors.

Doors Opening: A Positive Approach to AIDS. Santa Monica: Hay House, 1985, 55 min, video.

In this program Louise L. Hay demonstrates her alternative healing program of meditation, nutrition and exercise.

Drugs and AIDS: Getting the Message Out. National Institute on Drug Abuse. Rockville, Md.: Public Health Service, 1988, video and program guide, GPO item no.: 467-A-2.

Videotape on the transmission of AIDS through intravenous drug abuse.

An Early Frost. Cowen, Ronald, et al. New York: NBC Productions, 1985, 120 min, video.

TV docudrama portraying the emotional effects of AIDS on a person with AIDS, his lover and family.

Facts about AIDS. Public Health Service. Rockville, Md.: Public Health Service, 1986, GPO item no.: 569-C-3, 3 videos.

Videotapes providing general information on AIDS.

Fear of Caring. Chicago: American Hospital Association, 1986, 20 min, video.

In-service training video for hospital employees covering care of AIDS patients in hospitals, handling blood and equipment, and reporting incidents.

For Our Lives. Gay/Lesbian Community Services Center; Modern Media Firm. New York: MultiFocus, 1984, 25 min, video.

Program provides general information on AIDS with a focus on the social aspects, especially for gay and lesbian people.

The Frontiers of AIDS Treatment. Princeton, N.J.: Films for the Humanities and Sciences, 1989, 26 min, video.

Program explores the latest progress in AIDS research and treatment. Examines the slow process for the development and approval of drugs and how the urgency of AIDS is affecting this process.

General Series on AIDS. Centers for Disease Control. Atlanta: Centers for Disease Control, 1983, 23 slides.

Slide presentation designed for classroom use gives general information on AIDS.

International Impact of AIDS. Quinn, Thomas C. Baltimore: Johns Hopkins University School of Medicine, 1986, 132 min, 4 audiocasettes.

Audiotapes cover the worldwide impact of AIDS: reporting on occurrence, etiology, prevention, control and transmission of the disease.

The Intimate Epidemic. Princeton, N.J.: Films for the Humanities and Social Sciences, 1985, 24 min, video.

Reports on recent developments in detecting, treating and preventing further spread of AIDS.

Kids with AIDS. Princeton, N.J.: Films for the Humanities and Sciences, 1988, 28 min, video.

By 1991, it is estimated that 31,000 youngsters will have AIDS and another 20,000 will be infected by the virus. Program shows families taking care of AIDS-infected children.

Killer in the Village. BBC TV. Chicago: Films Inc., 1983, 56 min, video.

Traces the AIDS disease from its first diagnosis to the present.

Life of an AIDS Patient. Princeton, N.J.: Films for the Humanities and Sciences, 1987, 19 min, video.

This program, which profiles Don Miller, examines how AIDS is transmitted and how it breaks down the immune system, paving the way for opportunistic infection.

Life, Death, AIDS. Farinet, Gene, and Tom Brokaw; NBC Films. New York: NBC Films, 1986, 52 min, video.

TV documentary on living and dying with AIDS.

Men, Women, Sex and AIDS. Brokaw, Tom, et al. Chicago: Films Inc., 1987, 60 min, video.

TV documentary on AIDS spotlights four areas of concern: changing sexual habits, education, cures and cost.

Nature and Transmission of AIDS. Princeton, N.J.: Films for the Humanities and Sciences, 1987, 20 min, video.

An explanation of how AIDS is transmitted and the activities that spread infection. Addresses how the AIDS virus weakens the immune system, giving way to opportunistic infections.

Not Ready to Die of AIDS. Princeton, N.J.: Films for the Humanities and Sciences, 1987, 52 min, video.

The personal story of a man diagnosed as dying of AIDS and how he copes with the disease.

Oprah Winfrey Show. Winfrey, Oprah, and Debra DiMaio; ABC TV. New York: American Broadcasting Co., 1987, 47 min, video.

AIDS

Oprah Winfrey Show aired Feb 18, 1987 discussing AIDS and the present and future impact of the disease.

Our Worst Fears: The AIDS Epidemic. Saslow, Nancy, and Robert Hartnett. Los Angeles: Group W Broadcasting, 1985, video.

Documentary on the AIDS epidemic and the anxiety associated with it.

Psychosocial Interventions in AIDS. Tross, Susan; Carle Foundation; Norman Baxley and Associates. Urbana, Illinois: Carle Medical Communications, 1987, 22 min, video.

Explains the medical, psychological and social complexities that challenge and contribute to the emotional distress of people with AIDS.

Remember My Name. Princeton, N.J.: Films for the Humanities and Sciences, 1989, 52 min, video.

The story of the AIDS quilt, and the epidemic itself, is told through 11 individual chronicles reflecting how the disease has affected children and society.

Safe Sex. Princeton, N.J.: Films for the Humanities and Sciences, 1987, 28 min, video.

In this specially adapted "Phil Donahue Show," panelists, ranging from an educator to a brothel owner, discuss safe sex.

Safer Sex. Princeton, N.J.: Films for the Humanities and Sciences, 1988, 19 min, video.

This program examines the prevention of AIDS and investigates a dating club that offers its members an HIV test for screening prospective sexual partners.

Sexual Roulette: AIDS and the Heterosexual. Princeton, N.J.: Films for the Humanities and Sciences, 1988, 26 min, video.

Explains the risk factors affecting the heterosexual spread of AIDS: factors include geographic areas, types of sexual behavior and drug abuse.

Sexually-Transmitted Diseases. Princeton, N.J.: Films for the Humanities and Sciences, 1987, 19 min, video.

An examination of AIDS with emphasis on prevention and early detection through new diagnostic tests.

Teaching Sex Ed in High School. Princeton, N.J.: Films for the Humanities and Sciences, 1988, 14 min, video.

Newsman Ed Bradley introduces a sex education teacher who addresses the issue of instructing a class on sexual abstinence and the consequences of sexual activity.

Teens, Sex and AIDS. Princeton, N.J.: Films for the Humanities and Sciences, 1988, 28 min, video.

Teen group discussion on AIDS with dramatization of teens dealing with decisions about sex.

Telling Teens about AIDS. Princeton, N.J.: Films for the Humanities and Sciences, 1987, 52 min, video.

Program explains the AIDS virus and how it develops in an effort to tell teenagers of the importance of personal responsibility and choice.

Treating and Preventing AIDS. Princeton, N.J.: Films for the Humanities and Sciences, 1987, 20 min, video.

A heterosexual drug user describes what it is like living with AIDS. He and other victims make recommendations on how to avoid contracting AIDS.

Treating the Gay Patient. Audio Video Digest Foundation. Glendale, Calif.: Audio Video Digest Foundation, 1983, 57 min, video.

Videotape for primary care physicians outlining the special needs of gay patients.

Truth about AIDS. Educational Dimensions Group. Stamford, Conn.: Educational Dimensions Group, 1985, 2 filmstrips, 2 audiotapes and a teacher's guide.

Educational kit on AIDS.

Understanding AIDS. Cygnus Corp. Edina, Minn.: Cygnus Corp, 1985, 25 min, video.

Video providing general information on AIDS.

Update on Acquired Immune Deficiency Syndrome, Moral Problems Surrounding AIDS: The Patient, the Health Professional, and the Public Good. Purtilo, Ruth Bryant; Creighton University Biomedical Communications. Omaha: Creighton University Biomedical Communications, 1986, 35 min, video.

Program on AIDS and the moral problems surrounding patient care. For health professionals.

AIDS

What If the Patient Has AIDS: What Everyone Should Know about AIDS.
Public Health Service. Capital Heights, Md.: National Audiovisual
Center, 1984, 20 min, video.

General information on AIDS.

When Facts Are Not Enough: Managing AIDS in the Workplace. Chicago:
American Hospital Association, 1986, 24 min, video.

Videotape teaches hospital managers and supervisors how to educate
workers about AIDS; helps them develop policies; and reviews labor
laws that support the policies.

Women with AIDS. Princeton, N.J.: Films for the Humanities and Sciences, 1987, 28 min, video.

Video is adapted from Phil Donahue program and focuses on women
at risk of getting AIDS.

CHAPTER 7

███

ORGANIZATIONS AND ASSOCIATIONS

There are several thousand national, state and local organizations now involved in various ways with the AIDS epidemic. Their activities range from research and the development of drug therapies to prevention, education, counseling and outreach services. This chapter is a listing of organizations that are a source of educational materials and information on AIDS. They include government agencies, professional associations, foundations, and community facilities and groups. National organizations are accompanied by a brief synopsis of their involvement in AIDS issues and the types of information they make available. Similar abstracts are not provided at the state and local level because the services and activities of these organizations change frequently.

ORGANIZATIONS

NATIONAL

AIDS Clinical Trials Unit
2300 Eye Street, Suite 202
Washington, DC 20037
(202) 994-2417
Maintains current information on developments in medical research that may delay or halt the progression of AIDS.

American Foundation for AIDS Research (AmFAR)
9601 Wilshire Boulevard
Beverly Hills, CA 90210-5294
(213) 273-5547
Raises funds to support biomedical research about the causes of AIDS and its early diagnosis and treatment. Promotes AIDS education and understanding of the history and nature of the disease.

American Hospital Association
840 North Lake Shore Drive
Chicago, IL 60611
(312) 280-6000
Involved in research, educational programs, and administrative and legislative matters pertaining to AIDS and hospitalization.

American Medical Association
535 N. Dearborn
Chicago, IL 60610
(312) 645-5000
Major national professional medical association. Provides a range of AIDS educational programs and informational materials for the public.

American Red Cross, AIDS Education Program
1730 E. Street N.W.
Washington, DC 20006
(202) 639-3223
Conducts an extensive AIDS public awareness and education campaign. Source of wide range of information and materials on AIDS.

Centers for Disease Control
1600 Clifton Avenue
Atlanta, GA 30333
(800) 342-AIDS
(404) 330-3020 (statistics)
Provides a broad range of information on the epidemiology of AIDS. Maintains current statistics on the disease in the United States.

Gay Men's Health Crisis
132 W. 24th Street
New York, NY 10011
(212) 807-6655
Founded in 1982 as an AIDS education and support agency for the gay community. Source of numerous publications and materials on AIDS.

Lambda Legal Defense and Education Fund
666 Broadway
New York, NY 10012
(212) 995-8585
Provides legal services to protect the rights of gay persons in such areas as housing, employment and education. Prepares informational materials on the full range of AIDS legal issues.

The Names Project
2362 Market Street
San Francisco, CA 94114
(415) 863-1966
(800) USA-NAME
Sponsors and provides information on the AIDS Memorial Quilt.

National AIDS Information Clearinghouse
P.O. Box 6003
Rockville, MD 20850
(800) 458-5231
A service of the Centers for Disease Control, the NAIC is a centralized source of information about AIDS services and resources. Reference specialists are available to answer telephone inquiries. The service operates data bases allowing access to a comprehensive range of educational materials.

National AIDS Network
2033 M Street N.W.
Washington, DC 20036
(202) 293-2437
Serves as resource center and networking agency. Provides education on direct services to AIDS sufferers.

National Association of People with AIDS
2025 Eye Street N.W., Suite 415
Washington, DC 20006
(202) 429-2856
Maintains a national system of self-empowering programs administered by and for people with AIDS. Promotes AIDS-related health care, social services and educational programs.

199

National Association of State Alcohol and Drug Abuse Directors
444 N. Capitol Street N.W., Suite 520
Washington, DC 20001
(202) 783-6688
Represents the interests of alcohol and drug abuse directors and their agencies before Congress and federal agencies. Fosters development of comprehensive drug abuse programs tailored to AIDS.

National Gay and Lesbian Task Force
1517 U Street N.W.
Washington, DC 20009
(202) 332-6483
Group that advocates elimination of prejudice against gay and lesbian persons and lobbies for gay civil rights. Source of information and materials on AIDS.

National Gay Rights Advocates
540 Castro Street
San Francisco, CA 94114
(415) 863-3624
Public interest law firm promoting equality for homosexuals. Operates AIDS Civil Rights Project. Provides advice and informational materials on AIDS-related legal issues.

National Institute of Allergy and Infectious Diseases
9000 Rockville Pike
Bethesda, MD 20892
(301) 496-5717
Maintains informational pamphlets, fact sheets and other materials on research into the causes, prevention and treatment of AIDS.

National Lawyers Guild AIDS Network
211 Gough Street, 3rd Floor
San Francisco, CA 94102
(415) 861-8886
Offers legal and educational assistance on AIDS issues.

National Leadership Coalition on AIDS
1150 17th Street N.W., Suite 202
Washington, DC 20036
(202) 429-0930
Provides information and resources on AIDS in the workplace: advises

those developing workplace AIDS policies; and encourages private sector involvement with the AIDS epidemic.

National Lesbian and Gay Health Foundation
1638 R Street N.W., Suite 2
Washington, DC 20009
(202) 797-7104
Promotes research on issues of gay and lesbian health care. Disseminates information on AIDS.

National Native American AIDS Prevention Center
6239 College Avenue, Suite 201
Oakland, CA 94618
(415) 658-2051
National clearinghouse for Native American AIDS information and educational materials.

Project Inform
347 Dolores Street, Suite 301
San Francisco, CA 94110
(800) 822-7422
Serves as an information clearinghouse for AIDS drugs. Provides extensive materials describing up-to-date treatment strategies and promising medications.

San Francisco AIDS Foundation
P.O. Box 6182, 25 Van Ness
San Francisco, CA 94101-6182
(415) 864-4376
Provides a variety of informational materials aimed at educating the public about AIDS. Participant in the major national AIDS issues and events.

United States Conference of Local Health Officers
1620 Eye Street N.W.
Washington, DC 20006
(202) 293-7330
An affiliate of the U.S. Conference of Mayors, the organization is involved in the development of AIDS prevention and education programs.

United States Conference of Mayors AIDS Program
1620 Eye Street N.W.
Washington, DC 20006
(202) 293-7330

Facilitates the exchange of information on AIDS among local governments and community organizations. Emphasis is on AIDS education.

United States Public Health Service
200 Independence Avenue S.W.
Washington, DC 20201
(202) 245-6867
The Public Health Service, Department of Health and Human Resources, oversees all federal AIDS medical and research programs.

World Health Organization
525 23rd Street N.W.
Washington, DC 20037
(202) 861-4353
International health organization under the auspices of the United Nations. Maintains worldwide AIDS statistics.

World Hemophilia AIDS Center
2400 S. Flower Street
Los Angeles, CA 900007-2697
(213) 742-1357
Serves as an information clearinghouse and international surveillance center for AIDS in hemophilia patients. Conducts international survey on AIDS and AIDS-related cases in hemophiliacs.

STATE AND LOCAL

ALABAMA

Alabama Department of Health
Room #900, State Office Building
Montgomery, AL 36130
(205) 261-5131

Mobile AIDS Support Services
P.O. Box 16341
Mobile, AL 36616
(205) 342-5092

Birmingham AIDS Outreach
P.O. Box 73062
Birmingham, AL 35253
(205) 930-0440
(800) 445-3741

Montgomery AIDS Outreach Inc.
P.O. Box 5213
Montgomery, AL 36103
(205) 284-2273

ALASKA

Alaska Department of Health
3601 C Street, Pouch 6333
Anchorage, AK 99502
(907) 561–4233

Alaskan AIDS Assistance
   Association
417 W. 8th Avenue
Anchorage, AK 99501
(907) 276–1400
(800) 478–AIDS

American Red Cross
Tanana Valley Chapter
626 2nd Street
Fairbanks, AK 99708
(907) 456–5937

Anchorage S.T.D. Clinic
825 L Street
Anchorage, AK 99506
(907) 964–4611

Fairbanks Health Center
800 Airport Way
Fairbanks, AK 99701
(907) 452–1776

Identity Inc.
P.O. Box 2000070
Anchorage, AK 99520–0070
(907) 276–3918

Municipality of Anchorage Department of Health and Human
   Services
P.O. Box 196650, 825 L Street
Anchorage, AK 99511–6650
(907) 343–4611

ARIZONA

Arizona AIDS Information Line
P.O. Box 16423
Phoenix, AZ 85011
(602) 234–2753

Arizona AIDS Project, Inc.
736 E. Flynn Lane
Phoenix, AZ 85014
(602) 277–1929

Community AIDS Council
P.O. Box 32903
Phoenix, AZ 85064
(602) 890–1776

Shanti Foundation of Tucson, Inc.
602 N. 4th Avenue
Tucson, AZ 85705
(602) 622–7107

Tucson AIDS Project, Inc.
151 S. Tucson Boulevard, Suite 252
Tucson, AZ 85716
(602) 322–6226

ARKANSAS

Arkansas A.I.D.S. Foundation
P.O. Box 5007
Little Rock, AR 72225
(501) 663–7833

Arkansas Department of Health
AIDS Prevention Program
4815 W. Markham
Little Rock, AR 72205–3867
(501) 661–2408

Washington County AIDS Task Force
P.O. Box 4224
Fayetteville, AR 72702
(501) 443–AIDS

CALIFORNIA

AIDS Education Project
Division of Northern California
  Coalition for Rural Health, Inc.
2850A West Center Street
Anderson, CA 96007
(916) 365–2559

AIDS Health Project
1855 Folsom Street, Suite 506,
  Box 0884
San Francisco, CA 94143–0884
(415) 476–6430

AIDS Positive Action League
1154 N. Lake Avenue
Pasadena, CA 91104
(213) 684–8411

AIDS Project Los Angeles
3670 Wilshire Boulevard,
  Suite 300
Los Angeles, CA 90010
(213) 380–2000

AIDS Project of the East Bay
400 40th Street, Suite 204
Oakland, CA 94609
(415) 420–8181

AIDS Response Program of
  Orange County
12832 Garden Grove Boulevard,
  Suite B
Garden Grove, CA 92643
(714) 534–0961

AIDS Services, County Health
  Care Services
300 N. San Antonio Road
Santa Barbara, CA 93110
(805) 681–5120

AIDS Services Foundation for
  Orange County
1685–A Babcock Street
Costa Mesa, CA 92627
(714) 646–0411

California Department of Health
  Services
Office of AIDS
P.O. Box 942732, 714/744
  P Street
Sacramento, CA 94234–7320
(916) 445–0553

Central Valley AIDS Team
P.O. Box 4640, 606 E. Blemont
Fresno, CA 93744
(209) 264–2436

Desert AIDS Project
750 S. Vella Road
Palm Springs, CA 92264
(619) 323–2118

Division of AIDS Activities/
  San Francisco
995 Potrero, SFGH, Ward 84
San Francisco, CA 94110
(415) 321–5531

Documentation of AIDS Issues
  and Research Foundation, Inc.
2336 Market Street, no. 33
San Francisco, CA 94114
(415) 552–1665

Gay and Lesbian Community
  Services Center
1213 N. Highland Avenue
Los Angeles, CA 90038
(213) 464–7400 ext 251

Humboldt County Department of
  Public Welfare
929 Koster Street
Eureka, CA 95501
(707) 445–6023

Inland AIDS Project
3638 University Avenue
Riverside, CA 92501
(213) 784–2437

Kern County AIDS Task Force
P.O. Box 10961
Bakersfield, CA 93389
(805) 397–8588, 328–0729

Los Angeles County Department
  of Health Services
AIDS Program Office
313 N. Figueroa Street
Los Angeles, CA 90012
(213) 974–7803

Los Angeles Shanti Foundation
9060 Santa Monica Boulevard,
  Suite 301
West Hollywood, CA 90069
(213) 273–7591

Mayor's Task Force on AIDS
San Diego Health Department
1700 Pacific Highway
San Diego, CA 92101
(619) 236–2705

Minority AIDS Project/
  Los Angeles
5882 W. Pico Boulevard, Suite
  210
Los Angeles, CA 90019
(213) 936–4949

North State AIDS Project
P.O. Box 4542
Redding, CA 96099
(916) 225–5252

Orange County Health Care
  Agency
511 N. Sycamore
Santa Ana, CA 92701
(714) 834–2015

People with AIDS/ARC of San
  Francisco
333 Valencia Street, 4th Floor
San Francisco, CA 94103–3597
(415) 861–6703, 864–4376

Placer County Health Department
11484 B Avenue
Auburn, CA 95603
(916) 823–4541

Project AHEAD
2017 E. 4th Street
Long Beach, CA 90814
(213) 439–3948

Riverside County Office of AIDS
 Coordination
P.O. Box 1370
Riverside, CA 92502
(714) 787–1608

Sacramento AIDS Foundation
1900 K Street, Suite 201
Sacramento, CA 95814
(916) 448–2437

Sacramento County Health
 Department, AIDS Unit
3701 Branch Center Road
Sacramento, CA 95827
(916) 366–2922

San Diego AIDS Project
3777 4th Avenue
San Diego, CA 92103
(619) 543–0300
(619) 548–0604 (Spanish)

San Francisco Department of
 Public Health, The AIDS
 Office
1111 Market Street, 3rd Floor
San Francisco, CA 94103
(415) 864–5571

San Joaquin AIDS Foundation
P.O. Box 8277, 4410 N.
 Pershing, Suite C-5
Stockton, CA 95208–8277
(209) 476–8533

San Luis Obispo County AIDS
 Education and Prevention
 Project
P.O. Box 1489, 12191 Johnson
 Avenue
San Luis Obispo, CA 93406
(805) 549–5540

Santa Clara County Health
 Department AIDS Program
2220 Moorpark
San Jose, CA 95128
(408) 299–4151

Santa Cruz AIDS Project
P.O. Box 5142, 1606 Soquel
 Avenue
Santa Cruz, CA 95062
(408) 427–3900

Shanti Project
525 Howard Street
San Francisco, CA 94105
(415) 777-CARE

Shasta County Public Health
2650 Hospital Lane
Redding, CA 96001
(916) 225–5591

Solano County Health
 Department, AIDS Program
355 Tuolumne Street

Vallejo, CA 94590
(707) 553–5401

Stanislaus Community AIDS
  Project
820 Scenic Drive
Modesto, CA 95350
(209) 572-2437

UCSF AIDS Health Project
P.O. Box 0884, 1855 Folsom
  Street, Suite 506
San Francisco, CA 94143-0884
(415) 476-6430

COLORADO

Colorado AIDS Project
P.O. Box 18529
Denver, CO 80218
(303) 837-0166

El Paso County Health
  Department Clinic
601 North Foote Street
Colorado Springs, CO 80909
(303) 578-3148

Colorado Department of Health,
  STD/AIDS Control
4210 E. 11th Street
Denver, CO 80220
(303) 331-8320
(800) 252-AIDS

Larimer County Health
  Department
363 Jefferson Street
Fort Collins, CO 80524
(303) 221-7460

Denver AIDS Prevention
  Program
605 Bannock Street
Denver, CO 80204-4507
(303) 893-6300

Southern Colorado AIDS Project
P.O. Box 311
Colorado Springs, CO 80901
(719) 578-9092

Weld County AIDS Coalition
1516 Hospital Road
Greeley, CO 80631
(303) 353-0639

CONNECTICUT

AIDS Project Greater Danbury
P.O. Box 91
Bethel, CT 06801
(203) 426-5626

AIDS Project/Hartford
30 Arbor Street
Hartford, CT 06106
(203) 523-7699

AIDS Project/Greater New
  Britain
P.O. Box 1214, 147 West Main
  Street
New Britain, CT 06050-1214
(203) 225-7634

AIDS Project: Middlesex County
Middletown Department of
  Health
Middletown, CT 06457
(203) 344-3482

AIDS Project New Haven
P.O. Box 636
New Haven, CT 06503
(203) 624–0947

AIDS Project/Norwalk
137 East Avenue
Norwalk, CT 06851
(203) 854–7976

Bridgeport AIDS Advisory
  Committee
2710 North Avenue
Bridgeport, CT 06604
(203) 336–AIDS

Connecticut Department of
  Health Services, AIDS Section
150 Washington Street
Hartford, CT 06106
(203) 566–1157

Danbury Health Department
  AIDS Program
20 West Street
Danbury, CT 06810
(203) 796–1613

Greenwich AIDS Task Force
101 Field Point Road
Greenwich, CT 06836–2540
(203) 622–6460

Mid-Fairfield AIDS Project Inc.
30 France Street
Norwalk, CT 06851
(203) 854–7979

New London AIDS Educational,
  Counseling and Testing Service
120 Broad Street, Health
  Department
New London, CT 06320
(203) 447–AIDS

Stamford Health Department:
  AIDS Program
888 Washington Boulevard, 8th
  Floor
Stamford, CT 06904
(203) 967–2437

Waterbury Department of Public
  Health, AIDS Program
402 E. Main Street
Waterbury, CT 06702
(203) 574–6883

DELAWARE

AIDS Program Office, Delaware
  State Division of Public Health
3000 Newport Gap Pike,
  Building G
Wilmington, DE 19808
(302) 995–8422

Delaware Lesbian and Gay
  Health Advocates Inc.
214 N. Market Street
Wilmington, DE 19801
(302) 652–6776

DISTRICT OF COLUMBIA

Dupont West Medical Center
2032 P Street N.W.
Washington, DC 20036
(202) 775–8500

Whitman-Walker Clinic Inc.
1407 S Street N.W.
Washington, DC 20009
(202) 797–3500

FLORIDA

AID Jacksonville
P.O. Box 19–0488
Miami Beach, FL 33119–0488
(904) 399–4589

AIDS Resource, Education and
Assistance
P.O. Box 160224
Altamonte Springs, FL 32716
(407) 843–4368

Bay CPHU
605 N. MacArthur Avenue
Panama City, FL 32401–3680
(904) 785–4384

Center One, Anyone in Distress,
Inc.
P.O. Box 8152
Fort Lauderdale, FL 33310
(305) 561–0807

Charlotte County AIDS Task
Force
514 E. Grace Street
Punta Gorda, FL 33950
(813) 639–1181

Collier County AIDS Task Force
P.O. Box 428
Naples, FL 33939
(813) 774–8200

Comprehensive AIDS Program of
Palm Beach County, Inc.
P.O. Box 3084
Lantana, FL 33465–3084
(407) 582–HELP

Health Crisis Network, Inc.
P.O. Box 42–1280, 1351 N.W.
20th Street
Miami, FL 33242–1280
(305) 326–8833
(800) 443–5046

HRS/Hillsbourough County
Health Department/AIDS
Program
1112B E. Kennedy Blvd
Tampa, FL 33675–5135
(813) 272–6155

Leon County Public Health Unit
2965 Municipal Way
Tallahassee, FL 32304
(904) 487–3186

Monroe County Health
Department, AIDS Education
Project
513 Whitehead Street
Key West, FL 33040
(305) 294–8302

North Central Florida AIDS
Network
1005-I S.E. 4th Avenue
Gainesville, FL 32601
(904) 372–4370

AIDS

Saint Lucie County Public Health
Unit
714 Avenue C
Fort Pierce, FL 34954
(407) 468–3945

Tampa AIDS Network
P.O. Box 8333
Tampa, FL 33674–8333
(813) 221–6420

GEORGIA

AID Atlanta
1132 W. Peachtree Street N.W.
Atlanta, GA 30309
(404) 872–0600
(800) 551–2728

AIDS Coastal Empire Foundation
P.O. Box 2442
Savannah, GA 31401
(914) 236–2489

Central City Network/Macon
P.O. Box 6452
Macon, GA 31211
(912) 742–2437

DeKalb County Board of Health
440 Winn Way
Decatur, GA 30030
(404) 294–3796

Georgia Department of Human
Resources, AIDS Project
878 Peachtree Street N.W., Room
109
Atlanta, GA 30309
(404) 894–5304
(800) 551–2728

Laurens County Health
Department
2121 Bellevue Road
Dublin, GA 31021
(912) 272–2051

Spalding County Health
Department
P.O. Box 129, Magnolia Drive
Griffin, GA 30224
(404) 227–5588

HAWAII

Gay Community Center
1154 Fort Street Mall, Suite 415
Honolulu, HI 96801
(808) 535–6000

Life Foundation/Honolulu
P.O. Box 88980
Honolulu, HI 96830–8980
(808) 924–AIDS

Kauai District Health Office
3040 Umi Street
Lihue, HI 96766
(808) 245–4495

Maui District Health Office
54 High Street
Wailuku, HI 92793
(808) 244–0336

Waikiki Health Center
277 Ohua Avenue
Honolulu, HI 96815
(808) 922–4787
(800) 321–1555

IDAHO

Idaho AIDS Foundation
P.O. Box 421
Boise, ID 83701–0421
(208) 345–2277

Idaho AIDS Program,
    Department of Health and
    Welfare
450 W. State Street
Boise, ID 83720
(208) 334–5937
(800) 833–AIDS

Southwest District Health Department
P.O. Box 489, 920 Main
Caldwell, ID 83606
(208) 459–0744

ILLINOIS

AIDS Care Network
401 Division Street
Rockford, IL 61104
(815) 962–5092

Chicago Department of Health
50 W. Washington
Chicago, IL 60602
(312) 744–7573

Cook County Department of
    Public Health
1500 S. Maybrook Drive
Maywood, IL 60153
(312) 865–6100

DuPage County Health
    Department
111 N. County Farm Road
Wheaton, IL 60187
(312) 682–7400 ext 7310

Franklin-Williamson Bi-County
    Health Department
Williamson County Airport
Marion, IL 62959
(618) 993–8111

Lee County Health Department
144 N. Court
Dixon, IL 61021
(815) 284–3371

Peoria City County Health
    Department
2116 N. Sheridan Road
Peoria, IL 61604
(309) 685–6181 ext. 208

Southern Illinois AIDS Task
    Force
P.O. Box 307
Murphysboro, IL 62901
(618) 684–3143

211

Tazewell County Health Department
RR 1, Box 15
Tremont, IL 61568–0015
(309) 925–5511

INDIANA

AIDS Task Force
1208 E. State Boulevard
Fort Wayne, IN 46805
(219) 484–2711

Evansville AIDS Task Force
111 N. Spring Street
Evansville, IN 47711
(812) 476–5437

Indiana State Board of Health
AIDS Activity Office
1330 W. Michigan Street
Indianapolis, IN 46206
(317) 633–0851

Marion County AIDS Coalition
1350 N. Pennsylvania Street,
Damien Center
Indianapolis, IN 46202
(317) 929–3466

Project AIDS Lafayette
810 North Street
Lafayette, IN 47903
(317) 742–2305

Terre Haute AIDS Task Force
201 Cherry Street
Terre Haute, IN 47807
(812) 238–8431

IOWA

AIDS Coalition of Northeast
Iowa
2530 University Avenue
Waterloo, IA 50701
(319) 234–6831

Central Iowa AIDS Project
2116 Grand Avenue
Des Moines, IA 50312
(515) 244–6700

ICON PWA Fund
711 Navajo Street
Council Bluffs, IA 51501
(712) 366–1791

Iowa Center for AIDS/ARC
Resources and Education
P.O. Box 2989
Iowa City, IA 52244
(319) 338–2135

Johnson County AIDS Project
1105 Gilbert Court
Iowa City, IA 52240
(319) 356–6040

Quad Cities AIDS Coalition
605 Main Street, Room 224
Davenport, IA 52803
(319) 326–8618

The Rapids AIDS Project
Box 2861
Cedar Rapids, IA 52406
(319) 395–7530

Scott County Health Department
Communicable Diseases
428 Western Avenue
Davenport, IA 52801
(319) 326–8618

KANSAS

Kansas AIDS Network
1115 W. 10th Street, Suite 8
Topeka, KS 66601
(913) 357–7499
(800) 365–0219

Office of Health and
  Environmental Education
Kansas Department of Health and
  Environment
Landon State Office Building
Topeka, KS 66620
(913) 296–1216

Topeka AIDS Project
P.O. Box 118
Topeka, KS 66601
(913) 232–3100

Wichita AIDS Task Force
P.O. Box 2652
Wichita, KS 67201
(316) 265–7994

KENTUCKY

AIDS Crisis Task Force/
Lexington
P.O. Box 11442
Lexington, KY 40575
(606) 281–5151

Community Health Trust of
  Kentucky
P.O. Box 363
Louisville, KY 40201
(502) 634–1789

Lexington Fayette County Health
  Department
650 Newton Pike
Lexington, KY 40508
(606) 252–2371

Lexington Gay Services
  Organizations
P.O. Box 11471
Lexington, KY 40511
(606) 231–0335

Northern Kentucky AIDS Task Force
401 Park Avenue
Newport, KY 41071
(606) 491–6611

LOUISIANA

Baton Rouge MCC/AIDS Project
Box 64996
Baton Rouge, LA 70896
(504) 929–8830

Central Louisiana AIDS Support
    Services
1771 Elliot Street, Suite B
Alexandria, LA 71315
(318) 443–5216

Foundation for Health Education
1219 Barracks Street
New Orleans, LA 70116
(504) 928–2270

Greater Louisiana Alliance for
    Dignity
P.O. Box 4523
Shreveport, LA 71104
(318) 222–4523

New Orleans AIDS Task Force
1014 Dumaine
New Orleans, LA 70116
(504) 899–0482

New Orleans Health Department,
    Delgado (STD) Clinic
320 S. Claiborne Avenue, 2nd
    Floor
New Orleans, LA 70112
(504) 525–0086

NO/AIDS Task Force
P.O. Box 2616
New Orleans, LA 70176–2616
(504) 891–3732

Terrebonne Parish Health Unit
600 Polk Street
Houma, LA 70361
(504) 857–3601

MAINE

The AIDS Project
22 Monument Square
Portland, ME 04101
(207) 774-6877

Bangor Health Department
103 Texas Avenue
Bangor, ME 04401
(207) 947–0700

The Clinic
200 Main Street
Lewiston, ME 04240
(207) 795-4357

Maine Department of Human
    Services,
Office on AIDS
State House Station 11
Augusta, ME 04333
(207) 289–3747

MARYLAND

Baltimore City Health
  Department
303 E. Fayette Street, 5th Floor
Baltimore, MD 21202
(301) 396–4448

Baltimore County Health
  Department
401 Bosley Avenue, New Courts
  Bldg, 3rd Floor
Towson, MD 21204
(301) 494–2711

Charles County Health
  Department
P.O. Box 640, Garrett Avenue
LaPlata, MD 20646
(301) 934–9577

Dorchester County Health
  Department
Route 1, Box 50, Woods Road
Cambridge, MD 21613
(301) 228–3223

Health Education and Resource
  Organization
101 W. Read Street, Suite 812
Baltimore, MD 21201
(301) 685–1180

Howard County Health
  Department
3450 Courthouse Drive
Ellicott City, MD 21043
(301) 992–2333

Maryland Department of Health
  and Mental Hygiene,
AIDS Administration
201 W. Preston Street, Room 308
Baltimore, MD 21201
(301) 225–5019
(800) 638–6252

Mayor's AIDS Study Group
111 N. Calvert
Baltimore, MD 21201
(301) 396–3851

Montgomery County HERO
100 Maryland Avenue
Rockville, MD 20850
(301) 762–3385

Prince George's County Health
  Department, Office on AIDS
3003 Hospital Drive
Cheverly, MD 20785
(301) 386–0348

Queen Anne's County Health
  Department
206 N. Commerce Street
Centreville, MD 21617
(301) 758–0720

Talbot County Health
  Department, AIDS Program
P.O. Box 480
Easton, MD 21601
(301) 822–2292

Wicomico County Health
  Department
300 W. Carroll Street
Salisbury, MD 21801
(301) 749–1244

AIDS

MASSACHUSETTS

AIDS Action Committee
131 Clarendon Street
Boston, MA 02116
(617) 437–6200

American Red Cross, Northeast
  Region
60 Kendrick Street
Needham, MA 02194
(617) 449–0773

Fenway Community Health
  Center
16 Haviland Street
Boston, MA 02115
(617) 267–0900

Lifeline Institute Inc.
664 Main Street
Amherst, MA 01002
(413) 253–2822

Massachusetts AIDS Task Force
150 Tremont Street
Boston, MA 02111
(617) 727–2700

Massachusetts Center for Disease
  Control
Division of Communicable
  Disease Control
305 South Street
Boston, MA 02130
(617) 522–3700

Massachusetts Department of
  Public Health,
Health Resource Office
150 Tremont Street
Boston, MA 02111
(617) 734–4246

Newton Health Department
492 Waltham Street
West Newton, MA 02165–1999
(617) 552–7058

MICHIGAN

Calhoun County AIDS Education
  Steering Committee
190 E. Michigan Avenue
Battle Creek, MI 49017
(616) 966–1210

Gay and Lesbian Community
  Information Center/Detroit
940 W. McNichols
Detroit, MI 48203
(313) 345–2722

Genesee County Health
  Department
310 W. Oakley Street
Flint, MI 48503–3996
(313) 257–3585

Grand Rapids AIDS Task Force
P.O. Box 6603
Grand Rapids, MI 49516–6603
(616) 459–9177

Jackson County Health
  Department
410 Erie Street
Jackson, MI 49203
(517) 788–4477

Kalamazoo County AIDS
  Prevention Program
418 W. Kalamazoo Avenue
Kalamazoo, MI 49007
(616) 383–8850

Michigan Department of Public
  Health
Special Office on AIDS
  Prevention
3423 N. Logan
Lansing, MI 48909
(517) 335–8371

Vida Latina
4124 W. Vernor
Detroit, MI 48209
(313) 843–2437

Washtnaw County Public Health
  Division
555 Towner Boulevard
Ypsilanti, MI 48198
(313) 485–2181

Wayne County Health
  Department
Wayne Westland Complex
Westland, MI 48185
(313) 467–3300

Wellness House of Michigan
P.O. Box 03827
Detroit, MI 48203
(313) 865–AIDS

Wellness Networks Inc.
P.O. Box 1046
Royal Oak, MI 48068
(313) 547–3783

Wellness Networks Inc./Flint
P.O. Box 438
Flint, MI 48501
(313) 232–2417

Wellness Networks Inc./Huron
  Valley
P.O. Box 3242
Ann Arbor, MI 48106
(313) 572–WELL

MINNESOTA

Hennepin County Medical Center
701 Park Avenue S.
Minneapolis, MN 55415
(612) 347–2693

Minnesota AIDS Project
1010 Park Avenue
Minneapolis, MN 55408
(612) 371–0180

Olmsted County Health
  Department
1650 4th Street S.E.
Rochester, MN 55904
(507) 285–8370

Red Door Clinic
527 Park Avenue
Minneapolis, MN 55415
(612) 347–3300

217

MISSISSIPPI

Mississippi State Department of Health
AIDS/HIV Prevention Project
P.O. Box 1700
Jackson, MS 39209
(601) 960–7723

MISSOURI

AIDS Project/Springfield
309 N. Jefferson Avenue, 254
  Landmark Building
Springfield, MO 65806
(417) 864–5594

Columbia/Boone County Health
  Department
600 E. Broadway
Columbia, MO 65205
(314) 874–7355

Four-State Community AIDS
  Project
P.O. Box 3476
Joplin, MO 64803–3476
(417) 625–2486

Good Samaritan Project
3940 Walnut Street
Kansas City, MO 64111
(816) 561–8784

Kansas City Free Health Clinic
5119 E. 24th Street
Kansas City, MO 64127
(816) 231–4481

Metropolitan Saint Louis Task
  Force on AIDS
P.O. Box 2905
Saint Louis, MO 63130
(314) 768–8100

Mid-Missouri AIDS Project
811 E. Cherry Street, Suite 320
Columbia, MO 65205
(316) 875–2437

Saint Joseph/Buchanan County
  Community Health Clinic
904 S. 10th Street
Saint Joseph, MO 64503
(816) 271–4725

Saint Louis Effort for AIDS
4050 Lindell Boulevard
Saint Louis, MO 63108
(314) 531–2847

MONTANA

Billings AIDS Support Network
P.O. Box 1748
Billings, MT 59103
(406) 245–2029

Montana State Department of
  Health
Health Services and Medical
  Facilities Division
Cogswell Building
Helena, MT 59620
(406) 444–4740

Yellowstone City-County Health Department
123 S. 27th Street
Billings, MT 59101
(406) 256–6821

NEBRASKA

American Red Cross AIDS
  Education Coalition of
  Nebraska
3838 Dewey Avenue
Omaha, NE 68105
(402) 341–2723

Douglas County Health
  Department
AIDS Activity
1819 Farnam Street
Omaha, NE 68183
(402) 444–7214

Grand Island/Hall County
  Department of Health
105 E. 1st
Grand Island, NE 68801
(308) 381–5175

Nebraska State Department of
  Health
Office of Disease Control
P.O. Box 95007
Lincoln, NE 68509
(402) 471–2937

NEVADA

Aid for AIDS of Nevada
2116 Paradis Road
Las Vegas, NV 89104
(702) 369–6162

Nevada AIDS Foundation
P.O. Box 478
Reno, NV 89504
(702) 329–2437

State of Nevada Health Division
505 E. King Street, Room 200
Carson City, NV 89710
(702) 885–4800

219

NEW HAMPSHIRE

Citizen Alliance Gay/Lesbian
Rights, AIDS Education
P.O. Box 756
Concord, NH 03229
(603) 228–2355

New Hampshire AIDS
Foundation
789 Maple Street
Manchester, NH 03104
(603) 595–0218

New Hampshire Division of Public Health Services,
AIDS Program
Health and Human Services Building, 6 Hazen Drive
Concord, NH 03301
(603) 271–4477
(800) 852–3345

NEW JERSEY

AIDS Education Project, New
Jersey Lesbian and Gay
Coalition
P.O. Box 1431
New Brunswick, NJ 08903
(201) 992–5666

CURA (Community United for
the Rehabilitation of the
Addicted)
61 Lincoln Park
Newark, NJ 07104
(201) 622–3570

American Red Cross of Northern
New Jersey
106 Washington Street
East Orange, NJ 07019
(201) 676–0800

East Orange Health Department
143 New Street
East Orange, NJ 07017
(201) 266–5498

Atlantic City Health Department
35 S. Martin Luther King
Boulevard
Atlantic City, NJ 08401
(609) 347–6457

Hyacinth Foundation AIDS
Project
211 Livingston Avenue
New Brunswick, NJ 08901
(201) 246–0204
(800) 433–0254

Caribbean Haitian Council Inc.
410 Central Avenue
East Orange, NJ 07018
(201) 678–5059

Jersey City Mayor's AIDS Task
Force
586 Newark Avenue
Jersey City, NJ 07306
(201) 547–5168

La Casa de Don Pedro, Inc.
21–23 Broadway
Newark, NJ 07104
(201) 483–2703

New Jersey State Department of
  Health
Communicable Disease Service
Room 702 CN 360
Trenton, NJ 08609
(609) 292–7300

South Jersey AIDS Alliance
1616 Pacific Avenue, Suite 201
Atlantic City, NJ 08401
(609) 347–8799
(800) 432–AIDS

NEW MEXICO

AIDS Prevention Program
1190 St. Francis Drive
Santa Fe, NM 87503
(505) 827–0086
(800) 454–AIDS

New Mexico AIDS Services Inc.
209A McKenzie Street
Santa Fe, NM 87108
(505) 894–0911

New Mexico Public Health Division,
District IV Health Office
200 E. Chisum
Roswell, NM 88201
(505) 624–6050

NEW YORK

AIDS Center of Queens County
113–20 Jamaica Avenue
Richmond Hill, NY 11418
(718) 847–1966

AIDS Comprehensive Family
  Care Center
1300 Morris Park Avenue, Room
  F-401
Bronx, NY 10461
(212) 430–4227

AIDS Council of Northeastern
  New York
307 Hamilton Street
Albany, NY 12210
(518) 434–4686

AIDS Education and Service
  Coordination Project
111 Westfall Road
Rochester, NY 14692
(716) 274–6114

AIDS Epidemiology Program/
  Albany
Corning Tower Building, Empire
  State Plaza, Room 668
Albany, NY 12237
(518) 474–6730

AIDS Prevention Research Center
622 W. 113th Street
New York, NY 10025
(212) 854–3035

AIDS-Related Community
  Services
214 Central Avenue
White Plains, NY 10606
(914) 993–0606

AIDS Resource Center
24 W. 30th Street
New York, NY 10001
(212) 481–1270

AIDS Rochester Inc.
20 University Avenue
Rochester, NY 14605
(716) 232–3580

Association for Drug Abuse
  Prevention and Treatment
85 Bergen Street
Brooklyn, NY 11201
(718) 834–9585

Brooklyn AIDS Task Force
22 Chapel Street
Brooklyn, NY 11201
(718) 596–4781

Central New York AIDS Task
  Force
627 W. Genesee Street
Syracuse, NY 13204
(315) 475–2430

Gay and Lesbian Community
  Center/Buffalo
647 W. Delavan Avenue
Buffalo, NY 14222
(716) 886–1274

Haitian Coalition on AIDS
50 Court Street, Suite 605
Brooklyn, NY 11201
(718) 855–0972

HEALTH WATCH Information
  and Promotion Service
3020 Glenwood Road
Brooklyn, NY 11210
(718) 434–5411

Hispanic AIDS Forum
853 Broadway, Suite 2007
New York, NY 10003
(212) 870–1902

Jefferson County Committee on
  AIDS Information
1020 State Street
Watertown, NY 13601
(315) 782–4410

Long Island Association for AIDS
  Care
P.O. Box 2859
Huntington Station, NY 11746
(516) 385–2451

Lower Eastside Service Center,
  AIDS Prevention Program
46 E. Broadway
New York, NY 10002
(212) 431-4160

New York City Department of
  Health, AIDS Education Unit
125 Worth Street
New York, NY 10013
(212) 566-8290

New York City Department of
  Health, AIDS Program
  Services
125 Worth Street
New York, NY 10013
(212) 566-7103

New York State AIDS Institute
Corning Tower Building, Empire
  State Plaza
Albany, NY 12237
(518) 473-7328

New York State Department of
  Health, AIDS Prevention
  Program
677 S. Salina Street
Syracuse, NY 13202
(315) 428-4728

People with AIDS Coalition Inc.
31 W. 26th Street
New York, NY 10010
(212) 535-0290

Rochester AIDS Task Force
153 Liberty Pole Way
Rochester, NY 14604
(716) 232-7181

Southern Tier AIDS Program
65 Broad Street
Johnson City, NY 13790
(607) 798-1706

Westchester County Department
  of Health
112 E. Post Road
White Plains, NY 10601
(914) 285-5100

Western New York AIDS
  Program
220 Delaware Avenue, Suite 512
Buffalo, NY 14202
(716) 847-2441

NORTH CAROLINA

The AIDS Services Project
P.O. Box 3203
Durham, NC 27705-1203
(919) 688-5777

AIDS Task Force of Winston-
  Salem
P.O. Box 2982
Winston-Salem, NC 27102
(919) 723-5031

GROW AIDS Resource Project
P.O. Box 4535
Wilmington, NC 28406
(919) 675–9222

NC AIDS Control Program
P.O. Box 2091
Raleigh, NC 27602–2091
(919) 733–7301

Lesbian and Gay Health Project
P.O. Box 3203
Durham, NC 27705–1203
(919) 683–2182

Stanly County Task Force
945 N. 5th Street
Albemarle, NC 28001
(704) 982–9171

Metrolina AIDS Project
P.O. Box 32662
Charlotte, NC 28232
(704) 333–2437

Triad Health Project
P.O. Box 5716
Greensboro, NC 27435
(919) 275–1654

Western North Carolina AIDS Project
2 Wall Street, Suite 220
Asheville, NC 28802
(704) 252–7489

NORTH DAKOTA

North Dakota State Department of Health, AIDS Program
State Capitol
Bismark, ND 58505
(701) 224–2378

OHIO

AIDS Volunteers of Cincinnati
P.O. Box 19009
Cincinnati, OH 45219
(513) 421–AIDS

Athens AIDS Task Force
18 N. College Street
Athens, OH 45701
(614) 592–4397

American Red Cross, Columbus
    Area Chapter
995 E. Broad Street
Columbus, OH 43205
(614) 253–7981

Auglaize County AIDS Task
    Force
P.O. Box 59
Wapakoneta, OH 45895
(419) 738–3410

Canton City AIDS Task Force
218 Cleveland Avenue S.W., City Hall
Canton, OH 44702
(216) 489-3231

Cleveland Area AIDS Task Force
2074 Abington Road
Cleveland, OH 44106
(216) 844-1000

Cleveland City, Department of Health and Human Resources
1925 St. Clair Avenue
Cleveland, OH 44114
(216) 664-2324
(800) 332-AIDS

Columbus AIDS Task Force
1500 W. 3rd Avenue, Suite 329
Columbus, OH 43212
(614) 488-2437

Columbus Health Department
181 S. Washington Boulevard
Columbus, OH 43215
(614) 222-7772

Dayton Area AIDS Task Force
P.O. Box 3214
Dayton, OH 45401
(513) 223-2437

Dayton Free Clinic and Counseling Center
1133 Salem Avenue
Dayton, OH 45406
(513) 278-9481

Erie County General Health District AIDS Task Force
420 Superior Street
Sandusky, OH 44870
(419) 626-5623

Greater Cincinnati AIDS Task Force
231 Bethesda Avenue
Cincinnati, OH 45267-0563
(513) 872-4701

Health Issues Taskforce of Cleveland
2250 Euclid Avenue
Cleveland, OH 44115
(216) 621-0766

HIV Education and Counseling Center
3101 Burnet Avenue
Cincinnati, OH 45229
(513) 352-3138

Lake County AIDS Task Force
105 Main Street
Painesville, OH 44077
(216) 357-2554

Mahoning County Area AIDS Task Force
City Hall, 7th Floor
Youngstown, OH 44501
(216) 742-8766

Montgomery County Health Department
P.O. Box 972
Dayton, OH 45422
(513) 225-6462

Northeast Ohio Task Force on
  AIDS
251 E. Mill Street
Akron, OH 44309
(216) 762–AIDS

Ohio AIDS Coalition
P.O. Box 10034
Columbus, OH 43201
(614) 445–8277

Ohio Department of Health,
  AIDS Activities Unit
P.O. Box 118
Columbus, OH 43266–01118
(614) 466–5480

Ohio Department of Health,
  AIDS Unit
246 N. High Street
Columbus, OH 43266–0588
(614) 466–5480

Southern Ohio AIDS Task Force
P.O. Box 1287
Portsmouth, OH 45662
(614) 353–3339

Toledo Area AIDS Task Force
151 N. Michigan Street, Suite 322
Toledo, OH 43624
(419) 242–4777

Toledo City Health Department
635 N. Erie Street
Toledo, OH 43624
(419) 245–1785

OKLAHOMA

AIDS Support Program Inc.
P.O. Box 57531
Oklahoma, OK 73157–2057
(405) 840–2437

Garfield County Health
  Department
2501 Mercer Drive
Enid, OK 73701
(405) 233–0650

Oklahoma State Health
  Department, AIDS Division
P.O. Box 53551
Oklahoma City, OK 73152
(800) 522–9054

Tulsa AIDS Task Force
1711 S. Jackson
Tulsa, OK 74107
(918) 743–4093

OREGON

Cascade AIDS Project Inc.
408 S.W. 2nd Street, Suite 412
Portland, OR 97204
(503) 223–5907

Douglas County Health and
  Social Services Health Center
621 W. Madrone Street
Roseburg, OR 97470
(503) 440–3500

Gay and Lesbian Alliance/
  Roseburg
P.O. Box 813
Roseburg, OR 97470–0166
(503) 672–4126

Mid-Oregon AIDS/Health/
  Education and Support Services
  Inc.
1115 Madison Street N.E., No.
  510
Salem, OR 97303
(503) 363–4963

Multnomah County Health
  Division AIDS Program
426 S.W. Stark
Portland, OR 97204
(503) 248–3406

Oregon AIDS Task Force,
  Research and Education Group
P.O. Box 40104
Portland, OR 92740–0104
(503) 229–7126

Phoenix Rising
333 S.W. 5th Avenue
Portland, OR 97204
(503) 223–8299

Willamette AIDS Council
329 W. 13th Avenue, Suite D
Eugene, OR 97401
(503) 345–7089

PENNSYLVANIA

Action AIDS Inc.
P.O. Box 1625
Philadelphia, PA 19105
(215) 732–2155

AIDS Activities Coordinating
  Office
City Hall Annex
Philadelphia, PA 19107
(215) 686–5070

AIDS Council of Erie County
4718 Lake Pleasant Road
Erie, PA 16504
(814) 825–0881
(800) 445–6262

AIDS Intervention Project/
  Altoona
P.O. Box 352
Altoona, PA 16603
(814) 946–5411
(800) 445–6262

AIDS Prevention Project/
  Pittsburgh
P.O. Box 7319
Pittsburgh, PA 15213
(412) 624–2008

AIDS Task Force of the Lehigh
  Valley
Allentown Health Bureau
723 Chew Street
Allentown, PA 18102
(215) 437–7742

Allegheny County Health
  Department
3333 Forbes Avenue
Pittsburgh, PA 15213
(412) 578–8026

American Red Cross, Erie
4961 Pittsburgh Avenue
Erie, PA 16509
(814) 833–0942

Berks AIDS Health Crisis
P.O. Box 8626
Reading, PA 19603
(215) 375–2242

BEBASHI (Blacks Educating
  Blacks About Sexual Health
  Issues)
1528 Walnut Street, Suite 1414
Philadelphia, PA 19102
(215) 546–4140

Congreso de Latinos Unidos, Inc.
704 W. Girard Avenue
Philadelphia, PA 19123
(215) 625–0550

Lancaster AIDS Project
P.O. Box 1543
Lancaster, PA 17603
(717) 394–9900

Northeast AIDS Council of
  Pennsylvania
P.O. Box 751
Scranton, PA 18501
(717) 342–6907

Pennsylvania Department of
  Health, AIDS Program
Health and Welfare Building
Harrisburg, PA 17108
(717) 787–3350

Philadelphia AIDS Task Force
1216 Walnut Street
Philadelphia, PA 19107
(215) 545–8686

Pittsburgh AIDS Task Force
141 S. Highland Avenue,
  Suite 304
Pittsburgh, PA 15206
(412) 363–6500

South Central AIDS Assistance
  Network
P.O. Box 11573
Harrisburg, PA 17108–1573
(717) 236–4772

York City Bureau of Health
1 Market Way West
York, PA 17405
(717) 849–2252

RHODE ISLAND

Rhode Island Department of
Health, AIDS Program
75 Davis Street
Providence, RI 02908
(401) 277–2362

Rhode Island Project/AIDS
22 Hayes Street
Providence, RI 02908
(401) 277–6545

SOUTH CAROLINA

AIDS Support Network of
Spartanburg
P.O. Box 4786
Spartanburg, SC 29305–4796
(803) 596–3400

Spartanburg County Health
Department
151 E. Wood Street
Spartanburg, SC 29305–4217
(803) 596–3334

State Department of Health and Environmental Control
Bureau of Communicable Diseases
2600 Bull Street
Columbia, SC 29201
(803) 758–5621

SOUTH DAKOTA

Brown County Health
Department
25 Market Street
Aberdeen, SD 57401
(605) 622–2373

Eastern Dakota AIDS Network
P.O. Box 220
Sioux Falls, SD 57101
(605) 332–4599

Public Health Center/Sioux Falls
1320 S. Minnesota Avenue
Sioux Falls, SD 57105
(605) 335–5020

South Dakota Department of
Health
Communicable Disease Program
523 E. Capitol
Pierre, SD 57501
(605) 773–3364

TENNESSEE

Aid to End AIDS Committee/
Memphis
P.O. Box 40389
Memphis, TN 38174
(901) 272–7827

AIDS Response Knoxville
P.O. Box 3932
Knoxville, TN 37927
(615) 523–AIDS

Carroll County Health
Department
126 W. Paris Street
Huntingdon, TN 38344
(901) 986–9147

Chattanooga Council on AIDS
Resources, Education, and
Support
715 E. 11th Street
Chattanooga, TN 37411
(615) 266–2422

Mid Cumberland Regional Health
Office
Ben Allen Road
Nashville, TN 37216
(615) 262–6100

Nashville Council on AIDS
Resources, Education, and
Services
P.O. Box 25107
Nashville, TN 37202
(615) 385–1510

Tennessee Department of Health
and Environment
AIDS Program
1233 S.W. Avenue
Johnson City, TN 37605–2966
(615) 929–5927

Tri-Cities AIDS Project
P.O. Box 231
Johnson City, TN 37605
(615) 282–2416

TEXAS

Abilene AIDS Task Force
P.O. Box 6903
Abilene, TX 79608
(915) 891–2400

AIDS Coordinating Committee/
Dallas
5740 Prospect, Suite 2004
Dallas, TX 75206
(214) 823–2891

AIDS Foundation Houston, Inc.
3927 Essex Lane
Houston, TX 77027
(713) 627–6796

AIDS Legal Hotline/Houston
1236 W. Gray
Houston, TX 77019
(713) 528–7702

AIDS Resource Center
3920 Cedar Springs
Dallas, TX 75219
(214) 521–5124

AIDS Services
1702 Horne Road
Corpus Christi, TX 78416
(512) 851–7298

AIDS Services of Austin
P.O. Box 4874
Austin, TX 78765
(512) 472–2273

Amarillo Bi-City County Health
Department
411 S. Austin Street
Amarillo, TX 79186
(806) 371–1100

Coastal Bend AIDS Foundation, Inc.
616 S. Tancahua
Corpus Christi, TX 78404–1416
(512) 883–5815

Dallas County Health Department, AIDS Prevention Project
1936 Amelia Court
Dallas, TX 75235
(214) 920–7916

El Paso City-County Health District
222 S. Campbell
El Paso, TX 79901
(915) 541–4511

Fort Worth Counseling Center, AIDS Project
659 S. Jennings
Fort Worth, TX 76104
(817) 335–1994

Fort Worth Public Health Department
1800 University Drive
Fort Worth, TX 76107
(817) 870–7346

Harris County Health Department
2501 Dunstan
Houston, TX 77005
(713) 526–1841

Hispanic AIDS Committee for Education and Resources
1139 W. Hildebrand, Suite B
San Antonio, TX 78201
(512) 732–3108

Houston Health and Human Services Department
AIDS Surveillance Program
8000 N. Stadium Drive
Houston, TX 77054
(713) 794–9320

Montrose Clinic
1200 Richmond
Houston, TX 77006
(713) 528–5531

Panhandle AIDS Support Organization, Inc.
4101 W. 34th Street, Suite C
Amarillo, TX 79109
(806) 358–2853

San Antonio AIDS Alliance
1747 Citadel Plaza, Suite 104
San Antonio, TX 78209
(512) 822–4333

San Antonio AIDS Foundation
3530 Broadway
San Antonio, TX 78209
(512) 821–6218

Southwest AIDS Committee
916 E. Yandell
El Paso, TX 79902
(915) 533–5003

Triangle AIDS Network
P.O. Box 12279
Beaumont, TX 77726
(409) 832–8338

West Texas AIDS Foundation
P.O. Box 93120
Lubbock, TX 79493
(806) 747–AIDS

AIDS

UTAH

AIDS Project Utah
457 E. 300 South, Carriage House
Salt Lake City, UT 84110–2576
(801) 359–2438

Southwest Utah District Health
Department
354 East S. Street, Suite 301
Saint George, UT 84770
(801) 673-4179

Utah State Health Department
P.O. Box 45500
Salt Lake City, UT 84145
(801) 533–6191

VERMONT

Vermont CARES
38 Converse Court
Burlington, VT 05401
(802) 863–AIDS

Vermont Department of Health
60 Main Street
Burlington, VT 05402
(802) 863–7286

VIRGINIA

The AIDS Support Group/
  Charlottesville
P.O. Box 2322
Charlottesville, VA 22902
(804) 979–7714

Richmond AIDS Information
  Network
1721 Hanover Avenue
Richmond, VA 23220
(804) 358–6343

American Red Cross, Roanoke
  Valley Chapter
352 Church Avenue S.W.
Roanoke, VA 24016
(703) 985–3535

Tidewater AIDS Crisis Taskforce
814 W. 41st Street
Norfolk, VA 23508
(804) 423–5859

City of Richmond Community
  Mental Health Center
501 N. 9th Street
Richmond, VA 23219
(804) 643–5301

Virginia Department of Health
101 Governor Street
Richmond, VA 23219
(804) 786–6029

WASHINGTON

American Red Cross, Seattle–
King County Chapter
1900 25th Avenue S.
Seattle, WA 98144
(206) 323–2345

Health Information Network
P.O. Box 30762
Seattle, WA 98103
(206) 784–5655

Northwest AIDS Foundation
1818 Madison
Seattle, WA 98122
(206) 329–6963

Southwest Washington Health
District
2000 Fort Vancouver Way
Vancouver, WA 98663
(206) 695–9215

Washington State Office on HIV/AIDS
Airdustrial Park, Building 14, Mail Stop LP-20
Olympia, WA 98504
(206) 586–0426

WEST VIRGINIA

AIDS Task Force of the Upper
Ohio Valley
P.O. Box 6360
Wheeling, WV 26003–6360
(304) 232–6822

Charlestown AIDS Network
P.O. Box 1024
Charlestown, WV 25324
(304) 345–4673

Mountain State AIDS Network
P.O. Box 1401
Morgantown, WV 26507
(304) 599–6726

West Virginia State Health
Department
AIDS Prevention Program
151 11th Avenue
South Charleston, WV 25303
(304) 348–2950

Western West Virginia Chapter of the American Red Cross
1111 Veterans Memorial Boulevard
Huntington, WV 25701
(304) 522–0328

WISCONSIN

Brady East STD Clinic
1240 E. Brady Street
Milwaukee, WI 53202
(414) 272–2144

City of Milwaukee Health
Department
841 N. Broadway
Milwaukee, WI 53202
(414) 278–3333

Eau Claire County Department of
Human Services
202 Eau Claire Street
Eau Claire, WI 54703
(715) 833–1977

Madison AIDS Support Network
P.O. Box 731
Madison, WI 53701
(608) 255–1711

Madison Department of Public
Health
210 Martin Luther King Jr.
Boulevard
Madison, WI 53710
(608) 266–4821

Milwaukee AIDS Project
P.O. Box 92505
Milwaukee, WI 53202
(414) 273–2437

Racine Health Department
730 Washington Avenue
Racine, WI 53403
(414) 636–9498

Wood County Health Department
604 E. 4th Street
Marshfield, WI 54449
(715) 387–8646

WYOMING

AIDS Coalition/Casper
1200 E. 3rd Street
Casper, WY 82601
(307) 777–7431

Wyoming AIDS Project
P.O. Box 9353
Casper, WY 82609
(307) 237–7833

Wyoming Department of Health
Hathaway Building
Cheyenne, WY 82002
(307) 777–7953

APPENDIX

APPENDIX A

ACRONYMS AND INITIALS

ACT-UP   Aids Coalition to Unleash Power

AIDS   acquired immune deficiency syndrome

AmFAR   American Foundation for AIDS Research

AMA   American Medical Association

ARC   AIDS-related complex

ARV   AIDS-associated retrovirus

AZT   azidothymidine (also named zidovudine; brand name Retrovir)

CDC   Centers for Disease Control

CID   Center for Infectious Diseases

CMV   cytomegalovirus

DNA   deoxyribonucleic acid

DOD   Department of Defense

ELISA   enzyme-linked immunosorbent assay

FDA   Food and Drug Administration

GLS   generalized lymphadenopathy syndrome

GMHC   Gay Men's Health Crisis

GRID   gay-related immunodeficiency disease

HHS   U.S. Department of Health and Human Services

HIV   human immunodeficiency virus

HTLV	**(-I, -II, -III)** human T-cell lymphotropic virus (types I, II, III)
IV	intravenous
KS	Kaposi's sarcoma
KSOI	Kaposi's Sarcoma and Opportunistic Infections (Task Force)
LAV	lymphadenopathy-associated virus
MMWR	*Morbidity and Mortality Weekly Report* (published by the CDC)
NAS	National Academy of Sciences
NCI	National Cancer Institute
NGRA	National Gay Rights Advocates
NGTF	National Gay Task Force
NIAID	National Institute of Allergy and Infectious Diseases
NIH	National Institutes of Health
PCP	pneumocystis carinii pneumonia
PCR	polymerase chain reaction
PHS	U.S. Public Health Service
PWA	Persons (living) with AIDS
RNA	Ribonucleic acid
SAID	simian acquired immunodeficiency disease
TAT-3	Trans-activator gene
WHO	World Health Organization

APPENDIX B

GLOSSARY

Acquired immune deficiency syndrome (AIDS): a fatal disease complex characterized by failure of the immune system to protect against opportunistic infections and certain cancers. The underlying immune deficiency in AIDS patients is caused by infection with HIV.

AIDS-associated retrovirus (ARV): the name initially designated by researchers at the University of California at San Francisco (UCSF) for the retrovirus that causes AIDS.

AIDS dementia: a progressive and insidious condition leading to deterioration of mental activity characterized by loss or impairment of certain intellectual functions. The condition is thought to be caused primarily by the direct effects of HIV infection on the brain. Opportunistic infections also can contribute to the erosion of mental function.

AIDS-related complex (ARC): an acquired syndrome related to infection with HIV that resembles AIDS, but lacks the presence of an opportunistic infection or KS. Symptoms may include swollen glands, fevers, weight loss, chronic diarrhea and localized infections less severe than those seen in AIDS patients. ARC, in some instances, develops into AIDS.

Antibody: a protein produced by the immune system when exposed to pathogens and other foreign substances. Antibodies work with other parts of the immune system to eliminate infectious microorganisms from the body.

Antigenic variation: the process in which a virus changes its protein coat.

Asymptomatic: having no symptoms of disease.

Azidothymidine (AZT): an experimental antiviral drug used in the treatment of AIDS patients; though still widely referred to as AZT, the drug is now properly called zidovudine. It is marketed under the brand name Retrovir.

B lymphocytes: a type of white blood cell that produces antibodies in response to stimulation by an invading microorganism.

Enzyme-linked immunosorbent assay (ELISA):   a blood test used to detect the presence of AIDS virus antibodies.

Epidemiology: the branch of medical science involved in tracking and discovering the cause(s) of an epidemic.

Generalized lymphadenopathy syndrome (GLS):   a condition related to infection with HIV, and characterized by enlargement of the lymph nodes.

High-risk: in the context of AIDS, the term used to describe the fact that certain patterns of behavior place individuals at jeopardy of contracting the AIDS virus.

Human immunodeficiency virus (HIV):   the virus which causes AIDS.

Human t-cell lymphotropic virus, Type III (HTLV-III):   the name given initially by researchers at the NCI to the retrovirus that causes AIDS.

Immune deficiency: a condition in which the immune system does not function properly. In AIDS, the immune deficit is caused by infection with HIV.

Immune system: the combination of specialized cells and proteins in the blood and other body fluids that works together to eliminate disease-producing microorganisms from the body.

Kaposi's sarcoma (KS):   a previously rare cancer of the skin and lymph nodes that occurs frequently in persons with AIDS.

Lymphadenopathy-associated virus (LAV):   the name given initially by researchers at the Pasteur Institute to the retrovirus that causes AIDS.

Lymphocytes: a class of white blood cells. Two major types, B and T lymphocytes, are vital components of the immune system.

Macrophage: a type of white blood cell found in the blood, brain, mucous membranes, semen and cervical fluid that fights infection by attacking and ingesting invading pathogens.

Opportunistic infection: an infection caused by a microorganism that rarely induces disease in persons with normal immune defense mechanisms.

Pathogen: a disease-causing microorganism. There are four types: viruses, bacteria, fungi and protozoa.

Pneumocystis carinii pneumonia (PCP):   an unusual form of pneumonia caused by a fungus, it is the most common life-threatening opportunistic infection diagnosed in AIDS patients.

Polymerase chain reaction (PCR):   a recently developed and highly sensitive test to detect the presence of HIV in cells and tissue. This process works by magnifying traces of actual genetic material of the AIDS virus.

Retrovirus: a class of viruses, such as HIV, that contains an RNA core and has the capability to copy this RNA into DNA once inside an infected cell.

Reverse transcriptase: an enzyme found in retroviruses that allows them to produce a DNA copy of their RNA. This is the initial step in the retrovirus's natural cycle of reproduction.

Seropositive: the condition in which a person is found to have antibodies to HIV, indicating prior exposure to the AIDS virus.

Syndrome: a group of symptoms and signs that together characterizes a disease or medical disorder.

T helper lymphocytes (T4 cells):   also called CD4 cells, this subset of T lymphocytes acts as overall regulator of the immune system. T4 cells seem to be the primary targets of HIV.

T lymphocytes (T cells):   a type of lymphocyte crucial to immune response and principally involved in the direct attack upon invading, infectious microorganisms.

T suppressor lymphocytes (T8 cells):   a subset of T lymphocytes that helps to regulate immune function by deactivating, or "turning off," other cells.

Vaccine: a preparation administered to stimulate the body's immune system, and thereby protect an individual against contracting a specific disease.

Virus: a microorganism capable of causing disease, it consists of a core of genetic material, either RNA or DNA, surrounded by a protein coat. A virus depends on the cell it invades for its ability to reproduce.

Western blot: a test designed to detect exposure to the AIDS virus by identifying the presence of AIDS virus antibodies.

APPENDIX C

────────────■■■■■────────────

U.S. PUBLIC HEALTH SYSTEM

Within the United States Government, health agencies are part of the U.S. Department of Health and Human Services (HHS). The Secretary of HHS is a cabinet-level position.

The key scientific research agencies fall under the U.S. Public Health Service (PHS). The PHS is led by the Assistant Secretary for Health of the Department of HHS. This position is commonly referred to as the "Assistant Secretary of Health." The National AIDS Program Office falls under the PHS. Set up by Congress, it functions as the federal health service's liaison to the House and Senate on AIDS activities.

The PHS is composed of the Food and Drug Administration (FDA), the National Institutes of Health (NIH) and the Centers for Disease Control (CDC).

The FDA is directly involved in the AIDS epidemic in two capacities: as the regulatory agency for the nation's blood banks; and as the regulatory and approval authority for experimental drugs and medications.

Most of the federal government's laboratory research on health topics is done by the NIH. The National Cancer Institute (NCI) and the National Institute of Allergy and Infectious Diseases (NIAID) are the largest institutes at the NIH. They have been most involved in AIDS medical research.

The CDC is made up of constituent centers around the country that handle a variety of public health problems. The largest of these is the Center for Infectious Diseases (CID). The CID, through its Division of HIV/AIDS, is involved both in tracing the epidemiology of AIDS and in AIDS medical research. The Division of HIV/AIDS used to be named—from most recent to least recent—the AIDS Activities Office,

242

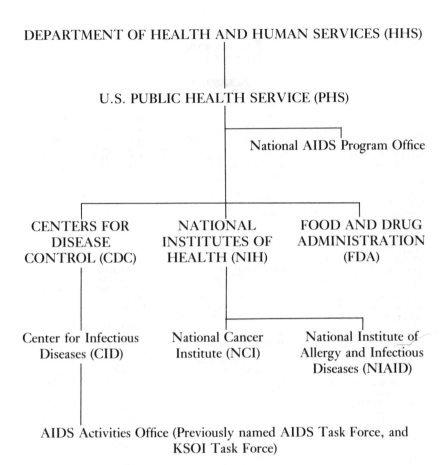

DEPARTMENT OF HEALTH AND HUMAN SERVICES (HHS)

U.S. PUBLIC HEALTH SERVICE (PHS)

National AIDS Program Office

CENTERS FOR DISEASE CONTROL (CDC)

NATIONAL INSTITUTES OF HEALTH (NIH)

FOOD AND DRUG ADMINISTRATION (FDA)

Center for Infectious Diseases (CID)

National Cancer Institute (NCI)

National Institute of Allergy and Infectious Diseases (NIAID)

AIDS Activities Office (Previously named AIDS Task Force, and KSOI Task Force)

the AIDS Task Force and the Kaposi's Sarcoma and Opportunistic Infections (KSOI) Task Force.

The U.S. Surgeon General is the principal advisor to the Department of HHS on public health issues. He is also the head of the health service's uniformed medical corps.

INDEX

Index

Index

Hemophilia and hemophiliacs 6, 20, 60–61, 89–90, 101
Hepatitis
  type B 60
  viral 6
Herpes zoster 17
Heterosexual Behavior in the Age of AIDS (book) 78–79
Heterosexuals
  HIV prevalence in 22
  HIV transmission by 19, 65
HHS—*See Health and Human Services, U.S. Department of*
Hispanics 22
HIV (Human Immunodeficiency Virus)
  blood testing for antibodies to 8, 32–33, 67–68
  genetic structure of 10–11
  immune system devastation by 12–14
  infection statistics and projections 29–30
  isolation (discovery) of 7–8, 64–67, 102, 104
  legal rights of the infected 44–47
  naming of 73
  and neurological disorders 17, 29, 67, 73
  related conditions 16–18
  risk groups 21–22
  transmission 18–21
    by prostitutes 65, 82
  vaccine development 27–28
  viral reproduction arrest report 79
HIV-2 53, 77, 80
HIV/AIDS Surveillance Report 114
HIV antibody positivity (seropositivity) 18
Hoffman, William M. 50
Homosexuals
  attitudes towards 42
  mobilization by 34–36, 47–48
  as risk group 21
Horne, Ken 58
HPA-23 24, 67, 69, 100
HTLV—*See Human T-Cell Leukemia Virus*
HTLV-I 7
HTLV-II 7
HTLV-III (former name for HIV) 8, 66–67, 102
Hudson, Rock 36, 48, 52, 68, 83–84, 89, 102
Human Immunodeficiency Virus (HIV)—*See HIV*
Human T-Cell Leukemia (Lymphotrophic) Virus (HTLV) 7–8, 62–63
Hyman, Harold 88–89
Hypodermic needles
  HIV transmission via 18

I

Idaho: organizations 211
Illinois 85
  organizations 211–212
Immigration and Naturalization Service, U.S. (INS) 55, 84
Immune system 4–5, 11–14

Imreg-1 25
Incubation period 12
Indiana
  organizations 212
  Ryan White case 89–91
Infections
  acute 18
  opportunistic 14–16
Inmates—*See Prisoners*
In re District 27 Community School Board v. Board of Education of the City of New York 88–89
INS—*See Immigration and Naturalization Service, U.S.*
Institute for Immunological Disorders (Houston, Texas) 72, 77
Insurance 31, 45, 71
Interferon 24
Interleukin-2 25
International Conference on AIDS
  First (1985, Atlanta) 68
  Second (1986, Paris) 71
  Third (1987, Washington) 75
  Fourth (1988, Stockholm) 80
  Fifth (1989, Montreal) 26, 28, 84
Intravenous (IV) drug users
  HIV transmission by 19–20
  and needle-exchange efforts 31–32
  as risk group 6, 22, 31
In utero transmission 20
Iowa: organizations 212–213
Isoprinosine 25, 66
IV drug users—*See Intravenous drug users*

J

Jaffe, Harold W. 59, 62, 100, 102
Japan 9–10, 79
John, Elton 69
John Paul II, Pope 83
Johns Hopkins University (Baltimore, Maryland) 79
Johnson, Virginia E. 78–79
Joseph, Stephen C. 102–103
Journal of the American Medical Association 62
Justice, U.S. Department of 71, 82, 93

K

Kansas: organizations 213
Kaposi's sarcoma (KS) 4, 16, 57–58, 60, 100, 105
Kaposi's Sarcoma and Opportunistic Infections (KSOI) Task Force 37–38, 58–61, 100, 243
"Kaposi's Sarcoma and *Pneumocystis carinii* Pneumonia among Homosexual Men—New York and California" 59
Kentucky: organizations 213
Kissing 75
Klatzmann, David 62
Knight, Gladys 69
Koop, C. Everett 26, 39, 49, 73–74, 77, 103
Kramer, Larry 36, 50, 68, 103
Krim, Mathilde G. 35, 64, 69, 102–103, 105

KS—*See Kaposi's sarcoma*
KSOI Task Force—*See Kaposi's Sarcoma and Opportunistic Infections Task Force*

L

Lambda Legal Defense and Education Fund 35, 113–114, 199
Langone, John 112
Latin America 52–53, 84
Laubenstein, Linda 57
LAV (Lymphadenopathy-Associated Virus) (former name for HIV) 7, 64–66
Lawrence, Dale N. 103
Legal issues 44–47
Leibowitch, Jacques 59–60, 103, 105
Lenox Hill Hospital (New York City) 63
Leonard, John 112–113
Lesbian and Gay Health Conference and AIDS Forum 81
Leukemia, feline—*See Feline leukemia*
Levy, Jay A. 8, 80, 103–104
Liberace 52
Living Daylights, The (film) 52
Los Angeles 4–6, 58
Louisiana: organizations 214
Lundberg, George D. 112
Lymphadenopathy-Associated Virus (LAV)—*See LAV*
Lymphocytes 11—*See also B lymphocytes; T lymphocytes*

M

MacLaine, Shirley 69
Macrophages 12–14, 17, 29, 80
Maine: organizations 214
Mann, Joseph M. 104
Mapplethorpe, Robert 50–51, 104
Maryland: organizations 215
Mason, James O. 66, 104
Massachusetts 83, 97
  organizations 216
Masters, William H. 78–79
Mayberry, W. Eugene 39, 76, 104, 106
McKinney, Stewart B. 75
Medicaid 30–31
Methodist Hospital (Houston, Texas) 76–77
Michigan: organizations 216–217
MicroGeneSys Company 28, 76
"Midnight Caller" (television series) 51
Mildvan, Donna 57
Mine Shaft (bar in New York City) 70
Minnelli, Liza 69
Minnesota: organizations 217
Mississippi: organizations 218
Missouri: organizations 218
MMWR—*See Morbidity and Mortality Weekly Report*
Monette, Paul 50, 113
Monkeys, African green 9–10
Monkey viruses 65, 101
Montagnier, Luc 7, 62, 64–65, 72–73, 98, 102, 104

246

Index

Index

Reagan, Ronald
  advisory commission
    report/10-point response
    (1987-88) 39–40, 43, 74–76,
    80–81, 106
  call for extensive testing 75
  medical wastes legislation 34
  policies deemed inadequate
    42–43, 83
  public education plan (1987) 74
  surgeon general's report (1986) 39
  virus discovery dispute resolution
    74, 98
Red Cross 32, 66, 114, 198
Rehabilitation Act (1973) 43, 93–95
Resources 109–114
  basic sources 112–114
  card catalogs 109–110
  government documents 111–112
  indexes 110–111
Retinal spots 15
Retrovir—See Azidothymidine
Retrovirus 7, 62
  definition 10–11
Reverse transcriptase 10–11
Reynolds, Burt 69
Rhode Island: organizations 229
Ribavirin 24, 67, 73
Risk groups 21–22
RNA 10–11
Rozenbaum, Willy 58–60, 104–105
Rubinstein, Arye 59
Rumania 54

S

SAID—See Simian Acquired
  Immunodeficiency Disease
St. Clare's Home for Children
  (Elizabeth, New Jersey) 75
Saliva 66, 75
Salk, Jonas E. 28, 105
San Francisco, California
  bathhouse closings 40, 64, 66–67,
    70
  early cases 4–6, 58–59
  gay activism 63
  health care impact 61–62
San Francisco AIDS Foundation 201
School Board of Nassau County v. Arline
  74, 89, 93–96
Semen
  HIV in 19
Senate, U.S. 74
Sencer, David J. 67, 105
Seropositivity—See HIV antibody
  positivity
Sexual contact
  HIV transmission via 18–19
Sexual promiscuity 5
Shandera, Wayne 58, 102
Shilts, Randy 50, 63, 105, 112
Showtime (cable television network)
  50
Shuttleworth, Todd 70, 97
Silverman, Mervyn F. 64, 66–67, 105
Simian Acquired Immunodeficiency
  Disease (SAID) 9
Slim disease 54
Social Security 64, 76

Sodomy statutes 72, 91–92
South Carolina: organizations 229
South Dakota: organizations 229
South Florida Blood Service Inc. v.
  Rasmussen 97
State, U.S. Department of 73
Statistics and projections 29–30,
  55–56
Stockholm international conference
  (1988) 80
Sullivan, Louis W. 84–85, 105
Suppressor T lymphocytes—See T8
  cells
Supreme Court, U.S. 48, 72, 74,
  91–94, 96
Suramin 24, 69
"Surgeon General's Report on
  AIDS" (1986) 103
Surviving AIDS (book) 113
Swine fever—See African swine fever

T

T4 cells 5, 11–14, 16–17, 25
T8 cells (suppressor T lymphocytes)
  12–13, 16–17
Tanzania 53–54, 82
Task Force on AIDS 63
TAT-3 gene—See Trans-activator gene
Taylor, Elizabeth 36, 69, 105
T cells—See T lymphocytes
Tears 69, 75
Tennessee: organizations 229–230
Teresa, Mother 48
Testing, HIV-antibody 32, 40–41,
  43, 62, 75, 83, 85, 99
Texas: organizations 230–232
"That's What Friends Are For"
  (song) 69
Thomas, James R. 85
T lymphocytes (T cells) 5, 11–14,
  16–17, 25, 58–59
Total parenteral nutrition 23
Toxoplasma gondii 15–16
Toxoplasmosis 60
Trans-activator (TAT-3) gene 11,
  102
Transmission modes 18–21
  blood exchange 19–20
  casual contact 20–21
  kissing 75
  saliva 66, 75
  sexual contact 18–19
    with prostitutes 65, 82
  tears 75
Treatment 22–26—See also specific
  drugs
Truth about AIDS, The: Evolution of an
  Epidemic (book) 112
Tuberculosis 60

U

UCLA—See University of California at
  Los Angeles
UCSF—See University of California at
  San Francisco
Uganda 53–54

"Understanding AIDS—A Message
  from the Surgeon General"
  (pamphlet) 39, 79
United Blood Services 97
United States Conference of Local
  Health Officers 201
University of California 65, 67
  at Los Angeles (UCLA) 58
  at San Francisco (UCSF) 59
Upjohn Company 100

V

Vaccine development 27–28
Vaginal intercourse
  HIV transmission via 19
Verhoef, Hans Paul 84
Vermont: organizations 232
Virginia: organizations 232
Viruses
  definition 10
Volberding, Paul A. 59, 105–106

W

Warwick, Dionne 69
Washington, D.C. 64, 71
  international conference (1987) 75
  organizations 209
Washington (state): organizations 233
Waste, medical 33–34
Wasting syndrome 23
Watkins, James D. 39, 76, 78–81, 106
Waxman, Henry A. 38, 61, 106
Weiss, Theodore S. (Ted) 38,
  64–65, 106
Western blot (HIV antibody test) 8
Western Europe 52
West Virginia: organizations 233
White, Byron R. 92
White, Ryan 68, 71, 89–91, 106
White blood cells 11
WHO—See World Health
  Organization
Windom, Robert 72
Wisconsin: organizations 233–234
Wonder, Stevie 69
World Health Organization (WHO)
  epidemic control efforts of 69, 73,
    82
  as international parley co-sponsor
    (1985) 68
  Jonathan Mann role at 104
  on organizations list 202
  surveys by 52, 65, 86
  on transmission modes 75
  travel curbs reported by 54–55
World Hemophilia AIDS Center 202
Worldwide perspective 52–55
Wyoming: organizations 234

Y

Young, Frank E. 81, 106

Z

Zaire 9, 66